PILGRIMAGE

A WELSH PERSPECTIVE

Nona Rees : Terry John

First Impression – 2002

ISBN 1 84323 081 X

This volume is published with the support of the Arts Council of Wales
and The Welsh Church Fund, Isla Johnston Trusts.

Printed in Wales at
Gomer Press, Llandysul, Ceredigion

CONTENTS

INTRODUCTION

CHRISTIAN pilgrimage in Wales is ancient: it reaches far back to post-Roman times, from the Age of Saints right up to the present day. The era that has left tantalising traces behind and on which much of modern pilgrimage is still based, is the Middle Ages. Pilgrimage was very much a part of daily life yet its driving forces, especially of the long-distance pilgrimage were life's exigencies. Geoffrey Chaucer's *The Canterbury Tales* memorably depicts a colourful cross-section of 14th-century society on pilgrimage with all its mixed motives; however, it was a world less cushioned than our own. The teachings of the Church about death and Judgement were immediate and terrifying. They were illustrated in sculpture and carving, wall-painting and stained glass in the simplest and the grandest churches. The reaction of the many who could not read was articulated by the 15th-century poet Francois Villon, writing for his mother:

> A painted paradise in church I see
> Where amid harps and lights the blessed dwell
> And lost souls burning in a painted hell.
> Fearful is one, the other fair to me

The harshness, uncertainty and brevity of life, sickness and old age, the fear of Purgatory and the pains of hell were compelling reasons to seek forgiveness of sins and cure of ills, and through the act of pilgrimage to beseech the help of Christ, the Virgin Mary and the saints.

Pilgrimages varied in length, from the long-distance pilgrimage – a major commitment though not mandated by the church, but sometimes used as a punishment for certain offences – to the local pilgrimage around the saint's 'parish', especially on the patronal feast day, with devotions made at stations along the way. The local pilgrimage was probably far more common, as in a poor, agricultural community in a difficult and mountainous country, few as individuals could have borne the expense of the long-distance pilgrimage. Medieval society was far more mobile than is often supposed however; within Wales itself, pilgrims would have travelled in groups and the poor would have been supported by the provisions made by church and community for their welfare; also charity to the wayfarer was considered part of Christian duty for everyone. There is evidence to suggest that the more ambitious pilgrimage to Rome might have been organised and led by priests from within a diocese.

After the conquest, the Normans added their own favoured saints from the apostolic or continental tradition to the native patrons of many Welsh churches, in which process some pre-Norman dedications were lost, but the Welsh persisted in venerating their own saints. There does not seem to have been the vogue for new saintly cults in medieval Wales as there was in England, and at the Reformation

Giraldus Cambrensis, modern statue, St Davids Cathedral

many of the relics and shrines facing destruction were those of the early Welsh saints.

Wales has passed through enormous changes in outlook since the curtain fell on a Catholic country at the Reformation and following centuries of suppression: Welsh Roman Catholics are still relatively few today. The world-view that nurtured medieval pilgrimage was abruptly severed in 1535, ironically at the hands of a Welsh dynasty, the Tudors. Wales entered a dark age, with her shrines, churches and monasteries laid waste, and until the translation of the Bible into Welsh in 1588, her language condemned, her religion denied. The great Welsh shrines that drew pilgrims from far and wide are now mostly Protestant-Anglican and the 'shrine' element is often muted, marginalised and half-forgotten.

This attempt to rediscover that lost land of Welsh pilgrimage takes two chief guides: the first and earliest is Gerald of Wales, in Latin, Giraldus Cambrensis and in Welsh, Gerallt Gymro. He journeyed around Wales in 1188 with Archbishop Baldwin of Canterbury gathering support for another great act of pilgrimage: the third crusade. Gerald's quick eye, boundless curiosity, ready wit and supreme self-confidence give us a unique, if journalistic, picture of 12th-century Wales. He wrote of all that attracted or fascinated the pilgrim: miracles, relics, penances, the blessings, curses and idiosyncrasies of the Welsh saints, and he had travelled with pilgrim bands on the continent. The second 'guide' is the information left by the Welsh bards, especially those of the mid-15th century to the Reformation, a period which saw a revival of both literature and art following the devastation left by a century of plague and war. Their patrons were often clerics and some of this religious 'praise poetry' has survived, extolling the saints, images, roods, shrines and relics, expanding on aspects of pilgrimage within Wales and beyond. Glanmor Williams has located about 90 poems addressed to individual saints or places of pilgrimage and points out the close connection existing between the two. An interesting late survival from north Wales indicated that the times appointed for pilgrimages may have been announced by a master poet or *pencar*, a corruption of the Welsh word *pencerdd*. We catch glimpses of a landscape with some familiar features but in many places altered beyond recognition, and of recognisable flesh-and-blood human beings who belonged to a different world order impossible to truly reconstruct. The Reformation changed the face of Wales inevitably and suddenly, within a few brief years. In the suppression of shrines and pilgrimages something of their nature was set down and preserved for posterity, but within a generation, as memories faded, much was lost.

The 'evidence' as such is fragmentary and has to be pieced together from tradition, the poetry of the Welsh bards, the survivals of church artifacts and illustration in paint, stained glass, wood and stone, the few and often fragmentary remains of shrines, pilgrim paths, stones, hospices and holy wells. Dafydd ap Gwilym described the hazards of estuaries for the pilgrim along Cardigan Bay. A fragment of a 10th-century Latin/Welsh phrase book survives, helping pilgrims negotiate their way through a mountainous and savage country. Pilgrim badges or little lead phials, ampullae for holy oil or water, are welcome evidence, and metal

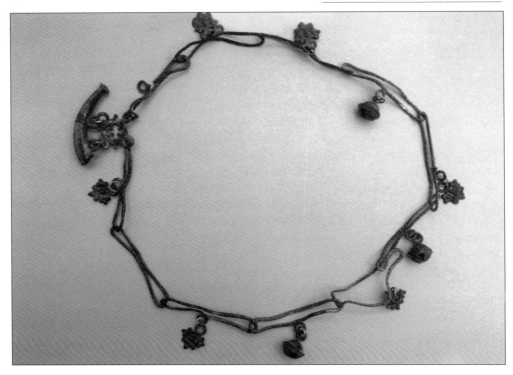

Pilgrim necklace, Pembrokeshire and details from necklace: Horn of St Hubert, Pilgrim bell

detectorists have unearthed a number in Pembrokeshire, though considerably more ampullae than badges. Surprisingly nothing has been found in St Davids until recently. It is not known if St Davids had a particular badge, but a suggestion might be the Virgin and Child image, reflecting the popularity of *Mair o Fynyw*, Mary of Menevia, in the 14th and 15th centuries when these pilgrim mementoes were most common. Two scallop shell ampullae have been found in the area, one near Rickeston Hall, Brawdy, and one near Porth Padrig on the south side of the cathedral. Sometimes an image survives, as in Llangynin church, or commemorating a long-dead pilgrim, as in Llandyfodwg, Glamorganshire and two in Haverfordwest. More nebulous are word-of-mouth traditions, like long-vanished

Pilgrim badges, Pembrokeshire. Two are of Virgin and Child.
Bottom row, left to right: bishop with crosier; St Thomas Becket; keys of St Peter, Rome; a king,
possibly Edward the Confessor

stones and tiles near St David's shrine worn smooth by pilgrims. For any serious researcher into Welsh pilgrimage, G. Hartwell Jones's *Celtic Britain and the Pilgrim Movement* contains an extensive collection of bardic poetry relating to pilgrimage and a breadth of general information. Peter Bartrum's *Welsh Classical Dictionary; Lives of the British Saints* by S. Baring Gould and J. Fisher, and Francis Jones's detailed investigation into the well cult in *Holy Wells of Wales* are valuable resources, and general background to the era is provided by Professor Sir Glanmor Williams's magisterial *Welsh Church, Conquest to Reformation.* One of the problems of attempting a history of Welsh pilgrimage is that so much material is still the subject of scholarly debate, and the translation of medieval Welsh poetry is a particularly difficult area. Confusion often arises from the enthusiasms of antiquarians of the 17th–20th centuries who remain a

Pilgrim image, Carmarthenshire

Pilgrim image on tombstone, Glamorganshire

necessary source of information. Pilgrimage traditions present a confusing mix of history and myth and rather than trying to disentangle the two, an attempt is made to present the information as it stands and to make clear where we are dealing with tradition which cannot be counted as factual. Also, the ground has to be walked, and evidence of ancient pilgrim traffic may still be lying undiscovered. A substantial part of this pilgrim search has been conducted in our native Pembrokeshire, and the shrine of St David of Wales seemed a good place to start. But in considering St Davids, the rest of Wales is immediately involved and with that, the place of Wales in the pilgrimages of Western Christendom. One shrine led to another: Holywell and St Davids were linked by the earliest direct north–south road in Wales; St Davids pointed the way to Glastonbury and to Santiago de Compostela.

Side by side with the so-called post-modern age, the pilgrim quest lives on. Today's pilgrims travel singly or in groups, but faster and with far greater ease. They perpetuate an ancient instinct. Wales itself has changed, but its remoter places, undiscovered churches and mysterious holy wells still embody a meaning, a place where contact can be made with something beyond and where prayers might yet be answered. The very act of going on pilgrimage has always given practical expression to life's hopes and fears, and what drew the pilgrims centuries ago has a resonance today.

PART I

The Pilgrim Journey

A deep penitence: the reasons for pilgrimage

A deep penitence (from a 10th-century English canon law)

IN March 1188, Gerald of Wales gave to Archbishop Baldwin a copy of his recently completed book, *Topography of Ireland*. Amongst the many legends and descriptions of Ireland that it contained was the story of Owain, one of the knights of King Stephen. This hardened warrior, during a journey to Ireland, was stricken with remorse for the many crimes he had committed during his lifetime. He was given penances to perform to atone for his sins and, by his own choice, made a number of pilgrimages, including one to the Holy Land.

The story of Owain was well known during the medieval period; there were several versions of it, as well as numerous other tales in which sinners atoned for their crimes through pilgrimage. Amongst the most famous British examples of atonement pilgrimages are those of Henry II to Canterbury following the killing of Thomas Becket. Murder, heresy, arson, the breaking of God's peace were all mortal sins for which a punishment of excommunication or death was decreed, but the sentence could be remitted and instead the guilty party was sent on a pilgrimage. During the reign of the English king Edgar (959–75), a canon law stated:

> *It is a deep penitence that a layman lay aside his weapons and travel far barefoot and nowhere pass a second night and fast and watch much and pray fervently, by day and by night and willingly undergo fatigue and be so squalid that iron come not on hair or nail.*

Such a journey involved first a confession, after which absolution was given. This freed a person from guilt, though punishment of the sin would still take place in purgatory or hell. The condemned were allowed to dress as pilgrims and were given safe conducts to a particular shrine, often following an organised itinerary. Others wandered from shrine to shrine. Those who had committed murder wore arm-bands forged from the weapons they had used. Glewus, a Lincolnshire man who had killed his brother with an iron pitchfork, travelled the roads of England for three years dressed in a hair shirt, with a ring made from the murder weapon clasped about his right arm. At Bury St Edmunds it cracked and the broken end continued to dig into his arm until the whole thing fell off at Norwich. Such was the sensation caused by this completed act of penitence that the bishop himself came to the spot and led a hymn of praise.

Towards the end of the Middle Ages, pilgrimage had become the punishment for secular crimes as well as for mortal sins. During the 14th century, for example, the Earl of Arundel promised to go on a pilgrimage to the shrine of St Richard of

Chichester after he had been found trespassing on the bishop's land at Hoghton Chase.

The majority of pilgrims were probably driven to make these long and hazardous journeys for much simpler reasons, namely a deeply held conviction that prayers uttered before a hallowed shrine would be more favourably heard and a belief that the journey there was in itself a remission of sin through the hardships endured. There were no doubt some who went on pilgrimage for more frivolous purposes; a journey to distant places offered a chance to break out of the day-to-day drudgery of life. There were new places to be visited, new people to meet and at some shrines jugglers, musicians and jesters entertained the crowds waiting for admission.

Some pilgrims were anxious to obtain a blessing on a marriage or a new business venture. Others begged their way from shrine to shrine in the hope of amassing enough money to live comfortably in the future. It was not unknown for a seemingly pious traveller to kneel and kiss a shrine, craftily sucking up the coins which lay there whilst doing so. Others went on pilgrimage in order to show their opposition to authority by praying at the tombs of a king's dead enemies.

Start out a pilgrim, return a whore (medieval proverb)

One of the oldest maxims concerning pilgrimage was, 'Start out a pilgrim, return a whore.' It acknowledged that there were moral as well as physical dangers to be overcome whilst journeying to a shrine. Many of the prostitutes in continental towns were rumoured to be of British stock, driven to sell themselves because they had run out of money whilst on pilgrimage. Even the most devout of pilgrims sometimes succumbed to temptation. A poem entitled 'To the Nun', *Caru dyn lygeitu lwyd*, written in the 14th century by an anonymous Welsh poet, ends with the words:

> *. . . And please don't be too pious.*
> *On the hillside we will free*
> *Our souls amongst the woodbines.*
> *God and the saints will pardon*
> *Such conjunction in true love.*
> *Does a well-born girl do worse*
> *Winning a soul in woodlands*
> *Than behaving as we have*
> *At Rome and Santiago?*

Sometimes, sexual temptation had unexpected results. A family of pilgrims on the road to Santiago de Compostela reached the town of Santo Domingo de la Calzada. They stayed at an inn where the innkeeper's daughter attempted to seduce the young son. Angry at his refusal to sleep with her, the girl hid a silver cup amongst his belongings. When it was discovered, the boy was hanged for theft. Grief-stricken, his parents continued on their way to the shrine of St James at Compostela, offering up many prayers for the soul of their son. During their return journey they had to pass the tree from which the body of the young man still dangled. They heard to their amazement their son's voice calling out to them. He explained that St James had been so touched by their devotion that he had restored the boy's life and had held him up by the arms until their return. The parents rushed into town to inform the authorities of what had transpired. The mayor was just sitting down to a meal of two roast chickens and angrily shouted, 'Your son is no more alive than these chickens.' Immediately the chickens leapt from the plate and began to flap around the room. The young man was taken down from the tree and continued on the homeward journey with his parents. The story of the miraculous resurrections soon spread throughout Europe and was retold in different versions for centuries, as well as being depicted in paintings as far away as Germany.

Promised pilgrimages

Belief in the curative powers of relics brought pilgrims flocking to shrines all over Britain. Some of these people were invalids who could barely walk and for whom special travel arrangements had to be made. Villagers living in the countryside around Hereford could hire litters in which to be carried to the cathedral. In 1300 another crippled pilgrim caused a stir at the same shrine by arriving in a wheelbarrow, having been pushed all the way from London by a companion. Others who had lost the use of their limbs used a sort of wheeled platform on which they lay, driving themselves forward with their arms. The blind were usually led along by a relative or friend, whilst those proceeding on crutches or on horseback might be given specially padded equipment to ease their discomfort. It was also possible for those too sick to visit a shrine themselves to send a proxy or to promise to make a pilgrimage as soon as they were healed. On 28 September 1443, Margaret Paston wrote to her husband John to let him know that during his illness her mother had 'promised another image of wax of the weight of yourself to Our Lady of Walsingham and she sent 4 nobles to the 4 orders of friars at Norwich to pray for you; and I have promised pilgrimages to be made for you to Walsingham and to St Leonard's'.

Margaret Paston was doing nothing unusual in arranging for pilgrimages to be made for her husband. Pilgrimage by proxy was a profitable business during the medieval period. Many people provided for this service in their wills, requiring close friends, trusted servants or even professional pilgrims to undertake the journey. Two examples will suffice: in 1433, Bishop Benedict Nicholls of St Davids left ten pounds in his will to Master Henry Wells and Lord John Sutton to visit in his name the shrines of St John at Bridlington and Beverley and the shrine of St Mary at Walsingham. The money was to be paid out as soon as possible after Benedict's death so that the pilgrimages could take place without delay. Sir Morgan Herbert made a similar provision in his will, dated 19 July 1526. Although of an

old Montgomeryshire family, Sir Morgan does not appear to have lived in the
county and directed that his body should be buried in Ribbesford churchyard,
Worcestershire. He specified that his servant, Howell Gethin, should have his black
gown and should go on certain pilgrimages for him, offering 4d at the following
places: Llandrinio, Llansantffraid, Pennant Melangell, Llandderfel, St John the
Baptist at Carno and the Holy Rood of Trefeglwys. The will is particularly
interesting as it provides late evidence of other active pilgrimage centres in
Montgomeryshire as well as the better-known ones of Pennant Melangell and
Llandderfel (in south Montgomeryshire).

In extreme cases, proxy pilgrimage might involve a voyage to the Holy Land,
Rome or Santiago de Compostela, though often a shrine closer to home was
nominated. The proxy, usually a male, might carry with him a message or a plea
written in by the person he represented, to be left at the shrine; alternatively he
might carry a piece of clothing or personal property, which was pressed against the
shrine or saint's relic and which was then carried back to the owner waiting at
home, in the hope that a blessing or a cure might be returned with it.

In some cases cures were effected immediately. At St Frideswide's church in
Oxford a woman was cured of her blindness at the church doors; at Canterbury a
crippled woman who had been kneeling at prayer rose to her feet healed of her
affliction. Sometimes the cure took place whilst travelling to a shrine or even some
time after returning from it. If a pilgrim did not obtain a cure at one shrine, the
journey might be continued to other holy places until at last health was regained:
one particularly determined man visited no fewer than eighty-seven shrines until he
was cured.

Indulgences

From the 12th century onwards, the sale of indulgences became common. These
were basically written certificates that stated that a period of suffering in purgatory
as a punishment for sin had been remitted. The first plenary indulgence was issued
by Pope Urban II in 1095. It gave remittance to all those who confessed their sins
and joined the first crusade. In the centuries that followed most shrines came to
offer indulgences to those who visited them. Remission of punishment from sin
was obtainable at a price and would cover a fixed period of anything from a few
days up to several years. St Peter's in Rome offered visitors indulgences of up to
9,000 years. When Gerald of Wales visited Rome towards the end of the 12th
century, he attended 395 masses in the shortest possible time in order to obtain a
total of 92 years' worth of indulgences. When he realised that he was only eight
years short of a century of remission, he enrolled in the Confraternity of the Holy
Spirit, which offered an indulgence of one-seventh of all penance due for his sins.

Prominent people could buy remissions on a regular basis. The royal families of
Europe were given annual remissions, though sometimes indulgences were granted
on a more frequent basis. In 1504, Lady Margaret Beaufort, the mother of King
Henry VII, was sent an indulgence in the form of a confessional letter. It allowed

both the king and Lady Margaret remission of sins every six months at the discretion of whichever confessor they chose.

Indulgences could also be used to release unwilling travellers from a vow of pilgrimage. In March 1518 William Yeman (or Yeomans) of Llandaf petitioned the Pope for several indulgences for himself, his wife and their children, requesting that:

1. A confessor chosen by themselves may have power (they being contrite in heart and having made confession with their lips) to absolve them even from sins reserved for the Papal Tribunal.
2. Any vows they may have made of pilgrimage to the threshold of the apostles Peter and Paul in Rome, or to the shrine of Saint James at Compostela, may be commuted into other works of piety.
3. They and any of them, on visiting one or two churches or two or three altars, on Lenten or other Station-days of the city of Rome, may gain the like indulgences as if they had made the Stations at Rome itself.

William's petition was granted on the application of the bishop of Leighlin, papal penitentiary.

The pardoner

An infamous figure on the pilgrim roads of Europe was the pardoner. These men were licensed to sell papal pardons and indulgences and they travelled from shrine to shrine pedalling their wares. When the custom originally began, the money was collected through official channels and was frequently used to help the poor and needy. By the 14th century, however, the pardoners often kept much of the money for themselves and shamelessly conned the more gullible pilgrims by producing an impressive array of relics to back up their claims.

> What! Do you think, as long as I can preach
> And get their silver for the things I teach,
> That I will live in poverty, from choice?
> That's not the council of my inner voice!
> No! Let me preach and beg from kirk to kirk
> And never do an honest job of work,
> No, nor make baskets, like St Paul, to gain
> A livelihood. I do not preach in vain.

> 'The Pardoner's Tale', *The Canterbury Tales*, Geoffrey Chaucer

The pardoner was often to be seen on the pilgrim roads of Europe, selling indulgences and relics to pilgrims

Chapter 2

My gown of glory: process and preparation

My gown of glory (from *The Pilgrimage* by Walter Raleigh)

FOR the medieval pilgrim, the prospect of a journey to a distant shrine was a daunting one. Many dangers lay in store: strange lands and customs, difficult terrain, robbers and the possibility of illness or death in unfamiliar surroundings. It was therefore wise to make careful preparations, leaving as little as possible to chance.

Application was first made to the local bishop, who granted written permission for the pilgrimage to be made. These letters, or *testimoniales*, were vital: they gave the pilgrim full rights to all the privileges to which a number of church decrees entitled him or her. Without them, a traveller risked arrest as an impostor or a trickster. So seriously were the *testimoniales* regarded that an ordinance of King Richard II, enacted in 1388, recommended the arrest of any pilgrim who could not produce them.

Once the bishop's permission had been obtained, pilgrims put all their affairs in order. A will was made, all quarrels were settled, debts were paid or collected and any unjustly held property was returned to its rightful owner; merchants and landowners appointed a trustworthy steward to oversee matters. Gerald of Wales records that Welsh pilgrims prepared for their journey by amending their ways and by donating to the church a tenth of all their worldly goods, including cattle, sheep and other livestock. This division of property was called the Great Tithe and two-thirds of it was given to the church in which they had been baptised, whilst the remaining third went to the bishop of their diocese. It was also not unknown for pilgrims to take an oath not to shave their beards or cut their hair until the conclusion of their pilgrimage.

A pilgrim in his pilgrim garb: the red cross sewn onto his tunic indicates that he is travelling to Jerusalem

One of the most difficult things to deal with would have been the constant stream of callers to the pilgrim's house. Once news of the intended journey had been noised abroad, people came to offer their best wishes for a safe return, but many also pressed upon the pilgrim written prayers and supplications, gifts and donations which they were anxious to have offered at the saint's shrine on their behalf. Special prayers for a safe passage were made for several days, if not weeks, before the journey began, and it was thought that good or bad fortune could be forecast through signs and omens. Even commonplace events foretold the future: to medieval people, a sneeze at the beginning of a journey indicated bad luck. It was also not unknown for the choice of destination to be made by lot. A favourite method was to light three candles, each one named for a different saint or sanctuary. The first one to burn out determined which shrine was to be visited. A common method in Wales, according to William of Canterbury, was to draw twigs instead of lighting candles.

Another consideration was whether to make the journey on horseback, by donkey or on foot. There was more merit in walking the entire distance and pilgrims were admonished to endure discomfort whilst travelling. The 13th-century preacher Jacques de Vitry advised his listeners during one sermon that there was 'nothing more efficacious and satisfying than the labour of pilgrimage'. One who chose to walk to Rome was the Icelandic outlaw, Flosi Thordarson, who had been involved in several killings. Flosi undertook to make a pilgrimage to Rome in reparation for these misdeeds. After staying for a while in Wales, Flosi made his way to France and then walked all the way to Rome, where he received absolution from the Pope himself.

If a pilgrim elected to walk the whole way, a further decision had to be made: should the journey be made barefoot? There is evidence that many people went shoeless for at least the last section of the way. In 1398, on the day of his consecration, Guy Mone, Bishop of St Davids, walked barefoot from Capel y Gwrhyd to the cathedral, a distance of more than a mile and there is little doubt that he was following a long-established tradition.

Many people, probably the wealthier ones, chose the easier method of travel and purchased mules or horses on which to make their journey. As early as 793, King Offa, whilst on his way to Rome, bought a number of fields in Flanders and instructed that they should be used by pilgrims who needed fodder for their animals. Many of the characters described in Chaucer's *The Canterbury Tales* are making their journey on horseback, and a number of accounts left by real pilgrims mention the stabling and care of their horses.

The day of departure

When the day of departure dawned, a special ritual was followed. The traveller made his way to his or her parish church, where other pilgrims had also gathered. It was important that the pilgrims first confessed their sins. They then lay prostrate before the altar whilst certain psalms and prayers were said over them. Once they had risen to their feet, they were given their pilgrim garb. Contemporary pictures and descriptions give us a clear idea of what this looked like: a long grey woollen gown, loosely gathered at the waist, with a monk's cowl stitched to the neck and a black or grey broad-brimmed hat. There are also a number of carved memorial slabs that depict pilgrim garb: they include a grave slab at Llandyfodwg church, where the pilgrim is shown wearing a loose, knee-length robe; a large effigy in St Mary's church at Haverfordwest and a much eroded slab at Llangynin church in Carmarthenshire.

If the pilgrim was bound for Jerusalem, both hat and robe were decorated with red crosses. The privilege of placing them there, if not of sewing them on, was reserved for bishops. The crosses were then consecrated and holy water was sprinkled over them.

Two of the most important items carried by the pilgrim were a stout wooden staff and a scrip or satchel. These were also consecrated and sprinkled with holy water and the scrip was placed about the pilgrim's neck with the words, 'In the name of our Lord Jesus Christ receive this scrip, the habit of thy pilgrimage that after due chastisement thou mayest be found worthy to reach in safety the Shrine of the Saints to which thou desirest to go; and after the accomplishment of thy journey thou mayest return to us in health.' The traveller was admonished to place all his money and other possessions in the scrip, but it was always to be left open and should never be padlocked or tied shut.

The figure on this slab at Llanfihangell Abercowyn wears clothing similar to pilgrim garb

More prayers followed as the staff was placed in the pilgrim's hand. This was a very important piece of equipment, used for support over difficult terrain or as a weapon in case of attack. The Worcester pilgrim, whose grave was discovered in Worcester Cathedral in 1986, had been buried with a 155-centimetre-long staff of ash. At the bottom of this was an iron collar with a double-pronged iron spike 6 centimetres long, whilst the top bore evidence that it had once been finished with a knob or finial. Similar staffs can be seen in contemporary illustrations.

The staff also had a symbolic meaning and was regarded as an extra limb, representing the protection of the Holy Trinity, which could be claimed by all truly penitent pilgrims against the wiles of the devil.

The pilgrims were then licensed and if they were going to Jerusalem, Rome, Santiago de Compostela or St Davids, they were led out in procession from their parish. In the 12th century, their departure was marked by the chanting of an intercession: 'Oh Lord, Heavenly Father, let the angels watch over thy servants that they may reach their destination in safety . . . that no enemy may attack them on the road, nor evil overcome them. Protect them from the perils of fast rivers, thieves or wild beasts.'

The Sarum Missal, written in the 13th century, describes a much more elaborate ceremony, which may have been used in some cathedrals and in the larger churches if the pilgrims were setting out for a destination such as Jerusalem.

The missal recounts how a small castle was erected in the nave of the church. This temporary structure represented the house of Emmaus where, in the Gospel, the risen Christ broke bread with two travellers. Two priests representing pilgrims emerged from the vestry and processed to the western porch of the church where they joined a group of choristers. They were then challenged by a third priest who, echoing the words of Jesus in the Gospel of St Luke, asked them, 'What manner of communications are these that ye have one to another, as ye walk and are sad?'

The two replied, 'Art thou only a stranger in Jerusalem, and have not known the things which are come to pass in these days?'

'What things?'

'Concerning Jesus of Nazareth, which was a prophet mighty in deed and word before God and all the people.'

The three then entered the castle of Emmaus and ate together. The third priest was recognised as the Lord and vanished from sight, whilst the others, singing sorrowfully, made their way to the pulpit where they chanted more verses. The performance ended with the emergence of another priest, whose head was muffled like a woman's. He paused before the door to the choir and threw down two cloths, possibly representing Christ's discarded grave cloths, and sang 'Christ is risen'. The procession then returned to the choir and the service ended.

A service such as this had a three-fold purpose: it reminded pilgrims of the importance of their undertaking and instructed parishioners in the tales of the Bible, as well as involving them in the drama of pilgrimage. It is worth emphasising that not all pilgrims seem to have gone through such an elaborate ceremony, nor were they always given their equipment before setting out from their home parish. Nikulas Bergsson, the Abbot of Munkathvera in Iceland, made a journey to Rome in the 12th century and describes how other Icelandic pilgrims received their scrips and staffs in Utrecht.

The path whereon I go

Before setting out on their journeys, pilgrims spent some time and money in finding out something about their destination. Several guidebooks were available, especially for the journey to Rome. The earliest were known as itineraria, and may have been based on Roman military maps and tax archives, though there were also a number of chronicles written by travellers in succeeding centuries. These covered not only journeys within Britain, but also the routes to Compostela, Rome and Jerusalem. One of the first of them dates from AD 333 and was compiled by a writer known as the Bordeaux Pilgrim; it gives a list of the principal stops in the land route from Bordeaux, where passengers from Britain came ashore, to the Holy Land. One of the most famous, the first guidebook ever printed in English, was the *Informacon for pylgrymes unto the holy land,* produced in 1498.

In addition to these guides, a phrase book for Welsh pilgrims was also available. It contained a list of useful Latin phrases, including the following:

> Get up, wake from your sleep. Fasten your belt so that we can get an early start, for the day is short and the way is long.
> Give me my cloak and shoes, hand me my staff to support me.
> O brother, show us the right road if you can.
> Have you heard if there are robbers on this road?
> Light a fire quickly, for I am worn out by the journey and by the long, muddy road.
> Give us warm water to wash our feet before sleeping.
> Innkeeper, bring us a pot of ale or mead.
> O best of girls, give me a kiss.

There were also a large number of maps, although only the wealthy could have afforded these. Most of them were intended for the general traveller as well as for the pilgrim and showed not only roads, but rivers and streams, which in the early medieval times were main routes of communication. Later, as the roads became dotted with inns and hospices for travellers, many of them became established pilgrim routes and were depicted as such. Eventually, special road maps were prepared, on which a particular long-distance route was drawn on a lengthy ribbon of paper, which could be unrolled as needed. Important geographical features such as mountains and hills were recorded as individual skylines, which could be recognised from a distance; bridges, churches, castles, towns, wayside crosses were all plotted in their correct places along the way, so that travellers could work out at any time where they were.

Silver over seas (*Piers Plowman*)

For pilgrims travelling beyond the confines of Britain, ready cash was a problem. The dangers of carrying large sums of money were obvious, so many people made special arrangements with foreign merchants. The most popular place to do this was at Winchester Fair, held every year from 1–5 September, to which foreign traders and pilgrims flocked from all over the continent. Drafts could be organised for money to be drawn by pilgrims at any of the main stops along their routes, though it was not always easy to obtain this cash once the nominated town had been reached. Gerald of Wales, on a journey to Rome in 1203, had great difficulty in recovering at Faenza the twenty gold marks he had purchased from Bolognese merchants at a fair in Troyes.

Costs could vary enormously, even taking into account the lengths of the journeys involved and the social status of the traveller. The wealthy often travelled with large retinues, which added to the cost, whilst poorer pilgrims had to shift for themselves. The sub-prior of St Augustine's in Canterbury, for example, was allowed five shillings for a journey of fifty miles in the 12th century, though not long afterwards a pilgrim bound for Compostela carried the same sum to cover the whole return journey.

Currency restrictions were sometimes enforced. Pilgrims embarking at Dublin for Santiago de Compostela were asked to swear on the Eucharist that they would only take as much gold as was reasonably required for the journey.

A pilgrimage might be delayed whilst enough money was saved up to cover the cost. A well-known story in medieval times was that of a man named Ralph who, with his wife, brewed up and sold beer to finance their travels. Others swore to beg for food and shelter along the way, however long the journey, and made a point of relying on whatever charity might be offered them. It was regarded as a noteworthy act to donate alms to begging pilgrims and richer travellers often took along with them a bag of small change to hand out along the way. Beggars caused considerable irritation along most of the pilgrim routes in Europe, even when all they required was food and drink. An exasperated inhabitant of Abingdon once turned on a group of begging pilgrims with the words, 'Not for the sake of Thomas, nor the Lord, nor the Blessed Virgin Mary, or any saint whatsoever. Not today, go away, you beggars'; whilst at the English Hospice in Rome it was estimated that the richer-paying guests were outnumbered three to one by 'pauper' guests.

The good ship *Le Saint Jacques*

The shipping of pilgrims overseas became a highly organised business during the medieval period. The Knights Templar and the Knights Hospitaller established large camps where pilgrims could be assembled not far from embarkation ports. Here they were fed and housed and as soon as possible they were loaded aboard ships which ran regularly to continental ports. These boats also carried cargo, especially on the return journey.

The Sarum Missal describes one of these voyages. The good ship *Le Saint Jacques* of Pembroke sailed for Spain with a group of pilgrims bound for Compostela and the Holy Land. Bargains had been struck with the captain, in which he agreed for a charge of forty ducats a day to provide two meals a day and, equally as important, to protect the passengers from harm by the galley slaves.

The pilgrims, a mixture of Welsh, Irish and English, included two noblemen with a retinue consisting of a barber, a musician, an old soldier who doubled as a manservant, another servant, a cook and two couriers; there was also an ex-trader who acted as an interpreter, and a preaching friar.

Ships such as this carried pilgrims to destinations overseas

At the time of departure the priests amongst the passengers were called forward and they led the ship's complement in the singing of 'Veni, Creator Spiritus'. Once out at sea, the Le Saint Jacques joined up at a pre-arranged location with a number of other vessels all bound for the same destination. These included the Le Lenard of Bristol. Off Cornwall the little fleet was augmented by the La Charite, The Galliotte and The Little Nicholas of Paignton, Le Petre and The Katherine of Dartmouth, La Marie, The Pylgryme and The Dorcette from Southampton, whilst Le Thomas came from Saltash. Huddling together across the Bay of Biscay, on constant look-out against attack by pirates or Saracen galleys, the fleet came at last to safety on the northern coast of Spain where the pilgrims disembarked at El Padron for the final trudge to Compostela.

Conditions aboard the *Le Saint Jacques,* as aboard any pilgrim ship of the time, was probably cramped, smelly and terrifying. Rhys Nanmor, who made the journey in the mid-15th century, sailed with other pilgrims from Haverfordwest to Spain and described his vessel as 'a sinister, ill-omened pirate ship'. Welsh bardic poetry contains many allusions to the Bay of Biscay, referring to it as *Môr Iago Lwyd,* Holy James's Sea, or as *Môr Sant Ialm,* St James's Sea. Lewis Glyn Cothi takes an altogether more romantic view of a pilgrim ship than Rhys Nanmor, likening it to the 'fair swallow on the crest of the wave . . . *gwennol deg yn ael y don'.*

Sea voyages were much feared, especially the journeys around the Cornish and Pembrokeshire coasts. Although *Le Saint Jacques* seems to have headed straight across the Bay of Biscay to Spain it was not unknown for pilgrims to land on the northern coast of Pembrokeshire and walk across to the southern side, where they took ship for Somerset or Devon. Once these counties had been traversed, the pilgrims would board ship again on the southern shores to resume the voyage to Spain. A landing might be made at Bordeaux in south-west France, which had good travel facilities thanks to a brisk wine trade with Wales and Pembrokeshire and the remaining distance to Compostela was covered on foot. The whole journey would then be repeated in reverse on the way home.

For those who chose to travel to the Holy Land via France and Italy, the embarkation port was Venice. Here it was possible to book a passage on galleys sailing eastwards. Pilgrims would gather before St Mark's church, where a number of banners had been raised. These banners were white, emblazoned with a red cross and they corresponded with the number of ships waiting to sail for the Holy Land. Several servants stood by, representing the captains of the various vessels and they loudly boasted of the superior merits of their own ship. Once a choice had been made, the pilgrims and the ship's captain would hammer out an agreement acceptable to both sides. These contracts would outline the cost per head of the voyage, the times of sailing, the destination port and the number of meals to be served each day during the journey. The agreements were usually signed and sealed before various witnesses in the palace of the Doge of Venice.

There was often a delay of at least a few days before the ships set sail. The pilgrims would spend this time in shopping for whatever extras were needed during the sea crossing. A good set of bedding was advisable; at a cost of three ducats, a mattress, pillows, a feather bed, two sheets and a quilt could be purchased. At least one spare set of clothing was also a necessity, plus perfumes to block out the stenches that were all too frequent in the close confines of the communal decks. In order to supplement their diet, many pilgrims purchased additional food. Long-lasting cheeses were a favourite, as well as smoked or salted meats and medicines such as syrup of ginger to comfort an upset stomach.

During the days leading up to a departure from Venice, most travellers stayed in the city inns. These were inspected regularly by the *Cattaveri,* a committee of the Senate. The *Cattaveri* controlled prices, listened to visitors' complaints, and licensed hostels and inns. Proprietors were expected to keep a list of the names of their guests, which was to be handed to the appropriate authorities within three days of arrival in Venice. The *Cattaveri* also appointed guides whose task it was to help pilgrims make their purchases, show them about the city and help them with finances. These guides were known as *tholomarii*, who were expected to be of irreproachable character. Upon taking up their duties, the *tholomarii* swore a solemn oath to observe the very strict rules laid down for their conduct. As they existed only to help the pilgrims, with no thought of self-advancement, the guides were not allowed to accept tips from visitors or bribes and commissions from merchants and shopkeepers. There were up to twelve *tholomarii*, who worked in shifts, with two on duty during the daylight hours and a rota system for night-time emergencies.

Most pilgrim traffic in the Middle Ages, particularly in the Mediterranean, was carried by galleys, not by the heavier, slower cogs which were used for cargo. Some of the vessels were specifically built for the pilgrim trade and were owned and manned by members of Venice's nobility. The oarsmen, or *galeotti*, were not slaves. During the 15th century they were recruited from the free men of the Venetian republic. Men between the ages of twenty-five and forty could sign on at one of the recruiting stations set up in the Piazza. The length of service varied from a single voyage to a period of several years. In addition to regular pay, the *galeotti* could indulge in business for themselves, selling goods to the passengers or the inhabitants of the ports they visited. They were also expected to fight if their ship came under attack and many were expert bowmen. This was necessary, particularly during the 15th century, because the Turks regularly attacked shipping in the Mediterranean and enslaved the passengers and crew of any boat they captured. A further danger was the likelihood of being becalmed far from land. There are several tales of ships drifting for days on a brassy sea, waiting for the wind to pick up again, whilst food and water ran short.

The galleys sailing out from Venice made a habit of putting into port every night to rest the oarsmen and for protection. This gave passengers the chance to eat and sleep onshore, as well as seeing the local sights. There were fast, 'express' ships sailing direct to Syrian ports and back, but passengers had to carry food for the whole trip. They paid a cheaper fare and existed in the most basic conditions.

Even if things went well, a pilgrim had to be ready to face the unexpected. Felix Fabri, a Dominican friar, travelled to Jerusalem in the 1480s and later wrote an account of the voyage from Venice. The journey started badly: the captain of the vessel had stored planks in the pilgrims' quarters and there was hardly any room to move. A furious row ensued before the planks were taken away. Several of the travellers, kept awake by burning lights, doused them by hurling chamber pots at them, whilst others got drunk and fell into the hold. A necessary daily task was the search for lice and vermin, with which all the passengers were infected, so a good insecticide, often concocted from herbs, had probably been purchased before the ship left port.

Perils on land

Any pilgrim setting off on a long journey would hope for the intercession of the Archangel Raphael, who was believed to have pilgrims in his special care. A prayer for good weather might also be wise, as heavy rain or snow could make roads impassable. Lurid tales abounded of travellers who had frozen to death in the mountain passes of the Alps and the Pyrenees.

The old Roman roads, together with the later medieval trade routes, provided a network of communications between the cities of Europe, though some of the continental pilgrim centres lay far from the original Roman roads and the tracks which led to them were not kept in good repair. A journey along them could be something of a nightmare, as described by a 10th-century traveller from Constantinople to Lepanto in Greece, five hundred miles away:

> On mule-back, on foot, on horseback, fasting, suffering from thirst, sighing, weeping, lamenting, I arrived after forty-nine days.

Attacks by robbers were much feared and pilgrims often travelled in large groups in the hope of discouraging brigands. In districts that were known to be infested by bandits, travellers were in the habit of chanting verses from the Bible as protective charms. One of the most popular of these was the following verse from the Book of Exodus, Chapter 15, verse 16:

> Fear and dread shall fall upon them; by the greatness of thine arm they shall be as still as a stone; till thy people pass over, O Lord, till the people pass over, which thou hast purchased.

The buildings where pilgrim robberies were committed were often destroyed by the authorities and offenders could be excommunicated, exiled or locked up in a monastery. In the same way, a pilgrim's possessions were regarded as sacrosanct and this extended to property left at home. Welsh law stated that no claim could be made against a person who was absent on pilgrimage until a year and a day had passed since the beginning of the pilgrimage. Furthermore, it was 'not right, according to law, to disturb the condition, or possession, of a person who might be constrained to seek customary remission of a deed, committed within the period when he might return'.

An outbreak of war was another hazard and areas where fighting was likely were, if possible, avoided. If the worst happened and war broke out in a country through which a pilgrim was journeying, he or she could always rely on their special status for protection. There were a number of official treaties and agreements between the rulers of various states that promised safe conduct to those on pilgrimage. As early as 794, in a letter to King Offa, Emperor Charlemagne gave immunity to anyone travelling to the Tombs of the Apostles. Similarly, King Canute, returning from a pilgrimage to Rome, bought free passage for pilgrims at many toll points.

In 1388 an Englishman was taken prisoner by French soldiers at Cahors, but when they realised that he was a pilgrim he was straightaway set free. His captors no doubt knew of the decree issued by a council of Pope Gregory VII, which punished the seizure of a monk or a pilgrim with excommunication.

The badge of pilgrimage could, in fact, offer protection not only to individuals, but to whole nations. King Philip Augustus of France gave assurances that he would not attack the realm of Richard I of England whilst that monarch was on pilgrimage, nor for forty days after his return so that a defence might be prepared.

Matters were not always helped by one's travelling companions. The governments of the day and the great banking houses often sent secret dispatches or money orders by way of messengers disguised as pilgrims. If the local authorities suspected the presence of a spy amongst the party, the whole group might be detained and searched until the culprit was revealed. This was particularly likely to happen in the periods of schism in the church, when pope and anti-pope vied for supremacy. Samson, Abbot of Bury, disguised himself as a Scot to avoid detection whilst carrying an appeal to Pope Alexander III in 1161. This did not prevent him from being searched by soldiers of the anti-pope Victor IV, but they overlooked the appeal, which Samson had hidden in a cup.

Janglers, tale-tellers and liars (William Thorpe, 15th-century Lollard)

At the very least, travelling companions could become embarrassing. Margery Kempe, a remarkable woman born about 1373 at Lynn, where her father was mayor, became famous as a mystic and made pilgrimages to Compostela, Rome and Jerusalem. Her account of her travels is one of the very few written down by female pilgrims.

Such was the fervour of her religious devotion that the sight of a shrine, or even the act of prayer itself, could set her off into fits of sobbing and shouting. On one occasion, she was banned from attending the sermons of a particular friar because of her noisy demonstrations of piety. Whilst returning from a pilgrimage to Jerusalem, she teamed up with a woman who carried with her a chest containing an image of Christ. Every time they entered a town along their route the women took out this statue and set it on the laps of respectable wives, who would kiss it and treat it with the utmost devotion. At the sight of such reverence, Margery inevitably burst into tears.

As Margery herself was well aware, her journeyings and her fame as a visionary earned her friends and enemies in equal measure. It is worth recording that, as well as her extravagant outbursts of religious feeling, Margery often gave away all her money as alms and visited the sick in the towns through which she passed. During her pilgrimage to Rome, she lived for six weeks in absolute squalor whilst nursing a sick old woman. She had no bed to sleep in and her cloak served as a blanket. She became infested with vermin and had to beg for food and drink for herself and her patient.

Some pilgrims were not above rowdiness whilst worshipping at a holy place. Visitors to Chichester fought to be the first to kneel before the shrine on St

Richard's Day and used their staffs to settle the argument. Bishop Storey was forced to issue strict regulations about visiting the shrine in 1487: no staves were allowed and only banners and crosses could be carried.

Groups of pilgrims often caused a considerable disturbance in the towns and villages through which they passed. In the early years of the 15th century, Archbishop Arundel of Canterbury was told by William Thorpe, an itinerant Lollard preacher:

> I know well that when divers men and women will go thus after their own wills, and finding out on pilgrimage, they will ordain with them before to have with them men and women that can well sing wanton songs and some other pilgrimages will have with them some bagpipes; so that every town they came through, what with the noise of their singing and the sound of their piping, and with the jangling of their Canterbury Bells, and with the barking out of dogs after them, that they make more noise than if the king came that way, with all his clarions and many other minstrels. And if these men and women be a month out in their pilgrimage, many of them shall be half a year after great janglers, tale-tellers and liars.

Sacred circuits and Creed Stones

In describing the difficulties of planning and completing a pilgrimage, it is easy to forget that not all such journeys were long and arduous. Some were very short and were made in a person's own locality; they usually lasted no more than a day or two, but nonetheless had a spiritual value.

There might be many reasons why it was impossible for a journey to be made to a distant shrine: illness, family or business commitments, a lack of time or money. It was therefore acceptable for someone to make a local pilgrimage, or round, as these sacred circuits were known. A number of holy places could be visited in a set order. These might consist of a string of chapels and wells, all contained within one parish, or the pilgrimage might be no more than a perambulation around a single churchyard. It was important that the pilgrim approached the task in a suitable frame of mind and that appropriate prayers and offerings were made at each stop.

The stopping places on the circuit might be marked with crosses. These were sometimes elaborately carved free-standing crosses of some size, although many were no more than cross-shaped incisions on a boulder. The pilgrim would place his or her finger in the incision and trace the shape of the cross over and over again whilst continuously repeating the Lord's Prayer. For this reason the stones came to be known as Creed Stones. Several of them existed along the pilgrim routes in Wales and were famous in themselves as holy places. Two of the best known were Cefn Bannog Maen Cred and St Beuno's Stone.

When eventually the habit of praying before these stones died out, the older generation of believers insisted that the nation was becoming irreligious because the incised crosses were slowly filling up with lichen.

Chapter 3

Hospices: shelter and care

I<small>T</small> was rare for travellers to have to sleep by the roadside during their journey, unless that was their choice. A network of inns, hospices and monasteries sprang up along the pilgrim roads of Europe because the church, from the earliest days of pilgrimage, had recognised the importance of providing organised accommodation for visitors to the holy shrines. In some places, clergymen were bound by the terms of their appointment to provide a resting place for the weary traveller, but the local monastery or abbey usually provided shelter.

Originally, the inspiration for this had been the idea of caritas, or Christian mercy, by which the faithful were expected to give succour to fellow believers in need. Bishops, in their pre-Norman vow of consecration, promised to care for and protect the sick, the needy and pilgrims. Even in the later medieval period, it was an ideal to which churchmen still aspired, as witness this extract from the statutes of St David's Cathedral, dated 12 May 1385:

> I (Bishop Adam Houghton) with the consent of the Chapter decree and ordain that all men and women, as well as my own as of any other diocese, who for the purpose of a devout pilgrimage shall come at any time of the year to my church or the City of St David's shall have free ingress without any impediment by me or any other person. And during the time of such pilgrimage, I take them into my special protection and especially enjoin all my officers peacefully to admit all pilgrims into my lordship and not permit them to suffer any molestation, damage or insult. And if they shall suffer any annoyance, satisfaction shall be made to them for it without delay under the blessing of God, St David and the Bishop.

The idea of caritas was especially important to the monastic orders. When in the 7th century, St Benedict drew up the set of rules which he believed should regulate monastic life, he specifically referred to the words of Christ which appear in St Matthew's Gospel (Chapter 25, verses 35, 36): 'I was a stranger and ye took me in . . . I was sick and ye visited me'. It was this philosophy which shaped not only the forms of hospitality on offer but the layout of the monasteries themselves.

In some of the larger religious houses there was permanent accommodation for the poor or a hospital for the sick, in addition to shelter for pilgrims. Free hospitality was usually given to travellers for two days and they were made welcome at the monastery's guesthouse, which stood in the outer courtyard. Wealthy pilgrims slept in the guest house itself, which was 'kept clean of spiders-webs and dirt and strewn with rushes under foot, (with) a sufficient quantity of straw in the beds; keys and locks to the doors and good bolts on the inside, so as to keep the doors securely locked while the guests are asleep'.

Poorer pilgrims were taken to the almonry, which was usually situated by the gatehouse. From this building old clothing and food were regularly handed out to the poor, with larger portions being reserved for pilgrims, palmers, chaplains, beggars and lepers. The accommodation offered to the poor in the almonry was spartan, often no more than a bed of rushes on a stone floor.

The care of the sick and elderly at a monastery was usually the responsibility of the infirmarer, whose domain, the farmery or infirmary, generally lay to the east of the cloister. In the houses of the Augustinian, or Black monks, this building often resembled in plan a church, with an aisled 'nave' and a 'chancel'. The 'nave' of the building was the hall, the beds of the sick being placed in the side aisles, and the 'chancel' was the farmery chapel. Here, aged and infirm monks were cared for and, since blood-letting was seen as a way of relieving stress and reducing the symptoms of a variety of illnesses, it was also here that the brethren were bled up to six times a year and were allowed to recuperate on a nourishing diet. The nursing role of these infirmaries was gradually extended to include not only the monks themselves, but the laybrothers, the abbey tenants and visitors. The abbey of Strata Florida, for example, which lay on the pilgrim road to St Davids from north Wales, came to care for lepers, as well as its own members.

The infirmarer headed a small team of nursing servants and gardeners, whose job it was to care for the sick and grow the medicinal plants that were required. A set of rules drawn up for the Augustinian priory of Barnwell in Cambridgeshire has survived and gives a clear idea of what was expected of an infirmarer.

He should, for instance, 'have the care of the sick, ought to be gentle, kind, compassionate to the sick and willing to gratify their needs with affectionate sympathy. It should rarely or never happen that he has not ginger, cinnamon, peony and the like, ready in his cupboard, so as to be able to render prompt assistance to the sick if stricken by a sudden malady.'

Similar instructions were laid down for those who did the actual nursing: they should 'endure without complaint the foulness of sick persons, whether in vomiting or in other matters; when they die he must . . . get their bodies ready for burial'.

The infirmary servants must also 'go to the town apothecary and get medicines and collect the garden herbs for decoctions, and under physician's orders, make tisanes'.

Adjacent to the monastery were the infirmary gardens, in which were grown a variety of medicinal plants and herbs, as well as vegetable supplies. A well-planned garden might be stocked with 'physic' plants such as kidney beans, savory, horsemint, cumin, lovage, fennel, tansy, lily, sage, rue, flag iris, fenugreek, mint and rosemary. Vegetables would include onions, garlic, leeks, shallots, celery, parsley, coriander, chervil, dill, lettuce, radishes, parsnips and carrots.[1]

---

[1] It is interesting to note that the recent excavations at Haverfordwest priory have revealed a number of formal garden beds, which may have been herb beds used for medicinal purposes. If so, the priory could have provided accommodation for pilgrims visiting the town. There was certainly a hospitium at the bottom of Merlin's Hill, the ruins of which were photographed at the beginning of the 20th century.

Another plant frequently grown was comfrey. It is believed to have been introduced into Britain by returning crusaders, who had learned of its medicinal properties from Eastern doctors. It was used as a salve on wounds, but its principal purpose was for bone-setting. The large hollow-crowned roots could be pounded up into a mush; the juice was used to wash out the wound, whilst the pulp was strained through a linen cloth and packed round the broken bone which had been placed in a wooden trough splint. Lettuce also had its medicinal use. The medieval variety, similar to today's cos lettuce, was ground up for its milky juice, which was dried into brown cakes and used as a narcotic for those about to undergo surgery. Monk's rhubarb also grew in monastery gardens, for use as a laxative, whilst calamint was brewed into a strong tea and served hot to those suffering from chest colds. A further monastic favourite was bistort of which both the leaves and roots were taken as an antidote to poison. The root also 'stayeth all manner of inward bleeding or spitting of blood and any fluxes in the body of either man or woman, or vomiting. It is also very available against ruptures or burstings, against all bruises or falls, dissolving the congealed blood and easeth the pains that happen thereupon; it also helpeth the jaundice.' In 1914, this plant was growing in abundance in the vicinity of the holy well at Penrhys, though it grew nowhere else in the locality; according to local legend it had been introduced by the monks.

In addition to the monastic houses, separate places of shelter were built for pilgrims, though many of them also catered for the elderly, the poor and the sick, especially lepers. Medical care of some sort was available at these places, which were known variously as hospitiums, hospices, hospitals or infirmaries. In Welsh the term was generally *ysbyty* (hospit-ty) and there are still many places in Wales called ysbyty, spite or spittal, where these buildings once stood.

Some of these hospices were daughter houses of local monasteries and were usually managed by one of the monks or by lay brothers. A surprisingly large number were founded by private individuals, often in the hope of earning remission of sins. In order to finance the running of the hospices, they were usually endowed by their founders with grants of either money or, more frequently, with lands which brought in annual rents or an income from the sale of produce. Because of their associations with the sick and those who suffered from leprosy, the hospitals were frequently built well beyond the town boundaries and away from any suburbs.

One of the greatest of the medieval founders in Wales was Bishop Bek of St Davids (1280–93); he is thought to have constructed pilgrim shelters at Llandrudion and Spittal, both in Pembrokeshire. He also established a hospital or priory at Whitewell, overlooking St David's Cathedral, to care for 'sick and infirm clergy and for hospitality towards others', and endowed it with property worth £5.

In 1287, he founded yet another hospital in which 'pilgrims, orphan paupers, infirm, old and feeble persons and imbecile strangers and wearied travellers may be entertained'. This stood at the western limits of the newly established borough of Llawhaden, near Haverfordwest. Dedicated to the Virgin, St Thomas the Martyr and Edward the Confessor, it is probably the same hospital as the one mentioned in a grant recorded in the Calendar of Welsh Rolls on 18 September 1291, when the bishop of St Davids and the master of the hospital of St Edward were given by the king 'for ever in common all the king's demesne woods in the county of Kardigan, so that they may fell and carry away underwood, oak for timber and other trees at their pleasure and make their advantage thereof as may seem most expedient to them'. It was endowed with lands at Cotlande, Kilvayne, as well as four and a half acres in Llawhaden itself.

The hospice flourished until the Reformation, though its history was not entirely scandal-free. In February 1406/07, its prior or warden, Richard Wythlokes, was 'not troubling to reside in his said priory, but at Tenby, openly keeping in his house one Gladusa Meuric, his concubine . . .' The two of them led a life which was dissolute and eventually Richard was instructed to cast out Gladusa, and never to admit her or 'any other woman' to his dwelling, or to accept the consequences.

Today, all that is left of the hospice at Llawhaden is the chapel, standing behind the village hall and adjacent to fields known as the Chapel field and Priory field. The buildings of these various hospices were often planned along similar lines. The ground floor was taken up with stabling for animals, whilst an outside staircase led up to a large first-floor dormitory, which could be divided up into smaller areas by movable wooden partitions. If there were no partitions, then the travellers would settle down to sleep around a raised hearth in the middle of the chamber. Plaited beds of straw or rushes were available, with raised rims to keep out the draughts. A small chapel, similar to the one at Llawhaden, was often attached to the main building, into which the pilgrims would crowd to give thanks for a safe arrival at

This building, said to be the chapel, is all that remains of the hospice at Llawhaden

the end of a day's journey, and to pray for similar blessing as they set off the next morning.

A grazing paddock and a smithy were usually adjacent to the hospice, which would also have had a large garden. There was probably also a bake house, a brew-house and a malt-house, all housed in a separate block, with stables, a barn and even a mill in the vicinity.

It is not possible to estimate the number of travellers who would have passed through these small establishments. The summer, with its promise of better weather, would have been the busiest season, but there were always people seeking accommodation. This could prove to be a problem: in 1338, so many Welsh pilgrims flocked to the shrine of St John of Jerusalem at Slebech in Pembrokeshire, that the preceptor of the hospital there complained bitterly of the demands they made upon his resources.

This is at first glance surprising: Slebech belonged to the Knights Hospitaller of St John of Jerusalem, one of the military orders set up to protect pilgrims. The Order was rich in lands and possessions and the commandery at Slebech had an annual income of £307 1s 10d, a considerable amount at that time.

Some of this income, £6 16s 4d, was used to pay the wages of the servants, for the commandery was one of the larger hospices in west Wales. It employed twenty-one people, who included an armiger (an esquire who was a skilled farrier and armourer), a chamberlain, a steward, a cook, a baker, a baker's boy, an overseer, a reaper, a porter, a gardener, a swineherd and his boy, and a cowherd.

It was the food bill that swallowed up most of the income. Eighty quarters of wheat at 4s a quarter were used annually for the baking of bread, whilst the brewing of beer accounted for a further 80 quarters of barley-malt at 2s a quarter, plus 120 quarters of oat-malt at 1s 6d a quarter. It has been estimated that, taken together, the barley-malt and the oat-malt would produce seventy gallons of beer a day. A further 80 quarters of oats were required to feed the horses of the preceptor and his guests.

In addition, the kitchen allowance for food amounted to 5s a week. In 1338 the stores of meat, game and fish consumed were valued at £13. Forty quarters of barley at 2s a quarter and fifteen quarters of beans and peas at 1s 4d a quarter were set aside for yearly distribution to the poor. This may not have been entirely an act of charity: a piece of ground on the opposite side of the river to Slebech was known as Beggar's Land and it is possible that beggar pilgrims were expected to work there in return for their food.[2]

---

[2] The commandery drew most of its supplies from the lands farmed on the opposite, southern side of the river. Over 360 acres of land were cultivated near Minwear, as well as most of the land on the south bank up to Canaston Bridge. The daily carriage of supplies across the tidal reaches of the river caused immense problems. During the 15th century it was suggested that parishioners should construct a causeway across the river to Slebech. The Hospitallers appealed to the Pope to allow alms to be collected to help with the work. Permission was granted in 1419 for a period of ten years. Anyone undergoing penance was exempted from their punishment if they contributed towards the project. There is no evidence that construction ever began.

A lack of resources, particularly monetary resources, was a difficulty faced by many hospices as the Middle Ages drew to a close. The Black Death, a slump in rents and other adverse economic conditions, were amongst the causes which prevented hospitals from operating effectively. The fate of two of these establishments may suffice as an example.

In 1332, Henry de Gower, Bishop of St Davids, founded the hospital of St David within the township of Swansea. He endowed it with lands he had inherited at Pennard, adding to the grant a collection of properties bought or acquired from other landlords in the area, including thirteen burgages or half-burgages within the town itself. The new foundation thus became one of the most important landlords in Swansea. The rents from these lands, 330 acres in all, were intended to support a warden and six priests to celebrate divine services, together with an unknown number of poor and infirm priests or laymen. It quickly became clear that such a large establishment could not be supported on income from the land grants alone, so the parish church of Swansea was added to its endowments.

In 1403, a petition was addressed to the Pope. This outlined the fact that, even with extra revenues appropriated from the parish churches of Llangiwg and Oystermouth, the hospital could no longer support itself in the manner envisaged by Bishop Gower. The six chaplains had been reduced to four. By 1546, after the Reformation, there were only two priests in service and only two of the four places available for poor people had been filled. The hospital's income stood at £40, half of which went to the warden as a stipend. This was a comfortable income by Tudor standards and seems to have ensured that a high number of churchmen held the office. Despite the fact that the wardenship had once been a residential post, it was now often held by absentees.

The same decline is evident in the history of the hospital of St John at Tenby. Built in the later half of the 13th century by William de Valence, Earl of Pembroke, to care for the poor and sick of the town, it seems by 1484 to have been failing in its traditional role. King Richard III granted the burgesses of Tenby the 'free disposition and rule' of both St John's and the nearby hospital of St Mary Magdalene. The revenues of both foundations, together with income from the hermitage of St Daniel's in Pembroke, were used to support the local almshouse.

Jasper Tudor, Earl of Pembroke, later restored the post of master of St John's, appointing his own nominee. The master in 1535 was the vicar, Robert Collins, who gave £4 of his revenues of £6 to four sick people. In 1546 the revenues stood at £9 3s 11d, most of which was Collins' stipend, £2 10s 0d being used to support one pauper.

During the reign of Queen Elizabeth I, the lands of both St John's hospital and St Mary Magdalene were leased by the crown to the Recorde family, though the borough of Tenby was subsequently awarded the custody and government of St Mary Magdalene's hospital and of the almshouse, together with their properties, the income from which was to be used for their upkeep.

Chapter 4

The Welsh pilgrim overseas

Jerusalem, Rome and Santiago de Compostela – Tair ffynnon gwynion ... i'r drugaredd – the three blessed fountains ... of mercy

Lewis Glyn Cothi, 15th-century

Jerusalem – the pioneers

She is situated in the centre of the world, in the middle of the earth, so that all men may turn their steps towards her.

Jean de Vitry, Bishop of Ptolemais. 13-century

JERUSALEM, Rome and Santiago de Compostela were considered to be the three great pilgrimages of Christendom and continued so down to the Reformation. A small but revealing detail in the records of the diocese of St Asaph indicates their importance in the eyes of the church: in 1433, Andrew Holles, Archdeacon of Anglesey, Canon of St Asaph and Papal Chamberlain was granted a faculty to hear confessions of his parishioners and to commute all their vows of pilgrimage except those of the Holy Land, Saints Peter and Paul (Rome) and St James of Compostela.

Jerusalem was the first place in Christendom to attract pilgrims in numbers both vast and continuing – the Holy City, where crucial events in the life of Jesus took place, in particular those leading up to his crucifixion, burial and resurrection. Here pilgrims could experience the most vivid re-enactment possible of these events by walking the Via Dolorosa, following the 14 stations of the Cross which marked out that last journey of Jesus. In the words of St Francis they would seek 'to enter into the mind and body of the crucified Christ and to take on Christ's sufferings in their own person'.

Pilgrimage to the Holy Land was pioneered by St Helena, mother of Emperor Constantine, who in her declining years had explored Jerusalem, AD 326–28, and discovered the cross on which Jesus was crucified. The 'True Cross' as it came to be called, was one of the most important relics of Christendom; portions of it were distributed among the churches and some found their way to Wales. Soon after this, in 333, the Bordeaux Itinerary, *Itinerarium Burdigalense*, was written, guiding pilgrims from the central French port of Bordeaux to the Holy Land. The Itinerary took an overland route to Jerusalem, well maintained by the Roman Imperial post, paved with smooth slabs to a width of 20 feet with convenient inns and staging posts. In the early 5th century, Egeria, a Galician nun, left a vivid account of her extensive pilgrimage in the Holy Land culminating in a celebration of Easter in

Jerusalem. From the 5th century, bands of Irish monks (*peregrini*) embarked on pilgrim wanderings across the continent, founding monasteries as they went. The pilgrimages to Rome and Jerusalem were well-worn paths by the time the Welsh saints David, Teilo and Padarn made their acclaimed pilgrimage thither at some time in the 6th century, described by St David's biographer Rhygyfarch, *c.* 1080. The patriarch at Jerusalem bestowed gifts of a bell, staff, altar and a golden tunic on the saints – these later became revered relics – and consecrated David archbishop. During the 10th century there was a substantial increase in pilgrimages to the Holy Land as a result of the widely held belief that the second coming of Christ was due a thousand years after his death, resulting in anxiety for many over the salvation of their souls. Travellers in the Mediterranean faced appalling conditions. It was not unknown for 500 to be jammed below deck on boats only 100 feet long, though in the later Middle Ages a highly competitive service developed from Venice.

The crusaders

> *The Scotchman and the Welshman left their hunting, the Dane his drinking bout and the Norwegian his raw flesh.*
>
> William of Malmesbury, 11–12th century

The crusades were pilgrimages and regarded as such by contemporaries, but pilgrimages with a difference and under arms. The first crusade was initiated by Pope Urban when in 1095, he called for the delivery of Jerusalem and specifically the Christian Holy Places from Muslim control. These 'holy wars' continued spasmodically until 1270, resulting in much bloodshed and brutality and ultimately failing in their endeavour although access to the holy places was secured for Christian pilgrims. To crusaders, the Pope offered not only a plenary indulgence, substituting danger and effort for normal ecclesiastical penance, but also legal protection by the church of property, lands and person. Welshmen were evidently involved: the *Brut* recorded that in 1143, 'some pilgrims from Wales were drowned on the sea of Greece, in going with the Cross to Jerusalem' '*Y vlwydyn honno y bodes (o Gymry) pererinyon ar vor Groec yn mynet achroes y Gaerussalem*'. In 1145 the *Brut Gwent* recorded that so many Welsh pilgrims went from Wales to Jerusalem that their absence was severely felt: '...*niferoedd mawrion o'r Cymry ym ymhererindawd i Gaer y Salem oni weled diffyg yn fawr o hebddynt.*' Documentary evidence indicates Welsh involvement up to the end of the crusades.

The sign Pope Urban gave to identify a crusader was a cross of cloth, blessed and attached to the right shoulder. In 1188, when Gerald of Wales and Archbishop Baldwin travelled the length and breadth of Wales preaching the third crusade, Gerald recorded this practice in Cardigan. The two churchmen preached sermons designed to whip up zeal and to heighten the emotional and spiritual pressure to join the crusade. Throughout Wales, about 3,000 men of military age were 'signed with the cross', which placed them under an irrevocable vow, enforced by a penalty of excommunication. Those too old to enlist gave money. Among the notables who took the Cross were Gerald, Bishop Peter de Leia of St Davids and Bishop Gwion of Bangor, to the dismay of his flock. Archbishop Baldwin, not a young man when he journeyed around Wales, perished in the Holy Land in 1191 and Bishop Gwion died in the same year, but where is not recorded. However, Gerald and Bishop Peter sought and achieved absolution from this vow as also did 'other Welshmen', on the death of Henry II at whose instigation they had taken the Cross, on condition that 'they should make contribution to those going to Jerusalem out of the possessions that God has given them and should bestow their labour and their aid upon the repair of the Church of Mynyw'. Another Welsh bishop, Anian of St Asaph, was confessor to Prince Edward, later Edward I, in the Holy Land after a particularly brutal massacre at the capture of Nazareth.

One of the recorded miracles of St David concerned a Welshman 'from the episcopal see of Menevia captured by Saracens and held with iron chains to labour along with a German'. The Welshman called repeatedly the words '*Dewi wared*' and shortly after this appeal effected a successful escape. The German to whom he had been bound, was suspected of complicity and scourged and decided to try the strange words for himself. He too was mysteriously released and transported home. He decided to find out their meaning and travelled to Paris where he found Welsh clergy who translated them: *Dewi wared*, 'David deliver (me)' and told him of the widespread fame of St David. As a result of this the German went on pilgrimage to St Davids arriving at Pentecost where Bishop Iorwerth (1215–29) was celebrating the feast with the clergy and a great crowd of people. The Welshman's miraculous escape had already been marvelled at and when he recognised his co-prisoner they greeted each other with embraces and tears. 'The bishop rejoiced, the clergy were happy, the people applauded . . . and praised the miracles of God'.

Although pilgrimage to the Holy Land continued throughout the Middle Ages – expense, wars, plague, the problems of a long absence from home – all the considerable risks of foreign travel caused it to decline. The rising star was Italy, the 'spoilt child of Europe', with so much in its favour: relative accessibility, equable climate, treasures of antiquity and the eternal city, Rome, Threshold of the Apostles.

Rome

> *Of all pilgrimages (the Welsh) prefer going to Rome and they pray there most devoutly when they reach St Peter's.*
>
> Giraldus Cambrensis, 12th–13th century

The medieval 'Lives' of the Welsh saints emphasised their pilgrimages to Rome. On their way to Jerusalem the 'Three Blessed Visitors of the Isle of Britain', Dewi, Padarn and Teilo, were said to have visited Rome and such was Teilo's sanctity that the bells of Rome rang out of their own accord at his approach. St Cadog was buried in Italy and his followers erected a basilica or church over his body, which no Briton (Welsh) was allowed to enter lest his relics be stolen. Saints Cybi,

Misericord, St Davids Cathedral, said to portray St Govan being seasick on his return journey
from Rome

Cawrdaf and Brynach made pilgrimages to Rome. St Govan nearly died of
seasickness on his return journey. The 7th-century *Life of St Samson* told of Irish
pilgrims landing on Caldey when returning from Rome. Another band of Irish
pilgrims passed through St Davids on their return journey and it was reported in a
15th-century collection of miracles of St David, that they managed to carry away
with them a large statue of the saint, which miraculously returned to its chapel of
its own accord. King and lawgiver Hywel Dda made a pilgrimage in 928. Gerald of
Wales journeyed to Rome on four occasions, sometimes travelling with bands of
pilgrims and experiencing many dangers. On his fourth and final journey, between
Epiphany and Lent, he went 'solely by way of pilgrimage and devotion', staying at
the English College or the Hospital of the Holy Spirit as it was also known,
established by Pope Innocent III. William of Malmesbury recorded Welshmen
leaving relics behind at Glastonbury on their way to Rome, perhaps as propitiatory
offerings for the journey.

The way there was long and hard and families left behind suffered acute and
endless anxiety, a fact lamented by several Welsh poets. But continental travel,
despite the vicissitudes of war, plague and highway robbery had never deterred the
pilgrim. The sturdy Roman highways were still in use and the later roads were
trade routes traversing the continent from as far afield as Iceland and Scandinavia.
A number of medieval itineraries survive including a comprehensive one through
France by Matthew Paris in the 13th century on which he represents the Alps as a
swirling mass. A century earlier Giraldus Cambrensis described them as 'steep and

sheer mountains, so dreadful and perilous, no less on account of their snows than by reason of the robbers that haunt them'. The Alpine passes were equally challenging and although there were many hospices along the way, pilgrims could be snowed in for days. There is no evidence that the St Gotthard Pass was used before the 13th century but it was open when Adam of Usk made his way to Rome in 1402 and he described his horrible experience of crossing the pass. He was drawn in an ox-wagon along giddy heights 'half dead with cold' and with his eyes blindfold lest he should see its dangers. When he reached Rome, the city was experiencing a period of decline: Adam remembered wolves howling at night outside his house and fallen buildings blocking the narrow streets.

The attractions of Rome were boundless and numerous indulgences were on offer, especially in a Jubilee year. After the sack of Constantinople, Rome was the privileged possessor of an unrivalled collection of relics. Apostles Peter and Paul were buried there and their heads preserved. John Capgrave described them: St Peter's was 'brood . . . with much hair on his berd and that is of grey colour betwixt white and black. The hed of Paule is a longe face, balled with red hair both berd and hed.' The three wells which rose in the places where St Paul's head rebounded at his execution were popular with Welsh pilgrims and mention is made of them by Dafydd ap Gwilym, Lewis Glyn Cothi, Lewys Morgannwg and Lewis Trefnant and other poets. Famous too was the Vernicle or *Sudarium*, the napkin with which St Veronica wiped the face of Christ on his way to Calvary and which thereafter bore the imprint of his features. It was described in 1471 by Francesco Ariosto as a thin, fragile, almost transparent veil of silk, bearing the features of a bearded man. All these and more were celebrated in medieval Welsh poetry. Rome drew enormous crowds of pilgrims who made their way through the narrow streets and over the bottlenecks of bridges, often far more than the city could control or support resulting in frequent disasters causing injury and death to many a pilgrim.

Evidence of Welsh pilgrimage has been collected from entries in the guestmaster's register of the English College in Rome in the pre-Reformation period from 1471 to 1514; the entries for this period are incomplete and often hastily written. Post-Reformation pilgrim entries date from 1584 to 1738. Welsh pilgrims, or those with a Welsh connection have been extracted from a much greater total. Before the Reformation Easter appears to be the most popular festival: 41 poor people, *in forma pauperum*, five of whom were women, from the dioceses of Llandaf, Menevia and St Asaph, with Bangor particularly well represented, accompanied by three priests, were signed into the college between 22 March and 1 April in 1507, when Easter Day fell on 4 April. Numbers indicate that Pentecost was the next most popular festival; however, a decline sets in after the Reformation and no real pattern of pilgrimage is evident. How they travelled is not recorded. Pilgrims came from Montgomery, Pembroke, Oswestry, Knighton, Wrexham, Caernarfon, Holyhead, Bardsey, Denbigh, Crickhowell, Cardiff, Glamorgan, Brecon and Carmarthen. A number were sick and some were looked after for a considerable time, such as Richardus Hugon of Carmarthen who was there for 28 days on account of infirmity.

Santiago de Compostela, the Field of Stars

In the Middle Ages the tomb of St James the Great, brother of St John, like those of Saints Peter and Paul, was believed to be in Europe – in Galicia in north-west Spain. As told in the Middle Ages, St James was sent to Spain by the Virgin Mary after the ascension of Jesus into heaven. He made a brief and unsuccessful attempt to evangelise the country and a vision on the plain of Saragossa led him to build a church there which was the beginning of the Santiago legend. In AD 44, James was beheaded by Herod Agrippa, becoming the first apostle martyr. His disciples returned his body to Spain by sea, landing at El Padron, the nearest port today to Santiago. After a series of adventures the saint's body was buried and over the centuries, the grave was lost and the site forgotten, to be re-discovered early in the 9th century.

The legend which gave the place its name emerged from this period. A hermit was granted a vision of a field of stars, *campus stella[rum]* pointing the way to the long-lost tomb of St James, hence its name Santiago de Compostela, St James of the Field of Stars. From then on it joined the ranks of Rome and Jerusalem, becoming the third great pilgrimage of Christendom. In a tract on miracles performed in Santiago, Pope Calixtus II counselled the English that two pilgrimages to Santiago equalled one to Rome. The fame of the shrine was linked to Charlemagne in *Ystorya de Carolo Magno*, part of which was written by a monk of Santiago, about 1050. Within a hundred years it had been translated into Welsh, probably at Llanbadarn Fawr or Strata Florida, an illustration of how Wales was part of a much wider European scene of both faith and literature.

In the art and sculpture of the Middle Ages, St James is represented as the patron saint of pilgrims and is always dressed as one, distinguishing him from the other apostles. He was first depicted thus in Spain, carrying a staff which he once gave to a magician, Hermogenes, to protect him from devils, so legend goes. He wore a scrip or large purse with a strap across the shoulder, usually adorned by scallop shells. Later in the 13th century he was depicted wearing a hat.

The scallop shell is the emblem of St James, the pilgrim badge of Santiago and eventually the symbol of pilgrimage. Much of the lore and legend of the saint comes from a pilgrim guide written by Amery Picaud about 1130. St James is said to have come ashore in a scallop shell, and to have saved a rider and his horse from drowning; the pair emerged from the sea covered in scallops. Pilgrims used the shells as a scoop for water and a plate for food, signifying poverty and

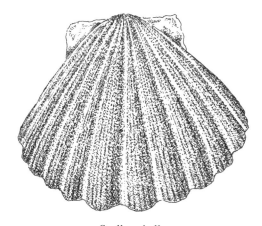

Scallop shell

renunciation of worldly things. Most powerfully evocative is the Christian symbolism: the two valves of the shell represent the two Great Commandments, 'Thou shalt love the Lord thy God with all thy heart, with all thy soul and with all thy strength and thy neighbour as thyself', and the ridges represent the fingers with which we do good works.

The shell was used as a motif on pilgrim badges, lead ampullae were modelled on it and it is sometimes found in heraldry. At the close of the 16th century it appeared in two insignia on the roof of the Lady Chapel in St Davids, of the families of Wogan, and Bateman impaling Maenyrch Goch, Lord of Brycheiniog: these no longer exist. Scallop shells can be found in a boss in St Mary's church, Tenby which must have witnessed many pilgrim departures. Scallop-shaped ampullae have been found by metal detectorists in the coastal areas of Pembrokeshire. The 14th-century relief carving of St James in the reredos of Holy Trinity chapel in St Davids Cathedral, shows him with a hat, scrip, staff and book. There is a late 15th-century carving of him on the font of Gresford church and an early 16th-century statue on the tower of St Giles's church, Wrexham.

G. Hartwell Jones has collected numerous bardic references to Santiago from Welsh sources and a (rare) written record survives of three Welsh pilgrims, Gruffydd ab Ieuan, Dafydd ab Ieuan and Gwilym ab Iorwerth leaving Welshpool for Santiago on the Monday following the feast of St Augustine, 26 May, in 1362, first taking leave of their neighbours in the church of La Pole. The old Welsh name for the Milky Way, more brilliant in days before light pollution of roads, towns and cities, was Hynt Sant Ialm, St James's Way. A long way from Galicia a distant echo can be found in east Carmarthenshire near the village of Llanwrda: Rhiw/Lôn Cwmpastel (Compostela hill). It lies just off a Roman road and due south are the ports of the south Wales coast. Was this a pointer for the medieval pilgrim towards an embarkation point for the Field of Stars?

Chapter 5

The Knights of God,
the military orders, piety and protection

For pilgrims travelling to Jerusalem in the 11th and early 12th centuries the journey was perilous. The overland route through what were later to become the Balkans, Greece and Turkey, was arduous in the extreme and there was the likelihood of attack by bandits. The ocean voyage across the Mediterranean from Italy was no easier, with the ever-present threat of interception by pirates. The last leg of the journey, by land from Antioch to Jerusalem or from the seaports to the west of the Holy City, was recognised as the most dangerous. Many pilgrims were robbed or murdered on the way or were captured and sold off into captivity. Once Jerusalem had fallen to the crusaders and the Latin kingdom of Jerusalem had been established, it was inevitable that protection should be given to the increasing numbers of pilgrims who were arriving from Europe.

The Knights Hospitaller

One of the first hospices in Jerusalem had been built by Emperor Charlemagne during the early 9th century, but it had been destroyed in 1010. Thirteen years later, a group of traders from Amalfi were given permission by the caliph of Egypt, in whose territories the city lay, to build another hospice. This was dedicated to St John the Baptist. The most famous of all the hospitals, however, and the one which was to result in the foundation of the Order of the Knights Hospitaller, was established in about 1080. In that year the Benedictine abbey of St Mary of the Latins created a hospital on the southern edges of the compound of the Holy Sepulchre in Jerusalem. The abbey was the only Catholic church in the city at that time and its monks and lay brothers formed the staff of the hospital. So successful was the new foundation that by 1113, fourteen years after the capture of the city by the crusaders, it had become independent of the abbey.

The most important rule of the hospital was commitment to the service of the 'holy poor'. These included not only Christian pilgrims, but also Muslims and Jews who were taken ill in the city. The servants of the hospital frequently searched the streets to find those who were unable to reach the building themselves. The sick were accommodated in eleven wards, which could house a total of some 2,000 patients, each in a separate bed. The food served to the sick included white bread, rye bread, corn cakes, pork, lamb, chicken, eggs and fish, though shrimps, moray eels, beans and lentils were considered inadvisable. The immense running costs of the establishment were met by the church through donations and gifts of land.

By the 1160s, the Hospitallers had developed a military wing. This may have begun through the employment of armed mercenaries to protect pilgrims arriving in the Holy Land. It is also possible that a number of knights who were anxious to take up arms for their faith had voluntarily attached themselves to the hospital. Whatever the reason, these soldiers were incorporated into the Order to form a class of brothers at arms.[1]

Though the Hospitallers never introduced a military element into the oaths they took upon joining, vows of poverty, chastity and obedience were imposed upon them and they became known as the Brethren of the Hospital of St John the Baptist of Jerusalem.

Pope Calixtus II later added to their vows an extra one concerning 'The Knightly Defence of the Christian Religion'. The brethren were also expected to receive the sacrament thrice a year, were to hear mass once a day and were banned from trading, duelling and from taking sides in quarrels which might arise between the kings of Europe. The Order was re-christened the Knights of the Hospital of St John the Baptist of Jerusalem, and its members were otherwise known as the Knights Hospitaller or the Johannists. This improvement in status encouraged new entrants from the nobility in many parts of Europe.

The Hospitallers were divided into three classes. The first consisted of knights who were to protect pilgrims and defend the faith, the second was made up of chaplains and priests, whilst the third included those who made up the militia of the Order, including light cavalry, or turcopoles. Members had to be at least eighteen years of age, of able body, of pure Christian descent and of legitimate

The Knights Hospitaller observed the rules of the Benedictine and Augustinian orders and, like the monks, wore mantles of black

birth, though the illegitimate sons of kings and princes were acceptable. In time, the members of the Order became recognisable by their clothing, a red tunic with a white, eight-pointed cross.

The new Order was not viewed favourably by all Christians. The patriarch of Jerusalem had complained that 'at the very door of the Holy Resurrection' the

---

[1] There were also sisters of the Order. These were ladies of rank, including many widows, who had vowed to take care of the sick. An establishment of these sisters existed at Buckland in Somerset.

Hospitallers were constructing buildings 'which were more costly and lofty' than the church itself. He was equally displeased in 1153, when the sound of the bells from the hospital drowned out the sermon he was trying to preach in the chapel on the Hill of Calvary. On another occasion a group of knights entered the Calvary chapel and proceeded to use it as an archery range. Bundles of arrows were left to hang in the building as a reminder of the episode.

The steady increase in men and resources enabled the Knights Hospitaller to extend the range of their activities. Hospices known as commanderies were established in many of the maritime towns of Europe, where travellers could find rest and accommodation before embarking on the sea voyage to the Holy Land. This network of hospitals, depots and gifted estates was extended to many inland areas, so that it was possible for a traveller to move across vast tracts of Western Christendom without leaving the protection of the Hospitallers. It was said that in Europe alone, the Order possessed over 20,000 manors.

The Order owned extensive acres in Wales, the majority of which were gifts from the Norman lords, though after the crusading appeal of Gerald of Wales and Archbishop Baldwin in 1188, the Lord Rhys of Deheubarth also gifted certain lands in Ceredigion. These varied territories were mostly to be found in south Wales, particularly in the Gower and in Pembrokeshire and in Herefordshire and Shropshire. There were few Hospitaller properties in the Brecon and Abergavenny areas or in central Wales.

The Welsh estates were grouped into blocks known as commanderies, which roughly followed the existing diocesan boundaries. One of the first to be established was at Slebech, about eight miles east of Haverfordwest, on land donated by Wizo the Fleming, Lord of Wiston. A still-extant charter of Bishop Peter de Leia of St Davids gives details of the Order's estates that were attached to Slebech at the end of the 12th century. There were about ninety in all, situated within the present-day counties of Carmarthenshire, Ceredigion and Pembrokeshire and they included manors, churches, chapels, burgage strips in a number of towns, as well as mills and farmland.[2] A considerable revenue was generated through cattle, crops, rents, market and fair tolls, dovecotes, fisheries, woodlands and the profits of courts and the incomes of churches.[3] Much of this money was used for the upkeep of the commandery at Slebech.

Centres were also established at Mochrader and Dolwyddelan, whilst the hospice at Yspytty Ifan in Denbighshire became famous for its size, hospitality and

---

[2] A complete list of all the properties would be tedious, but as a partial example, in Pembrokeshire alone the Order held the churches of Ambleston, Boulston, Clarbeston, Cuffern, Letterston, Llanfyrnach, Martletwy, Minwear, Prendergast, Redberth, Rosemarket, Rudbaxton, Uzmaston and Wiston; in Ceredigion, the churches of Llansantffraid and Ystrad Meurig amongst others; in Carmarthenshire, the churches of Cilmaenllwyd and Llansteffan; on the Gower, the churches of Loughor, Port Eynon, Llanrhidian, Llandimore and Rhossili, whilst Breconshire churches included Llanfeigan, Llanfihangel nant Melyn, Ilston and Penmaen.

[3] The annual rent collected by Slebech from its tenants amounted during the 14th century to £33, a considerable sum at the time, indicating a large number of tenants.

charity.[4] Halston in Shropshire, close to the Welsh border, was the headquarters of the preceptory of Llanwddyn, on the shores of Lake Fyrnwy, with lands near Ellesmere and at Carno. The church at Carno was dedicated to St John, as were many of the churches associated with the Hospitallers. The Knights of Halston quickly became involved with the suppression of banditry, as pilgrims travelling from Strata Marcella to Pennant Melangell, Clynnog or Bardsey had been frequently robbed by outlaws.

The preceptories of the Order claimed for all their buildings the right of sanctuary and, for certain of their lands, immunity from legal invasion or encroachment. Various royal charters or papal bulls were cited in support of these claims and the places concerned were clearly named to reflect their function. At Amroth in Pembrokeshire, a tract of ground was called the Sanctuary, whilst buildings at Loughor, and at Penrice on the Gower, were similarly named.[5]

In addition to its rights of sanctuary, the Order also had free court of jurisdiction over its tenants, except in case of life or death. When one of the Hospitallers' tenants died, a specified share of the dead person's goods was forfeit to the Order. Most of its revenues came from land ownership or from gifts donated to it, but money was also raised through *confraria*, annual sums of money loaned out and recoverable by the seizure of a debtor's goods. The Hospitallers also had the privilege of 'free chase' on all crown lands in Wales.

With its vast wealth, its ownership of manors all over Europe and of castles in the Holy Land, its independence of diocesan jurisdiction and organisation and its great military strength, the Order became a powerful force within Christendom. Of all the military orders, only the Knights Templar equalled and surpassed it and the quarrels between the two are said to have been one of the factors leading to the downfall of the Latin kingdom of Jerusalem.

The Knights Templar

In the early years of the 12th century Hugh de Payans, a knight from Champagne in France, together with eight other knights of like mind, approached the patriarch of Jerusalem and begged to be allowed to dedicate their lives to the service of the Holy Land. They would do this by patrolling the roads leading to Jerusalem, by fighting the enemies of their religion and by protecting pilgrims. To prove their

---

[4] The function of the Hospitaller properties in Britain seems to have differed from that of the hospices on the pilgrim roads to the Holy Land. It has been suggested that the Eastern establishments were concerned with the welfare of pilgrims and the care of the sick, whilst the English and Welsh hospices were in the main involved with the provision of hospitality to travellers, including pilgrims. Each house would have contained a sick ward, but was primarily a hospice giving shelter, not a hospital.

[5] The original grant of William Herizon to the Hospitallers of land at Amroth mentions 50 acres of sanctuary land. Like all ground set aside by the Order as sanctuary, crosses would have been erected on the boundaries to indicate the purpose of the area. It was said that lights were always kept burning in the Order's churches for the same reason.

determination, they were prepared to take the same vows of poverty, chastity and obedience that governed the monastic orders. A base for their operations was needed, as well as some form of financial support. King Baldwin II of Jerusalem gave them rooms in the royal palace, the Templum Solomonis, the present-day Mosque of Al-Aqsa. The building was believed to stand on the site of the Temple of Solomon and from this the group took its name – *the Pauperes Commilitones Christi Templique Salomonis*, or the Poor Fellow Soldiers of Christ and the Temple of Solomon.

King Baldwin wrote to St Bernard of Clairvaux, who was a cousin of Hugh de Payens and a nephew of Andre de Montbard, another of the founding Templars, asking him to intercede with the Pope so that a formal rule might be drawn up by which the new Order could be governed. Accordingly, at a special meeting convened in 1128 at Troyes, the rule was formally promulgated.

The Knights Templar were divided into three classes. These consisted of knights, who had to be drawn from the knightly class and who wore white habits emblazoned with a red cross; the sergeants or mounted men-at-arms, who came from the bourgeoisie and who dressed in black or brown; and the Templar priests, who acted as chaplains. Because they were literate, the chaplains acted as clerks, keeping records and carrying out correspondence. They were awarded special privileges: the best robes were given to them and they were allowed to wear leather gloves. They could hear confessions and absolve their fellow knights of their sins, though there were five faults which could not be absolved. These were the killing of a Christian man or woman, an attack upon another brother, an attack upon a priest or a member of another order, the renunciation of

The Knights Templar were granted permission by the Pope to wear a white hooded robe similar to that worn by the Cistercian order of monks

the priesthood to become a Knight Templar and entering the Order through simony.

In addition to their vows of poverty, chastity and obedience, the Templars were regulated in their daily conduct by a complex series of rules that developed over the years. They were, for instance, allowed to eat meat three times a week, although fast-days were to be regularly observed throughout the year, and there were to be frequent times for prayer and meditation. No knight on watch duty would be called to prayer.

Married men were accepted into the Order on condition that they left a part of their estate to the Templars after death, though the remainder of their possessions should be reserved to support a widow during her lifetime. Married knights could not wear the Order's white habit. Contact with women was otherwise shunned. An unmarried knight could not embrace his mother, sister or aunt and was not to be alone in female company, 'for the company of women is a dangerous thing for by it the old devil has led many from the straight path to Paradise'.

The Templars' military role was not forgotten. They were trained to move quickly and to follow orders without question. They were expected to fight together, even on horseback. Surrender was not to be considered: a Templar must fight on until death and was never to retreat unless ordered to do so by his superior. The order to retreat should only be given if the odds were three to one against the Templar. If, by chance, a knight was taken prisoner by the enemy, no ransom was to be paid.

Underlining the fact that the Templars existed to serve God, the Order's motto was '*Non nobis Domine, non nobis, sed nomine tuo da gloriam*; Not unto us, Lord, not unto us, but to thy name give glory.'

The Grand Master of the Order had total control over the Templars. His was the sole decision-making power and he alone could alter or even overturn the governing rules. During the reign of Pope Innocent II (1130–43), a papal bull was issued which granted even more than this. No authority on earth, secular or temporal, was to have any authority whatsoever over the Order, except the papacy itself. This meant that the Templars were not subject to the rule of any king, archbishop or bishop, nor could anyone demand a change in their governing rules. No Templar could be asked to swear an oath and though the Order could collect tithes, it was exempt from paying them. This exemption caused so much resentment that it was later applied only to lands cultivated by the Templars themselves.

From the very inception of the Order, the Templars seem to have enjoyed a high reputation. Knights flocked to join it from all over Europe. The dedication to the service of Christ and the life of chastity and prayer was regarded as atonement for all misdeeds. St Bernard encouraged rapists, murderers, excommunicants and adulterers to enlist, so sure was he of the redemption of their sins. The penance imposed upon the murderers of Thomas Becket was to serve for fourteen years in the Holy Land with the Knights Templar. Poverty was no bar: Templars were allowed no personal property and newcomers were each given three horses, clothing, weapons, bedding and eating utensils.

Gifts of land and money flowed into the Order. Preceptories were set up across Christendom: these were gifted estates or manors that, through their revenues, supported the work of the Order. The men in charge were expected to extract the maximum amount of money from the land. After deductions for expenses, the remaining amounts were sent on to Jerusalem for the purchase of armaments and other necessities.

Amongst the knights of many nationalities who joined the Order were a number from Wales, including William Marshall, Earl of Pembroke and Regent for the youthful King Henry III; William was received into the Order shortly before his death. Other Welsh Templars included several members of the Wogan family from Pembrokeshire.

The Templars' lands in Wales included many estates in Pembrokeshire[6] and at Rhuddlan, as well as in Monmouthshire,[7] Glamorgan and the Gower. Their main preceptory was at Garway, on the borders of Herefordshire and Wales. On the closure of the Order in the 14th century, Garway became the property of the Knights Hospitaller, together with many of the Templars' other lands.

The Templars developed a network of bases across Europe, linked by pilgrim roads. Large camps were constructed near many of the maritime towns used as points of embarkation, at which pilgrims were collected, housed and fed before being shipped on to their destinations. To transport pilgrims and supplies, the Templars bought or built their own ships. They dealt in commodities such as sugar and cotton, which were kept in heavily guarded warehouses. The Order also stored other people's treasures and offered a range of loans and other financial services. To avoid falling foul of church laws against usury, the Templars ensured that their record of loans never mentioned interest rates. They were also used by the kings of Europe to collect or disperse tax revenues or to act as ambassadors. King Henry II of England, for example, as a penance for his involvement in the murder of Thomas Becket, began transferring large sums of money to the Holy Land for the Templars to guard. In 1187, the Master of the Order was using the money to hire mercenaries, who were to fight the Saracens under the English king's banner.

Other military orders

The Hospitallers and the Knights Templar were not alone in their desire to defend the Holy Land. As early as 1142, there was in existence a group known as the Knights of St Lazarus. As their name suggests, they included not only healthy knights, but also those suffering from leprosy. They may have had links with the famous hospital of St Lazarus, which was situated outside the Damascus Gate of

---

[6] The presence of the Templars in Pembrokeshire is also recalled by a number of places in the county named Temple Bar. One such existed between Saundersfoot and Jeffreston and there were others near Nevern and at Amroth, where, even in the 20th century, a piece of land and an inn bore the name. The little-known Red Castle, Castell Coch, now an impressive ruin in woodland near Canaston Bridge, has also been associated with the Order. Imble Close and Lane between Pembroke and Pembroke Dock may originally have been named Timble or Thimble, a corruption of Temple, though other origins for the name have also been suggested.

[7] The church at Kemeys, north of Usk, with 120 acres of attached land, may have been a gift to the Templars by William Marshall, Earl of Pembroke (1147–1219). It is interesting to note that, upon the fall of the Templars, Aymer de Valence, Earl of Pembroke (1307–24), took possession of the Order's chief house in London, together with the adjoining church and outbuildings. He may also have taken over some of the Templars' more remote Welsh estates, to which some Templars are thought to have fled following the closure of the Order. Is it possible that de Valence, at the same time as he enlarged his estates, also protected some of the refugees?

Jerusalem. There is no evidence that the knights played a military role in the defence of the Holy Land before 1244, but their contribution must have been considerable. In 1153, the Pope approved a change in their statutes allowing healthy members to succeed as grand master. Far too many of the lepers were being killed in battle against the Saracens.

The Knights of St Lazarus never enjoyed the independence accorded to the Templars. They seem to have been under the control of their diocesan bishops and, perhaps because of the stigma then attached to leprosy, their numbers never approached those of the better-known orders.

Another well-respected Order was that of the Knights of the Holy Sepulchre. This had been functioning as a secular confraternity since the first half of the 12th century, and was confirmed as a military order by Pope Innocent III (1198-1216). Its privileges included the right to marry, exemption from taxation and the right to cut down and bury the bodies of executed criminals. The core of the Order was resident in Jerusalem and one of its principal duties was the guardianship of the Holy Sepulchre, a magnificent church built in AD 335 by the Emperor Constantine on the alleged site of the tomb of Christ. Members were also expected to attend daily mass, recite the Hours of the Cross and to ensure the redemption of Christians from captivity amongst the Saracens, as well as caring for and protecting pilgrims. They were recognised by their white habit, embroidered with the Jerusalem Cross. This was a red-cross potent, with similar but smaller crosses in each of the four angles, the whole representing the five wounds of Christ.

The ceremony of admittance to the Order traditionally took place during the hour before midnight in the innermost chamber of the Holy Sepulchre and was sometimes witnessed by pilgrims visiting the shrine. At least two written descriptions of it have survived, one by Felix Fabri, who was there in 1483, and another by Roberto da Sanseverino, who had made a pilgrimage to the Holy Land some thirty years earlier. Two of Roberto's fellow travellers were admitted to the Order by the Father Guardian of the Mount Syon monastery, who had the authority to accept those whose nobility of birth and military skills made eligible. The knighthood was customarily conferred by another noble, in this case by John Tiptoft, Earl of Worcester, who was himself on a pilgrimage to Jerusalem.

After prayers and hymns, the candidates took the necessary oaths, promising to hear the daily mass, to risk their lives in defence of their faith, to abhor injustice, usury and homicide and to defend the unity of the church. They also took an oath to keep peace between Christian people, to defend widows and children and to lead a pure and Christian life. They were given the golden spurs that were part of their insignia, after which they received the kiss of peace from the Guardian.

Felix Fabri mentions that, during the ceremony that he witnessed, the knight knelt with his arms and breast resting on top of the tomb itself. He received a threefold accolade in the name of the Trinity and was raised with the words, 'May it be for thy good.'

The Order seems to have attracted many members from amongst aristocratic Welsh families. Of the forty-eight names of members of the Order known from inscriptions, manuscripts and bardic compositions, thirty-five are Welsh or of Welsh provenance. In the closing years of the 14th century Sir William Stradling, his son Edward and another relative went on pilgrimage to Jerusalem, where all three were received in to the Order. A scion of Pembrokeshire's Perrot family was also a member, along with Sir Elidir Ddu of Carmarthenshire, ancestor of Sir Rhys ap Thomas. It is recorded that amongst the soldiers of Emperor John of Constantinople was another Welsh Knight of the Holy Sepulchre, Sir Hugh Johnys of Landymore Castle in the Gower.

One of the better-known military orders was the Teutonic Knights, which more properly was known as the Order of the House of St Mary of the Germans in Jerusalem. This had been founded as a hospital community near Acre in 1190 by citizens of Lubeck and Bremen. By 1196 the community was living under religious rules and was famous for its care of the sick; its duties soon included military action. The knights were all drawn from German families and were easily identifiable by their white tunics emblazoned with black crosses.

The fall of Jerusalem and the end of the military orders

Almost from the moment of their inception, there had been criticism of the military orders. There were many people who felt that it was impossible to combine the role of a monk following a monastic rule with that of a warrior trained to kill. One of the most vociferous critics of the Templars was an Englishman, Walter Map, who was horrified by their ferocity in battle. Such scruples met with little general approval, some churchmen claiming that all opponents of the Orders must be heretics.

There were, nevertheless, genuine causes for concern. The Orders did not fit into the feudal system that operated in Europe and the Holy Land. The Pope was the only authority they recognised. This meant that they could be, and often were, rivals to church and state, and to one another. Despite the fact that the crusader states were under increasing pressure from the Saracens throughout the 12th and 13th centuries, the Orders sometimes fought amongst themselves and took sides in disputes between the crusaders.

During the 13th century the crusader states fell one by one to the Saracens. In 1244 Jerusalem was taken, reducing the kingdom of Jerusalem to a small coastal strip surrounding the city of Acre. This last remnant was finally stormed in May 1291, forcing the military orders to return to Europe.

The Knights Hospitaller went first to the island of Rhodes, which they held until driven out by the Turks in 1522. In 1530 they settled on Malta, where they remained until the end of the 18th century. The Order still exists today as a philanthropic organisation, carrying out charitable work across the world.

The Hospitallers lingered on in Britain until the reign of Henry VIII, when their estates and wealth were confiscated in the general suppression of the monasteries. The knights were ordered to abandon the White Cross, the symbol of the Order, and

The ruined church of St John at Slebech

in 1540 their famous preceptory at Slebech was surrendered to the crown. It was
the last of the monastic establishments in Wales to close and also one of the richest.
It was valued at £211 and when the official charged with overseeing the closure
arrived at the house, he was given a complete inventory of all its lands, money,
plate and relics. These were passed to the crown, which had already absorbed the
Hospitallers' border properties at Garway and Dunmore.

Within a few years, Roger and Thomas Barlow, the brothers of Bishop William
Barlow of St Davids, had purchased from the king several former monastic estates
in Pembrokeshire, including Slebech. An attempt was made to return these to the
Hospitallers in 1558, when Queen Mary I tried to revive the Order. She appointed
Richard Shelley as preceptor of Slebech and Halston, though he never seems to
have obtained the lands from the Barlows, perhaps because the queen died before
the transfer could be achieved. It is ironic that the Barlow family, who profited so
much by the Reformation, later abandoned their Protestant leanings and Slebech
became a centre of Catholic devotion in west Wales.

Today, apart from the ruined church of St John, there is no trace of the
commandery at Slebech. The present Slebech Hall is an 18th-century construction,
yet there are many traditions associating it with the Hospitallers. The eastern arm of
the Daugleddau flows past the hall and just offshore is a tiny island. It is said to be
the final resting place of the hearts of many knights who were killed in the Holy
Land. Another heart burial, contained in a casket, is reputed to be secreted within
the sealed vault of St John's church. A medieval sword was also discovered at

On this island in the Daugleddau at Slebech, the hearts of many Knights Hospitaller
are said to be buried

Slebech. It has been deposited with the National Museum of Wales and on occasion is loaned to the priory for Wales of the present-day Knights of St John for use in their ceremonials.

The Slebech sword being carried in procession at St Davids Cathedral

The Knights Templar met a particularly gruesome fate. After their return from the Holy Land, they came to be seen by the sovereigns of Europe as a possible source of danger. The Order was enormously wealthy and maintained a fighting force of highly trained warriors. In addition, it was a Sovereign Order, owing allegiance to no king and there was the possibility that it would take sides in disputes between nations. There were also several monarchs, including Philip IV of France, who were heavily in debt to the Templars.

What happened next shocked Europe. On 13 October 1307, almost every Templar in France, from knights to servants, was arrested on charges of heresy. It was said that their secret rites of initiation included a denial of Christ and that the cross was insulted, also that they desecrated the Holy Sacrament and that they worshipped satanic idols. Many of those now in captivity suffered dreadful tortures as the French authorities attempted to substantiate the claims. Ordinarily, the Templars, as a monastic order, would have been exempt from torture, but the exemption did not apply to heretics. In their agony, many of the knights admitted the charges.

At first, Pope Clement V refused to accept the Templars' guilt, but after several weeks of secret negotiations with the French king he issued a bull which recognised the accusations. He demanded the arrest of all knights of the Order in papal lands and insisted that other nations should follow his example. In the event, most ignored his orders: the kings of Spain and Portugal even declared the Templars of the Iberian peninsula to be their main bulwark against Muslim invasion and pronounced the Order to be innocent of all charges.

In France, there were wholesale executions of the Templars. On one occasion, fifty-four knights who had confessed to heresy under torture were burned at the stake outside Paris, but not before recanting their confessions. At Rheims and Rouen, a total of 120 others were executed. The destruction of the Templars culminated in the burning of Jacques de Molay, Grand Master, and Geoffroi de Charnay, Preceptor of Normandy.

All Templar treasures and goods in France were seized by King Philip. Those French knights who had escaped arrest were given a year to submit to justice or be declared heretics without right of appeal. Many of the properties belonging to the Order in England and Wales were transferred to the Hospitallers by papal bull and by Acts of the English Parliament in 1324 and 1334.

Though the Order of the Knights Templar had ceased to exist as such, it lived on in other guises. In Portugal, a new secular order was formed called the Order of Jesus Christ. It included former knights and properties of the Templars and in time it became an order of chivalry of the Portuguese crown. In Aragon, the Templars became the Order of Montesa, named after Our Lady of Montesa. In other kingdoms, the Knights Templar were quietly allowed to join other existing orders, including the Hospitallers; the ideals which they had sworn to uphold were not completely forgotten.

PART II

Saints and Pilgrims

Chapter 6

Shells from Gallice

As early as 1130, pilgrims to Compostela would have found a small market-place housed in a paved courtyard to the north of the cathedral. Here were gathered a number of stalls selling all manner of souvenirs, including shoes, purses, straps, belts, deer-skin bags, medicinal herbs and even casks of wine. Amongst the most popular items offered for sale were scallop shells, gathered from the beaches of Galicia. Few pilgrims left the city without having purchased one, which they wore sewn to their cloaks or hats.

As we have seen in Chapter 4, the legendary associations of these shells with St James were many and gave them a mystical significance. It was even said that the scallop possessed healing properties: a knight of Apulia was cured of a goitre by the touch of a shell carried home by a pilgrim.

Scallop shells very quickly became the recognised symbol of St James and, eventually, of all pilgrimage. They were later reproduced as metal badges and, during the later half of the 12th century, other shrines began to manufacture their own versions. By the end of the 15th century there was a bewildering variety, but there is little doubt that the emblems of the more famous shrines were instantly recognisable, even to people who had never visited them.

A pilgrim returning from Canterbury, the first English shrine to manufacture souvenirs, would have sported an image of St Thomas Becket. The martyred saint was depicted in several ways: mounted on a horse, as a standing figure, or head and shoulders only. Other Canterbury badges showed the murder of the archbishop or the sword that killed him. Badges from Walsingham and Salisbury often depicted the Virgin Mary, patron of both places. Letters of the alphabet bearing crowns were also used to denote certain shrines; a T for Thomas Becket and Canterbury, an M for the Virgin joined with a W for the shrine at Walsingham.

A badge depicting St Thomas Becket

Travellers who had been to the Holy Land wore a badge shaped like a palm leaf, symbolising Christ's entry into Jerusalem; these pilgrims were also known as 'palmers', and were much revered. They often attached the title 'Le Paumer', or 'The Palmer', to their names in token of their journey to the greatest of all shrines. A 14th-century grave slab still exists in the church of St Thomas in Haverfordwest, which bears the inscription F. RICARD LE PAVMER GIT ICI DEV DE SAALME EIT MERCI AMEN. Brother Richard the Palmer, whom it commemorates, may have been a monk at one of two small monastic houses established within the environs of the town. He had made the long and difficult journey to Jerusalem and, as a further reminder of his achievement, his memorial also bears a carving of a rolled-up palm leaf.

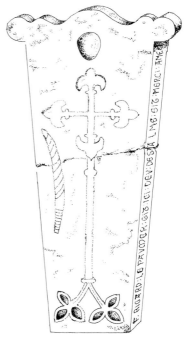

The gravestone of Richard the Palmer, showing a rolled-up palm leaf, symbolising his journey to Jerusalem

Circles and lozenges

The shapes of these souvenirs were often dictated by fashion. By the late 15th century, hat ornaments had become popular on the continent and many sanctuaries were producing badges that were circular, square, polygonal or shield- and lozenge-shaped. In Britain, there was more resistance to fashion, and production of irregularly shaped badges continued, though there was some attempt to conform to European styles, with the traditional shapes being placed within a square or rectangular frame.

There were also badges that included mirrors in their design. These seem to have come into fashion as a direct result of the huge increase in the numbers of pilgrims attending shrines on saints' days and holy days. To ensure that the maximum number of people could see the relics, they were often taken out of the shrines and exhibited publicly to the crowds. Pilgrims at the back of the multitude would hold up little mirrors in order to glimpse them and the belief grew that the mirrors themselves absorbed some of the powers of the relics. It was not long before shrines began to sell mirrors in pewter frames, or badges incorporating tiny mirrors.

A number of badges bore inscriptions: an example now in Salisbury Museum carries the words +IHS NAZARENVS; the first three letters are the initial letters of the name of Jesus in Greek, Ihsus. Canterbury badges were frequently inscribed

Sancta Thome ora pro me, words calling on the saint to intercede for the wearer. Another popular legend, translated from Latin, was 'Thomas is the best doctor of the worthy sick'. Others bore the words *Ave Maria Gracia Plena* or were inscribed with the names of the Three Kings. Some experts consider that these are not true pilgrim badges, but were sold instead as talismans to keep away ill-fortune.

Metals and moulds

At first the badges were made of jet, lead or pewter, but later enamel, silver and gold came to be used, though sometimes a flashing of tin was laid over the baser materials to give a bright silvery look. The more expensive versions were intended for the wealthier classes, though even the poorer pilgrims could afford the cheaper ones. They were sold in great numbers: in 1466, at the Swiss monastery of Einsiedeln over 130,000 badges were sold in a fourteen-day period. Thirty years later, 142,000 pilgrims passed through the gates of Aachen in a single day and even if only half of them bought badges, the income generated must have been considerable.

The manufacture of these badges was in the hands of the monastic houses and they were usually made in the same locality at which they were sold. Occasionally, the craftsmen of a town were allowed to produce them, either under licence or by hiring moulds from the church. Regulations controlling the production and sale of these items were carefully enforced because of the income involved.

The moulds from which the badges were made consisted of a fine-grained stone, such as slate, chalk or lithographic limestone, though bronze, clay, wood and even cuttlebone were used. The moulds were in two halves, which fitted tightly together; one half of the matrix, or design, of the front of the badge was cut in reverse. The other half contained the back of the badge, also in reverse, complete with pin. When the two halves were bound together, liquid metal was poured in through a tiny hole in the top. Once it had solidified, the mould was opened, revealing the completed badge, which was filed and polished into its final appearance.

Some badges were intended to be sewn onto the clothing rather than pinned. These usually consisted of wafer-thin sheets of brass, which had been stamped out on a die and included stitching holes along the edges.

The power of holiness

Most pilgrims brought home with them some souvenir of their visit to a shrine. Many found it necessary to do so, for an employer or a sponsor might require proof that the journey had been made; in a court of law, however, badges were not admitted as evidence that a pilgrim had completed a journey undertaken as punishment for an offence.

It was important that, once the souvenir had been purchased, it was pressed against the sides of a shrine or dipped in the waters of a holy well. In this way, some of the miraculous power of the saint was believed to pass into the badge; this was of great comfort to pilgrims for it gave reassurance that, in some measure, divine protection had been afforded to them. The badge was afterwards regarded as a holy relic in itself, with its own miracle-working powers. Several badges might be purchased, each one to be used for a different purpose.

Once a traveller had returned home, he could present his badge to his parish church, where it would be kept as a relic. Other badges were passed down through a family as heirlooms, or were buried with their owners. There is also evidence that the protective powers of these souvenirs were widely applied: they were nailed above the doors to houses, over beds, even on stable-doors, water-troughs, cowsheds, beehives, pigsties, chicken-coops and in dairies. Many were buried in fields to ensure a healthy crop and to keep away birds, rats and insects.

It was not unknown for a badge purchased at one sanctuary to be left at another as an offering, as the following tale illustrates. In 1486, a nine-month-old baby, Miles Febrygge, swallowed a badge depicting the head of Thomas Becket. Despite the frantic efforts of his father to recover the badge, it seemed that the child would choke to death. Prayers were made to the Virgin and to the murdered King Henry VI, who was widely believed to be a saint, though uncanonised. Miles immediately coughed up the offending item, which was then taken by his father to the king's tomb at Windsor, to be left as a votive offering.

Large numbers of pilgrim badges have been recovered from river fords all over Britain and in Europe. They cannot all have been lost accidentally, the numbers are too great, and it is more likely that they were deliberately deposited there by returning pilgrims as thank-offerings. If so, this is a continuation of a custom which may well have its roots in the Iron Age, when the Celts made gifts to the presiding spirits of rivers and wells.

Ampullae

Another type of souvenir, purchased in great numbers from the end of the 12th century, was the ampulla. This was a flask or phial made of lead or pewter, with small loops at the neck so that it could be worn around the pilgrim's throat or sewn to the hat. It contained either holy oil or water that had been blessed at a shrine or drawn from a holy well; both oil and water were believed to have healing or protective powers. In the case of ampullae purchased at Canterbury, they had been filled before being sealed with water from Becket's Well, into which the martyr's blood was said to have flowed immediately after his murder.

The ampullae were usually decorated, as were the badges, with scenes or symbols identifying the sanctuary from which they came; thus Canterbury's ampullae bore representations of St Thomas, though later examples from this shrine and many other sanctuaries in Britain depict the scallop shell motif.

Ampullae were regarded in much the same way as badges and once the pilgrim had returned home, he might donate his to the parish church, where it would be

Two pilgrim ampullae discovered in Pembrokeshire

hung as a relic before the altar. Because of their protective powers they were also fixed over the entrances to houses, cowsheds and barns, or were broken open and the contents scattered over the fields to ensure a good harvest, with the ampulla itself being buried beneath the soil. Examples have been found in the countryside surrounding Pembroke and a scattering of half a dozen, each bearing the stamp of a different shrine, was discovered on the outskirts of the town.

It was also not unknown for ampullae to be retained as family heirlooms and for them to be periodically sent back to the shrine from which they came, to be refilled.

The jangling of their Canterbury bells (William Thorpe, 15th-century Lollard)

The nuisance caused by pilgrims passing through the towns and villages on their way to a shrine has already been noted in Chapter 2. Many of them, in addition to badges, wore small bells, which jangled constantly and caused irritation to more than one observer. The ringing of bells was supposed to keep away evil spirits and to prevent storms. Pilgrims to the Holy Land dipped their bells into the sacred waters of the River Jordan in the certain belief that the jingling would afterwards protect them from the extremes of bad weather.

In addition to bells, worshippers at a shrine could also purchase tin or pewter whistles. Horns and trumpets were available at some sanctuaries and these were blown with deafening energy by the faithful during processions through the streets surrounding the shrine.

There were also other, quieter types of souvenirs, which sold in great numbers, but which have rarely survived into the present era.

Pilgrims could purchase whistles made of tin or pewter at many shrines

These were religious pictures, painted on parchment or paper, which depicted the martyrdom of a particular saint or the performance of a miracle. Devotional books, beautifully illustrated, were also on offer, but these were intended for the wealthier, literate pilgrim.

A stone of the Sepulchre

It is worth noting that some pilgrims preferred not to spend money on their souvenirs. In 1458, an English traveller to the Holy Land, William Wey, ignored all the notices posted up in Jerusalem forbidding the removal of objects from sacred sites and quietly pocketed stones from the Mount of Calvary, the Sepulchre, the hill of Tabor, the pillar that 'our Lord was stowrchyd too', and from the place where the cross had been hidden and discovered. He finished off the collection with a stone from the holy cave in Bethlehem.

An act of vandalism was recorded by Felix Fabri when he visited the monastery of St Catherine at Mount Sinai. One of his party broke off part of the altar with an iron bar. When the damage was discovered, the abbot demanded the return of the missing piece and threatened to refer the problem to the Arabs, who would settle the matter immediately. This caused great consternation amongst the pilgrims, but nobody would own up to the crime. At last the leader of the group promised that if the culprit would secretly hand him back the stolen portion he would placate the authorities without divulging the thief's identity. This was accordingly achieved and the little group left without ever learning the name of the guilty party.

Behaviour of this sort was common at most shrines and the church did its best, through strictly applied rules and even stricter supervision of visitors, to ensure that damage and theft was kept to a minimum.

Welsh badges

As this chapter has made clear, a wealth of information exists concerning the production of pilgrim souvenirs throughout Europe. Unfortunately, little of it is specific to Wales. Though tradition suggests that badges may have been manufactured in a few locations within Wales, the written sources do not support this idea. Furthermore, archives in Wales have scanty information concerning symbols representing local dedications.

There seems to be no reason why the Welsh shrines could not have made and sold their own tokens. The powerful Norman bishops would surely have been eager to promote the sale of souvenirs, especially if it improved the incomes of the cathedrals following large-scale rebuilding, or the translation of a saint's bones to a new and more costly shrine. Why did they apparently fail to do so?

It may be that Welsh tradition concerning the saints was markedly different from that of the Norman church. It was usual in the centuries before the Norman

Conquest to reverence the material possessions of the saints, rather than their corporeal remains. This could have resulted in the deliberate shunning of the trade in symbols.

It is also possible that the badges for Welsh shrines were produced outside Wales. These mass-produced items could have carried symbols common to a number of shrines. Representations of the Virgin, for example, or emblems associated with her, were popular in the Middle Ages, and were sold at numerous locations. It is likely that badges and ampullae bought at Welsh shrines have already been discovered, but as they bear no distinctively Welsh symbol, are thought to come from places outside the Principality.

Chapter 7

Saints and relics

Welsh saints and their festivals: Gwylmabsant

*There is not a land in all Christendom of comparable area having so
many saints within it as were found among the Welsh of yore.*

Y Drych Cristionogawl, 1585.

THE great saints of Wales's conversion, between AD 5 and 7 were numerous,
among them Dewi, Dyfrig, Deiniol, Teilo, Illtud, Beuno, Cawrdaf, Cadog,
Curig, Dwyn(wen), Melangell, Non, Gwenfrewi, Seiriol, Samson and Cybi. No
Welsh saint of this early period was officially canonised: the suffix 'sant' simply
meant 'holy' and their sainthood was by popular acclaim and authorised by the
bishop. Only two Welsh saints were officially recognised as such, St David and St
Winifred, but neither would have undergone the careful sifting of evidence of
sanctity, the usual first step in the process of canonisation, for which no official
procedure involving papal consent existed until the end of the 11th century. By the
time Gerald of Wales, Archdeacon of Brecon, attempted to get Caradog of St Issells
in Pembrokeshire canonised, actually investigating his miracles for Pope Innocent
III, the process involved lengthy judicial formalities and was ruinously expensive.
It is not surprising that the attempt failed as did many others.

Generally speaking, the early church in Wales buried its saints, preserving and
revering objects associated with them during their lifetime such as bells, books,
staffs and clothing. The Norman church brought a change of emphasis, venerating
the physical remains of saints and elevating their status as relics. In the early 12th
century, Bishop Bernard of Menevia searched fruitlessly for the body of St David
and was upstaged by Bishop Urban of Llandaf who in addition to having one of the
three bodies of St Teilo and that of St Euddogwy entombed in his cathedral, added
the body of St Dyfrig, translated from Ynys Enlli in 1120. This shift of emphasis
was paralleled in the formalising of the process of canonisation and in the
increasing importance of the written 'Lives' of saints and collections of miracles
attributed to them in establishing their reputation. In the case of the native Welsh
saints this could be seen as an opportunity to affirm their importance in the face of
Norman incursion and reorganisation. It is arguable that some of the 'Lives' of the
Welsh saints were written at least in part, with the motive of preserving the
individuality of the native church in the face of Norman pressure.

These saints were dear to Welsh hearts and their earthly homes were places
where their sanctity was still felt and had power to help and heal. To echo the
sentiments of Julian of Norwich, they were 'kynd neyghbours and of our

knowyng'. The places where they had settled and established early religious communities became part of the geography of Welsh pilgrimage. Here they were usually buried and their relics preserved. Their lives and exploits became part of sacred literature, read out in church on their saints' day, patronal festival or Gwylmabsant.

Gwylmabsant or patronal festival

Gwylmabsant drew together Welsh reverence for the local saint and the domestic pilgrimage; it was an expression of popular religion at its most exuberant. The earliest account of one such festival was written down in the 12th century, by Giraldus Cambrensis who described the form festivities took for the feast of St Eluned in Brecon where her chapel still stood in 1698. The ritual began with young men and maidens threading their way round the graves, singing as they went. This was followed by a highly theatrical re-enactment of the various ways in which they had broken the Sabbath commandment 'thou shalt do no manner of work': the cobbler at his bench, the tanner at his work and the weaver at her loom. Afterwards they were led into church where they made an offering and received a pardon.

Most of what we know of these festivals in Wales comes from the observations of antiquaries of the 17th–19th centuries describing post-Reformation survivals. Like other great festivals of the church's year, the saint's day was part of the agricultural calendar, reflecting the concerns of a society dependent for its existence on the success of crops and the well being of livestock. It was also the time when the saints were most powerfully present in their sanctuary. Part of the celebration would have involved the ritual of visiting certain sites or physical features within the sacred landscape of the saint's particular 'parish' with prayers marking the stations along the way, a practice known in Ireland and Brittany and a feature of medieval religious life in Wales. In many country parishes the sites are still known or at least have been recorded by antiquarians and it is possible to detect features of these sacred landscapes: the 'gwely' or 'myfyr' – the saint's bed or place of meditation; standing stones or rocky features; the holy well; the grave chapel and the path which the saint would walk. One of many instances is on the north Wales coast: St Seiriol was said to 'have caused' a pavement to be made over marshy ground from his island, Ynys Seiriol, to Penmaenmawr where he would go to pray and meditate. A cleft in the rock – Clippyn Seiriol – marked the approach to his chapel above which were his gwely and holy well. The chapel was reached by a rough path, at one time maintained by the efforts of a hermit, assisted by people from the adjoining parishes. There are many others, among them Pennant Melangell, Llanymawddwy (St Tydecho), Llanddwyn Island and in particular the area around St Davids.

In the form in which it survived the Reformation, Gwylmabsant consisted of three main elements: the sacred services, the traditional ritual, and the festivities which on occasion, fuelled by alcohol, bordered on the profane. The eve of the festival began with processions and wakes or all-night vigils held at the saint's tomb, holy well and other special sites associated with him or her. Before the Reformation the saint's day mass would have been celebrated in the early morning[1] and the relics brought out and carried in procession. Rituals would be enacted to promote health and healing in man and beast. Divinations over courtship and other matters were performed to determine the favour or misfortune of the coming year. Festivities included fairs, ball-games such as *cnapan* in Newport, Pembrokeshire, and feasting when special dishes were prepared, like the Trefin pasty in north Pembrokeshire; Bonny Clobby – a plum pudding – at Rhossili; in Llangenydd, White Pot – flour and milk boiled together and taken on St Cenydd's Day, 5 July, and in Llanmadoc, a pie of chopped mutton and currants.

The relative isolation of Anglesey and the Llŷn peninsula probably led to the late survival of saint's day devotions and celebrations into the 18th and 19th centuries. St Cybi's festival in Caergybi (Holyhead), lasted for three weeks and on the Relics Sundays, *Suliau'r Creiriau*, during that period, his bones were carried through the town. According to William Morris this practice had died out by the middle of the 18th century. At Llangybi on the Llŷn peninsula, elaborate rituals at the saint's holy well survived until the 19th century. The well chamber and the ruins of surrounding buildings are set in a lovely, secluded valley. St Cybi is linked in tradition with St Seiriol of Penmon. The two saints would walk daily to meet each other in the centre of Anglesey at Clorach where wells are dedicated to each of them. Cybi who walked into the sun on his outward and return journeys, was known as Cybi Felin (the suntanned) and Seiriol whose back was always against the sun as Seiriol Wyn (the fair). Seiriol was buried on Ynys Seiriol (Priestholme, Puffin Island, Ynys Lannog) and in the Middle Ages his remains were translated to the Priory church at Penmon and interred beneath the altar. Pilgrims entered the shrine by means of a stone staircase. The floor of the modern sanctuary is raised several feet above the original. St Seiriol appears with St Christopher in medieval glass taken out of the 15th-century east window of the chancel, restored and reset in the east window of the south transept. A holy well and footings of a hermit's cell, reputedly that of St Seiriol, are near the priory buildings. Both St Seiriol and St Curig were sufficiently popular for the mendicant friars to exchange small images of them for bacon, cheese and corn, according to Lewis Glyn Cothi. St Seiriol's image was effective against eye disorders – in Anglesey the periwinkle was known as *llygad Seiriol* – Seiriol's eye. St Curig's image was effective against skin disorders and the expulsion of evil spirits from farmhouses. At Llaneilian, there is a rare physical survival in the shape of the *cwpwrdd* or cupboard once used for a divinatory practice. It was kept in the grave chapel to the south-east of the church and set up as an altar when the chapel was restored in 1952. The chapel was known as Y Myfyr (the place of meditation), and during the wake 'all the people get into this

---

[1] The early morning service survives in Plygain (Latin *pulli cantus* – cockcrow), held at 6 am on Christmas morning in a few Welsh chapels.

Ynys Seiriol, St Seiriol's Island, off the north Anglesey coast

Penmon Priory church

St Seiriol and St Christopher,
15th century, Penmon,
Anglesey

Holy Well, Penmon

Y Cwpwrdd, the Cupboard,
Llaneilian, Anglesey

Y Myfyr, Llaneilian, Anglesey

box, and should they get in and out with ease, having turned round in it three times they will live out the year, but otherwise they will assuredly die'. The narrow apertures, now boarded over and the confines of the cupboard would exclude all but the slim and agile today! Other attractions of Llaneilian, apart from its famous cursing well, were 'to visit a dry skull, scrapeing of an old stone, and playing other Jugling tricks in the Myfyr and ye Cupboard' (27 July 1740, William Bulkeley).

Holy bones

Relics were the major attraction of medieval pilgrim centres and the visible, tangible evidence that supported and encouraged faith. The most important relics were those of the Holy Family. Because of his bodily ascent into heaven, corporeal relics of Jesus were rare. The umbilical cord of the infant Christ was said to have been preserved by Mary and the midwife in a pot of spikenard, kept in Rome. The blood and tears of Christ were preserved, and among many shrouds and grave cloths, the Shroud of Turin still challenges scientific investigation. Mary, like Jesus, was received bodily into heaven – in India, according to tradition – and the only physical remains were hair, nail clippings, milk, wedding ring and articles of clothing. She gave her girdle to the apostle St Thomas from heaven and it was celebrated in Welsh poetry by Iolo Goch, 1320–98, and Lewis Môn, *fl.* 1480–1527.

The bodies of some saints remained incorrupt, considered to provide incontrovertible evidence of sanctity. A Welsh example is St Caradog whose tomb is in St Davids Cathedral; Gerald of Wales wrote that his body was the cause of many miracles. His tomb was visited by William of Malmesbury around the year 1143, who attempted the semi-accepted *furtum sacrum* or sacred theft: he tried to remove one of the saint's fingers by way of acquiring a personal relic, but was foiled when the hand clenched and withdrew itself into its sleeve, to the dismay of the chronicler William. The remains of Caradog, no longer incorrupt, are believed to be still in his tomb.

Relics included fragments of bone, teeth, even flesh: the 'ear of Malchus that Peter stroke off' was observed in Wales by the bishop of Dover. Other relics were objects with which the saints had contact during their lifetime and if they had suffered and died for their faith, the instruments of their martyrdom. Another type of relic was a piece of cloth called a *brandeum*, plural *brandea*: a length of fabric, or scarf that had been sanctified by touching a primary relic of a saint such as the body or bones. Into a similar category came ampullae, small phials to contain fluids, either oil from lamps that burned above a shrine or altar, or water from a holy well. Early ampullae were made of earthenware and examples of these from St Menas' holy well in Egypt were found on the Welsh border at Meols, on the Wirral in Cheshire and also in Radnorshire. The shrine of St Menas was destroyed by Moslems in the 7th century and it is likely that these ampullae would have reached north Wales before AD 750. Other ampullae were made of wood and in the later Middle Ages, of metal. A number of these have been discovered by metal detectorists in Pembrokeshire in a scatter mostly in the south of the county. Like a holy energy source, a relic emanated the power of the saint which reputedly altered objects physically, making them slightly heavier. It could impart benediction and healing, but misused could bring down the wrathful curse of the saint, blighting where it would not bless.

The position occupied by relics in a church or cathedral was indicative of their importance. They were usually kept in, under, above or at any rate close to the altar. The high altar at Abbey Dore on the Welsh border near Hereford, has what appears to be a relic cavity in the centre of the west side, with a wooden cover. The cult of

Relic cavity in the altar at
Abbey Dore, Herefordshire

relics was in existence in the early centuries of Christianity and would have been absorbed by churches as an integral aspect of the faith. However, in the 7th century St Augustine provided a theological justification for the veneration of relics and in AD 787 the second Council of Nicea decreed that an altar could not be consecrated unless it contained relics. Centuries later, in the Counter Reformation, the Roman Catholic church worked out a detailed theology of relics, influenced by the writings of St Thomas Aquinas. The saints were present in their relics. The miracles were achieved by those relics, by which a saint's reputation would be judged, as instruments of God. The saints as friends of God, interceded for the living but honour paid to relics was an extension of that due to God alone.

'Bishops' Crooks, portable bells, holy books, the Cross itself and other similar relics' Giraldus Cambrensis

Gerald of Wales is our earliest authority on the medieval Welsh and their attitudes to the relics of their saints. He was of Norman and Welsh ancestry, born in Manorbier and spending his formative years in west Wales. He was highly educated and widely travelled but had to some extent shared the life of the ordinary Welshman which by his account was very basic and unsophisticated. He describes the Welsh as hospitable, generous, quick-witted, articulate, spiritually aware, but also, and sometimes paradoxically so, inconstant, greedy, quarrelsome, vindictive, bloodthirsty and violent.

Gerald is our witness to the material evidence of faith that drew Welsh pilgrims. He observed that the common people and the clergy revered 'bishops' crooks . . . encased in gold, silver or bronze . . . portable bells, holy books, the cross itself . . . and other similar relics of the saints'. But the power that emanated from them was not to be trifled with: those who broke their word sworn on relics lived to rue the day and those who scorned relics were punished severely. For instance, Gerald described St Patrick's horn, which was made of bronze 'if you hold the larger end to your ear, you will hear a sweet melody being played, as if you had left a harp uncovered and the breeze blew gently on it'. A poor Irish beggar wandered around Breconshire, wearing the horn round his neck as a relic and would offer it to the faithful to kiss, but one day it was snatched from him by Bernard, a priest

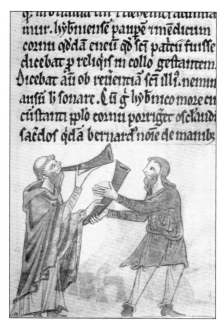

The priest Bernard unwisely blowing St Patrick's horn

who tried to blow it and appears to have had a seizure, from Gerald's observant account of his symptoms. 'Immediately he lost all use of speech . . . he went into a coma and immediately lost his memory altogether . . . He was in fact so injured in his memory that, as I myself saw, for many days afterwards he tried to memorise, as if anew, the Psalms, which before that he had off by heart perfectly.' St Cynog's gold torque was made of four sections, divided in the middle by a dog's head standing erect with its teeth bared; however, it bore the indentation of a hammer blow and the man who tried to break it for its gold lost his sight.

Bishops' crooks were the revered croziers of the major saints. Few survived the Reformation. St Baglan's crozier survived to the end of the 17th century, but many more must have met the fate of St Curig's staff with its healing powers. According to Gerald it was 'completely encased in gold and silver, and the top part of it (had) the rough shape of a cross'. It healed glandular swellings and tumours if pressed to the affected part and if an oblation of a penny was offered. It was preserved in St Harmon's church in Radnorshire but was burnt at the Reformation. More to be feared was St David's staff, once kept at Llanddewi Brefi, Ceredigion: the poet Gwynfardd Brycheiniog, *c.* 1170, advised 'flee from it as from fire'. St Padarn's staff was called Cyrwen:

> Much accomplishing, much loved it gives protection,
> Its holy power reaching the limits of three continents.
> No other relic can be compared with Cyrwen –
> A wonderful gift – Padarn's Staff.
>
> Ieuan ap Sulien, 11th century (Translated by Sir Ifor Williams)

The staff of St Cybi of Llangybi (Holyhead), decorated with leaves and nuts, profusely carved, was praised by Dafydd Llwyd ap Llewelyn (15th century).

Portable bells were important relics and some of these are preserved in museums. In their many different forms, bells have been used in religious rites and in many cultures for thousands of years to banish evil spirits and facilitate contact with the deity. The early saints inherited this use of the bell as talisman and focus of magical and sacred power. Each saint had his own hand bell and each bell its own personality, its potency increasing after the death of its owner. The surviving Welsh hand bells are the products of the pre-Norman church but are unlikely to have belonged to the saints whose names they bear. The earliest metal bells were made of iron and later ones cast in bronze. If danger threatened they were buried in

Medieval Welsh hand bell, north Wales

hallowed ground. This may have happened to St Gwyddelan's bell which was found buried on the site of the old church at Bryn y Bedd. St Gwynhoedl's was cast in solid bronze, as was that of St Cystennin from Llangystennin, making them the largest surviving casts from their period. St David's bell named Bangu (the dear loud one) was once kept at Glascwm, Montgomeryshire. St Hywyn of Aberdaron had a Cloch Wen (white or blessed bell). St Gildas, reputedly an expert bell-founder, made his own bell and bells for Saints Cadoc, Illtud and Brigid of Kildare. St Cawrdaf's book and bell attracted pilgrims to Abererch, Llŷn; Cloch Felen Beuno (St Beuno's yellow bell) was preserved up to the 18th century at the now vanished Tre'r Dryw house at Llanidan, Anglesey. There are numerous stories of the early saints and their bells.

Holy books. These had the aura of sanctity equivalent to that of a relic. Some of the earliest books were copies of the scriptures made by the saints themselves, such as the Gospel of St John, written by St David and completed by an angel 'in letters of gold'. As well as being Gospel books, some recorded grants of land or other gifts to a religious community and were also used in oath-taking. One of the major relics of Llancarfan was the Gospel of Gildas, a mass-book written by Gildas and offered to St Cadoc. 'The inhabitants of Wales hold this volume as a most valuable possession and dare neither to open it, nor look in it, nor to confirm peace and friendship between hostile parties unless it be present, set there for that purpose.'

The value accorded these hand-written and often beautifully illustrated books was immense. A recurring theme in the 'Lives' of the early saints is the miraculous survival of books that have been mislaid (St Beuno's was recovered by a curlew) or left out in the rain yet remained dry: St Aidan incurred the wrath of St David for

Carpet Page from the Lichfield Gospels

St John the Evangelist, with Welsh manumission
Lichfield Gospels

MAEN Y CHYFAN

Maen Achwyfan, Thomas Pennant, 18th-century engraving

such carelessness. It was reflected in their value: as recorded in early Welsh in the book itself, it cost one donor, a man named Gelhi, his best horse to acquire an illuminated Gospel book which for the benefit of his soul he offered to God on the altar of St Teilo at Llandeilo Fawr. This magnificent illuminated Gospel book, dated to the 8th century was in Lichfield by the 10th century where it is preserved today as the Book of St Chad or the Lichfield Gospels. In the high Middle Ages a book was said to be worth as much as a farm.

The Book of St Beuno was known for centuries as *Y Diboeth*, 'the unburnt', because of its escape from destruction when the church burnt down. It was last seen in 1594 by Thomas Williams of Trefriw, Anglesey. St Cawrdaf's book, kept at Abererch on the Llŷn peninsula was associated with the end of a three-year drought when, as a result of Cawrdaf's prayers and his pilgrimage to Rome, the first drops of rain fell on the saint's book.

The Cross itself. The events of the last few days in the life of Christ, his trial, crucifixion and resurrection, the whole period of Easter from earliest times, has always been the high point of the many festivals of the church's year. Central to this is the image of the cross, the emblem of Christianity. The veneration of the cross began in the 4th century with the discovery of the True Cross which was kept at Jerusalem and many portions were later distributed widely among the churches. Many practices developed which had the cross as their central theme. In 1229, William of Blois decreed, 'Let a handsome cross be erected in every churchyard to which procession shall be made on Palm Sunday.' Crosses were erected by the wayside, at the entrance to towns and at the end of bridges, and in Wales the dead were prayed for at crossroads: 'For thys reason ben crosses by ye waye, that when folke passynge see the crosses they shulde thynke on Hym that dyed on ye crosse and worshippe Hym above all thynge', *Dives et Pauper*, 1496. The finely decorated cross at Whitford (Clwyd) is known as Maen Achwyfan (stone of lamentation) – thought to be 10th–11th centuries. Other stone crosses in Wales were once known thus, in the form '*maen achwynfan*' where, it was said, penances were finished, attended by weeping and marks of contrition.

The Cross was a powerful protection against the dangers of a journey; Meini Cred, Creed Stones, were wayside guardians. Elias Owen recorded that the sign of the Cross was often used with the admonition '*Ymgroesa!*' – 'Cross yourself!' before starting out. There were many rituals associated with Holy Week. On Good Friday a special barefoot, penitential procession was made called 'creeping to the Cross'. In Tenby people walked barefoot to church on Good Friday 'so as not to disturb the earth', a practice which continued until the end of the 18th century. In the later Middle Ages there was an intense focus on the physical sufferings of Christ for humanity. In churches, the Cross, or Rood, was conspicuously placed high at the east end of the nave above elaborately carved rood screens and lofts, with attendant figures, the Virgin Mary, St John, saints and angels, and was seen as a source of healing and salvation in itself.

The Welsh bards were significant publicisers of roods as of other pilgrim attractions: from them we learn of roods at: Llangynwyd, Glamorganshire;

Restored screen and rood, Llanfilo, Breconshire

Llanbeblig, Caernarfonshire, and Strata Marcella. The great golden Rood of Brecon priory was celebrated by a number of bards, among them Hywel ap Dafydd ap Ieuan ap Rhys, 1450–80. The site of the medieval screen and the Golden Rood is at the head of the nave; doors to the screen and the stone corbels that held the beams are still visible. Pilgrims passed through one door to a bridge from which they touched the rood and descended on the other side. The Holy Cross of St John's church, Chester, just over the north-east Welsh border, drew many Welshmen. Maredudd ap Rhys, one-time Vicar of Ruabon, *fl.* 1450–84, was cured of lameness and another poet-priest, Ifan Brydydd, (enviably) cured of old age. Part of the 14th-century Rood of Tremeirchion near St Asaph, survives in St Beuno's College. Another rood placed in the grounds of the Dominican monastery at Rhuddlan in 1518 – Iesu Gwyn o Rhuddlan, the Blessed Christ of Rhuddlan – was the object of a special Easter-week pilgrimage. This was one of a different class of images which have come to be known as 'bound roods' and as the name suggests show Christ bound and awaiting his death on the cross. Survivals of this type of carving in Wales are rare: the only survivals are that at the church of St John Baptist, Newton Nottage near Porthcawl, and the figure in Bangor Cathedral known as the Mostyn Christ, named after the family believed to have concealed it at the Reformation and which could be the Rhuddlan figure. Gruffudd ab Ieuan ap Llywelyn Fychan, *c.* 1485–1553, eloquently described this beautiful, anguished image:

Draw mae delw drwm ei dolur
drwy waith Peilar wrth piler
duw gwiwlan diogelwr
dy ddelw a doddai alar.

Yonder is an image heavy with grief
Through the work of Pilate by a pillar
O holy, worthy, guardian God,
your image melts our grief.

The impact of these roods and figures, usually brightly painted and sometimes gilded, on the drab, uncomfortable lives of so many unlettered men and women can only be imagined. The salvation they promised and their miracle-working powers could draw pilgrims from far and wide. They were targets of the later reformers to whom veneration of such images and idolatry were one and the same, and therfore most did not survive the Reformation. It is interesting to note that parts of north Wales (once devoutly Catholic) remained intensely Protestant until the First World War, so much so that there were no crosses on the altars. Young men coming back from the war encountered altar crosses in particular in France and urged for them to be reinstated. In 1684, Thomas Dinely, travelling in north Wales, described a rood that had escaped destruction in Llanrwst church where 'lieth hid the ancient figure of the Crucifixion as bigg as the life, this is shown to none but the curious, and rarely to them'. Occasionally a precious rood figure was spirited away or hidden. Two such figures were discovered in Mochdre church, Powys, in 1867 and are preserved in the National Museum of Wales, Cardiff. Although time has taken its toll of the oak from which the figures were carved, the same emotional intensity is evident in Christ's features as on those of the Mostyn Christ, contrasting with the remote serenity on the features of the Virgin Mary.

Bound rood, the Mostyn Christ,
Bangor Cathedral

And other similar relics would have included items such as St Teilo's mitre, book, bell and comb[2] at Llandaf.

> *Ath gloch, mi yw vn oth gler,*
> *Ath grib ath lyfr iaith groewber.*

> And thy bell, I am one of thy poets, and thy comb and thy book of a language so clear and sweet.

One relic survived long into the post-Reformation period, possibly because of the isolation of the area. St Degan's cloak was preserved in a chapel on the edge of a cliff on Strumble Head in Pembrokeshire. Richard Fenton remembered hearing of it in his youth and referred to a letter dated 1720 describing it. 'There is a remarkable habit of this said St Degan preserved for several ages; the person that has it now having had it in his custody for forty years, to whom it was handed down by an elderly matron of upwards of ninety years of age. This habit, a piece whereof I have sent you enclosed, I had the curiosity to see; it is much in the form of a clergyman's cassock, but without sleeves. There were two of them of the same make near a yard in length, but having the like slit or hole at every corner on each end, and on the brim of each side were loops of blue silk.' According to Fenton, the relic was bought by a stranger and with its removal, the 'fame of his sanctity died away'.

Great Welsh relics – relics as power

Relics had the power to attract pilgrims in great numbers. There were fashions in relics; new wonders replaced old – the pilgrim trade was as fickle as any other – and churches were dependent on oblations, especially for building and repair. Gresford recorded a sharp decline in its prosperity when pilgrimages were forbidden at the Reformation. Competition between shrines was often keen and power-play and abuse inevitable. The medieval Welsh Laws required relics to be used in oath-taking: Gerald of Wales, not a man for half measures, made the abbot of St Dogmaels swear with 'his hand extended over the high altar of St David and all the relics' that he intended Gerald no harm in a wrangle over preferment. The tomb of St Teilo and the relics of Llandaf and Margam feature in references to oath-taking in the Episcopal Acta of Llandaf Cathedral. The relics of saints David and Cadoc were taken in procession throughout their respective territories to encourage support and tributes. From the melting pot of legal significance, economic advantage, spiritual devotion and patriotic fervour came political expediency.

Edward I

Ruthless, astute, devout, this king of England acknowledged the spiritual benefits of relics – a number were found on his body after death – and also had a shrewd

---

[2] A ritual comb was used by bishops to dress their hair before celebrating mass and for centuries was
  included among their ceremonial ornaments.

appreciation of how they could be used for political ends, especially in the unruly fringes of his kingdom. Patriotism and piety were a potent and dangerous brew and the Welsh of an earlier age had rallied under *Lluman Glân Dewi* (pure banner of David). When a new shrine was built to house St David's bones in his cathedral in 1275, Edward contributed open-handedly to its construction and in company with Queen Eleanor visited St Davids in November 1284. It is perhaps significant that the following year, King Edward led a solemn procession from the Tower of London to Westminster, bearing the head of St David and other Welsh relics, one of which may have been the great Croes Nawdd or Cross of Protection, thus spiritually disarming and demoralising the Welsh and asserting Edward's divine right to rule.

Croes Nawdd (Naid)

The intriguing story of this fragment of the True Cross and earliest-known non-native relic in Wales, began when according to legend it was brought into Wales from the Holy Land by a priest, Neotus. The relic was held by the princes of Wales and carried before them as a national shrine or palladium; its name means the Cross of Protection or Refuge. When Llywelyn ap Gruffudd the last Prince of Wales, was killed at Aberedw in 1282, the relic was found on his body. What happened next is obscure, but a document signed by Edward I at Rhuddlan on 25 June 1283, recorded its surrender. In the same year Edward gave thanks for the subjugation of the Welsh at the shrine of St Wulfstan and in 1285

Croes Nawdd/Naid, painted stone boss, South Choir Aisle, St George's Chapel Windsor. Kneeling figures: Edward IV and Bishop Beauchamp, *circa* 1475.

the king carried the Croes Nawdd in a procession in Westminster Abbey headed by the Archbishop of Canterbury and other prelates and accompanied by a vast concourse of people who chanted as they went. It was later kept in St George's chapel, Windsor and until the Reformation was an object of pilgrim devotion, celebrated by Welsh poets such as Dafydd ap Gwilym and Lewis Glyn Cothi. Four representations of it still survive in the chapel.

St David's Sapphire Altar

The first reference to this portable altar is in the *Life of St David*, written around 1080 by Rhygyfarch, of Llanbadarn Fawr, son of Bishop Sulien of St Davids, who described how it was consecrated and given to David by the patriarch when the saint visited Jerusalem and was later delivered to him at Llangyfelach (near

Swansea). It was described as 'potent with miracles' and after the saint's death was kept hidden, 'concealed by coverings of skins' and 'never seen…by men'. In the 1120s, William of Malmesbury wrote that the saint had bequeathed the altar to Glastonbury during his lifetime and that the case in which it had been kept remained in the diocese of Menevia. However, in a later *Life of St David* written at the end of the 12th century by Giraldus Cambrensis, the altar was apparently in Llangyfelach, claim and counter-claim suggesting keen competition for this relic. This Glastonbury altar was hidden in time of war and then rediscovered in a doorway of St Mary's church by Henry of Blois, d. 1171, who was Bishop of Winchester, Abbot of Glastonbury and brother of King Stephen. He adorned it richly with silver and precious stones, though history does not record who gave the magnificent sapphire after which it was named. It has been suggested that one of a pair of fine half-plaques of enamelled copper preserved in the British Museum depicts Bishop Henry holding a portable altar which may well be the famous Sapphire Altar (the Henry of Blois plaques, Mosan, around AD 1150, probably made in England). Two angels with thuribles are also depicted. Inevitably, on 25 May 1539 a 'superaltarre, garnished with silver and gilte, called the greate saphire of Glassonburye' was delivered to King Henry VIII.

Glastonbury's collection of relics was vast and priceless. William noted that Welshmen journeying to Rome left 'very many bodies of saints and reliques' before leaving Britain. He also gives a curious account of circumstances in St Davids which may have led to Glastonbury's claim to possess the body of St David[3] in the year 962 when the bishop was Bledud: 'a certain dame named Aelswitha, in the reign of King Edgar, acquired the said relics through a relative of hers, who at that time was bishop over the Ross [Rhos] valley when all that district was so devastated that scarce one mortal could be found in it, only a few women, and these in few places, and she placed the relics at Glastonbury'. The *Brut y Tywysogyon*, History of the Princes, recorded that Menevia was burnt in 810, 'destroyed' in 907 and Dyfed was ravaged in 952: the whole era was one of strife and unrest.

Phiol Sanctaidd Ystrad Fflur – The Nanteos Cup

Most Welsh relics disappeared at the Reformation and a line can be drawn under what is known of their history. Problems arise when what is believed to be a relic survives and skeins of legend form around it as with the Nanteos Cup. One version of its history has given rise to the belief that it was the Holy Grail, brought clandestinely by a small group of monks from Glastonbury to Strata Florida and thence to Nanteos as the dissolution of the monasteries spread. The tradition was handed down in the Powell family of Nanteos and first appeared in print at the beginning of the 20th century. Dr Juliette Wood has gathered together an extensive body of information on the Nanteos Cup and the 19th- and 20th-century traditions

---

[3] The location of St David's grave was evidently known in the early 11th century as it took a priest seven days to cut his way through brambles to the saint's tomb, after which the site seems to have been forgotten until its rediscovery in the mid-13th century.

The Nanteos Cup

and folklore connected with it. The cup is considered in the context of the typical development of legend and through its connection with a defined area of Cardiganshire and its gentry families as 'a later icon of social identity and power-sharing'. It was probably a mazer bowl, a medieval wooden cup often with a protective silver lip fitted over the rim. One survives in St Beuno's church, Clynnog Fawr dating from about 1485. Although it is preserved as one of the treasures of the church, no traditions attach to it.

The identity of the Nanteos Cup as the Phiol Sanctaidd (sacred phial) of Strata Florida has never been satisfactorily explained. T. Pierce Jones wrote that it was

Nanteos Mansion, Ceredigion

displayed to pilgrims as the Holy Grail, but does not give a source, and no reference is made to it in surviving bardic poetry. At the Reformation there was no record of it in the *Valor Ecclesiasticus* entry for the abbey – though if there had been its survival would have been most unlikely. In one version the cup was in the possession of the monks when the earliest monastery at Strata Florida was built, between 1164 and 1184. From 19th-century accounts it was assumed that the bowl or cup arrived at Nanteos mansion in the 18th century, probably as a result of a marriage and property transaction between the Stedmans of Strata Florida and the Powells of Nanteos. The earliest Stedman, said to have been an Arab called Stidmon – a legendary figure caught up in the romance of the crusades[4], was created Knight of the Holy Sepulchre by Richard I and came to England in 1191. The family was originally associated with Staffordshire and the only sources that record the existence of this man are the Welsh genealogies of his alleged descendants. The Stedmans were a leading family in the county of Ceredigion for 200 years and a descendant, John Stedman, bought the demesne lands and site of the dissolved monastery of Ystrad Fflur in 1571, building an imposing stone mansion with materials taken from the abbey ruins.

Once at Nanteos mansion, the cup and its healing powers soon became legendary. According to two 19th-century accounts, 1889 and 1895, it was believed to have been carved from a piece of the True Cross. The wood is said to be olive wood or wych elm. Judge David Lewis copied details of the pledges given for the loan of it and cures received from 1857 to 1889. There was an interruption when the cup was sent away for a crack to be repaired. The gold or silver hoop put round it adversely affected its healing powers and was removed. The cup remained at Nanteos until 1969 when the mansion and estate were sold and it was eventually taken to Herefordshire where it is kept today by the Mirylees family. The faithful who sought cures from the cup also bit out small pieces and what survives is an age-blackened wooden fragment.

The cup is an enigma. It could have been spirited away by monks of Strata Florida for safety until, as was said of it 'the church reclaims her own'. Precious relics were often well hidden at the Reformation, sometimes they were smuggled abroad or found their way into the houses of sympathetic gentry: secrecy was paramount. If the cup was believed to be the wood of the True Cross, then the memory of their ancestor, Stidmon, Knight of the Holy Sepulchre might give later Stedmans cause to ensure its preservation – and still, to this day, use it for healing, while keeping forever the secret of its mysterious past.

St Teilo's skull

The skull reputed to be that of St Teilo returned to Llandaf Cathedral on Dydd Gŵyl Deilo, 9 February 1994 after an absence of nearly 500 years, handed to the dean by

---

[4] The name is found in the *Black Book of St Davids* 1326, 179, 191, where it is recorded that a John Stedemon held lands at Lamphey. In some unpublished papers of Francis Jones the name is spelt 'Stidmon'.

Captain Mathew, the last hereditary keeper of the relic. The Mathew family connection with St Teilo has been woven into the family pedigree. The family had a long association with Llandaf and a shadowy ancestor of approximately the 11th century was appointed guardian of Teilo's tomb; Gruffydd Gwas Teilo (servant of Teilo) ap Aidan ap Gwaethfoed as reflected in his name and title, from then on an hereditary appointment within the Mathew family. In the middle of the 15th century, Sir David Mathew, active *c.* 1430, keeper and restorer of the tomb was rewarded by Bishop Marshall with the saint's skull, taken from the tomb and set in a costly reliquary. At the end of a long and active life in Llandaf Cathedral David Mathew was laid to rest there,

Penglog Teilo, St Teilo's skull, set in a modern reliquary stand, Llandaf Cathedral

where his tomb can still be seen. The skull remained in the family for seven generations until there was no longer a male heir to inherit it. In 1658 it was stripped of its mounting and left at Llandeilo Fawr by William Mathew and on his death in the same year was given into the keeping of the Melchior family at Llandeilo Llwydarth in Pembrokeshire where it was used as a drinking cup at St Teilo's Well near the little ruined church dedicated to the saint. Water drunk from the skull was said to cure whooping cough. In 1927 the skull was sold back to the Mathew family and it travelled from Winchester to Sydney, Australia, before being given to Llandaf Cathedral where it reposes in a niche, encased in a fine reliquary.[5]

---

[5] Archbishop Mathew, a descendant of the Irish branch and author of the article on the family in the *Dictionary of Welsh Biography*, researched the history of the relic extensively and produced an account of the history of the skull from the 15th century. Three head reliquaries were seized from Llandaf Cathedral at the Reformation, one of which would have been St Teilo's. It may have contained only part of the skull and it is possible that the keeper managed to conceal the brain pan which is what survives.

Chapter 8

Shrines and images

Welsh shrines and reliquaries

THE early saints of Wales were buried after death and their tombs venerated as early as the 6th century as noted by the monk Gildas whose account is the first we have. Welsh place names such as Merthyr, Bassaleg and Myfyr, derived from the Latin *martyrium*, *basilica* and *memoria*, indicate the presence of a church that in very early times would have contained major relics. The saint's grave would have been marked by an altar, low wall or a kerb of stones. Eventually a chapel would have been built. A few of these grave chapels (*capel/eglwys y bedd*) survive; many were separate from the main church as at Holyhead, Tywyn, Gwytherin, Clynnog Fawr and Llaneilian. In the two latter churches the connecting passages are post-medieval. At Pennant Melangell the grave chapel is attached to the church building.

In the later Middle Ages, the pressure of pilgrims led to the development of elaborate shrines into which the bodies and other relics of saints were 'translated', usually in the chancel but not necessarily on the site of the original grave. On festivals and other special occasions, relics of the saints would have been exposed. Shrines had apertures for offerings, sometimes these were big enough to crawl into; pilgrims could approach as close as possible to the sacred remains and in doing so, receive healing of body and spirit. Great shrines like that of St Thomas Becket at Canterbury were sumptuous, covered with gold, with canopies that could be raised to the sound of tinkling bells, glowing in the light of many candles and bright with gold and silver images and precious stones. In Wales no account books, or detailed descriptions have survived so we can tell relatively little about the appearance of shrines or rituals associated with their veneration. Only fragments survived Reformation, Civil War and Puritan suppression. Anything remotely 'papist' was seized and zealously destroyed. A few notable survivals and disappearances are described here.

One survival is part of the wooden reliquary and shrine of St Erfyl. It was probably made in the 15th century and once preserved the relics of a 6th-century female child saint, Erfyl, who is also commemorated by an early

St Erfyl's reliquary

inscribed stone in Llanerfyl church. A reliquary containing bones was found 2 feet beneath the altar of the church of Llanidan in Anglesey. Once one of the most important churches on Anglesey, dedicated to the 7th-century St Nidan, confessor to the priests of Penmon, it is now an atmospheric ruin. The reliquary has been moved to the new church of St Nidan in Brynsiencyn. Also in Anglesey is the shrine of St Gredifael in Penmynydd church which the saint founded, sometimes called Llanredifael. A healing ritual was performed using alabaster scrapings from a much later tomb close to the shrine, suggesting the common belief that anything placed close to a relic would absorb its sanctity and healing power. Scrapings were also taken from the pillars in St Beuno's grave chapel at Clynnog Fawr for a similar purpose. A stone reliquary which probably once held a relic of St Barruc was recovered from the ruins of the saint's church on Barry Island (Glamorganshire) 1967–68. St Cybi's shrine, kept in his church at Holyhead (Caergybi) succumbed to seaborne aggression from Ireland. Stephen Scrope, Deputy Lieutenant of Ireland landed at Holyhead in 1405 with an Irish army and devastated Anglesey in an attempt to put down the Owain Glyndŵr uprising. The jewelled shrine was snatched and placed on the altar of the church of the Holy Trinity, now Christchurch Cathedral, in Dublin. It disappeared about half a century later. Whilst in Holyhead church the shrine had been a considerable draw for pilgrims and the theft impoverished the church.

Pennant Melangell

The church of St Melangell, in a secluded Montgomeryshire valley was a pilgrimage site from the 12th century. The devotion to Melangell was restricted to this single church. A late 15th-century 'Life' of the saint and a wooden frieze carved on the rood screen of a similar period celebrated the picturesque legend of the forest maiden who protected a little hunted hare from the hounds of Prince Brochfael. The royal pursuer turned preserver and granted Melangell and the hare their woodland sanctuary. Fragments of a greyish sandstone from her shrine surviving in the masonry of the church building and the lychgate were put together in a conjectural reconstruction east of the altar in 1991. No evidence survives of the

Pennant Melangell church, Montgomeryshire

Pennant Melangell rood screen, drawing by John Parker, 1837

Gravestone of Melangell

precise appearance of the original shrine. The bones of St Melangell would have been preserved in a 'house'-shaped shrine above an ornate base. The Cell y Bedd or grave chapel is reached through an archway behind the shrine and a stone marks the grave believed to be that of Melangell. Her reputation for healing was recommended in strong terms to Hywel of Moelyrch who had wounded his knee in a fall from his horse, in a *cywydd* by the 15th-century poet, Guto'r Glyn.[1]

---

[1] Guto names several saints, some well known: Mary, Oswald, Martin, Gwenfrewi (Winifred), Silin, Curig, and two little-known saints – Ieuan of Gwanas and Saint Lednart ('our kinsman'). In another poem Guto calls on 'St Harry' (Henry VI who was promoted by the Lancastrians as a martyr) when he broke three ribs in a fall, and made an offering of a 'long torch' (candle), also wondering if the pains of old age would count as expiation of his sins!

Loomis, R. and Johnston, D. (translation) *Medieval Welsh Poems; an Anthology.* Medieval & Renaissance Texts & Studies, Binghamton, New York 1992.

Llanddwyn

Ruins of Llanddwyn church, Anglesey

One short pilgrimage route, famous in its time, can be identified on Anglesey: the tidal island of Llanddwyn on which stood a large church now ruinous.[2] At a time when the sea level was lower, St Beuno (7th century) walked the sands to preach on the island. St Dwyn or Dwynwen was a 6th-century saint who became famous as the Welsh patron saint of lovers. Her embellished legend and cult survived into the 20th century as one who could heal the pains of unrequited love, having suffered from a broken heart herself. As usual it is the poets who preserve the visual impressions of the medieval church and shrine. Dafydd ap Gwilym, not surprisingly, was familiar with her reputation for healing the lovesick:

> Dwynwen, your beauty like the hoar frost's tears
> from your chancel with its blazing waxen candles
> well does your golden image know
> how to assuage the griefs of wretched men.

[2] An excerpt from W. Bingley, *North Wales, its Scenery, Antiquities, Customs (etc)* 2 Vols, recounts the following disaster which happened to the big Abermenai boat in 1664: the boat had arrived at Abermenai and 'the passengers were about to land, when a misunderstanding occurred concerning a penny more than the people were willing to pay. During the dispute the boat was carried into a deep place, where it upset, and although it was at that time within a few yards of the shore, seventy-nine of the passengers perished, one only escaping. The country people believed that this was a visitation of heaven, because the boat was built of timber that had been stolen from Llanddwyn Abbey.' (This was the church: there was no abbey on Llanddwyn Island.)

What man soever would keep vigil in your choir
(a holy shining pilgrimage) [you with] Indeg's radiance
there is no sickness nor heart's sorrow
which he would carry with him thence from Llanddwyn.

Dwynwen deigr arien degwch
Da y gwyr o gor flamgwyr fflwch
Dy ddelw aur diddolurian
Digion druain ddynion draw
Dyn a wylio gloywdro glân,
Yn dy gor, Indeg eirian,
Nid oes glefyd na bryd brwyn
A el ynddo o Landdwyn.

A late 15th-century cywydd by Sir Dafydd Trefor described the saint's statue, miracles at the holy well and crowds of young people with candles and offerings. The one-time rector of Llanddwyn and Dean of Bangor, Richard Kyffin (Y Deon Du, the Black Dean, d. 1502), encouraged St Dwyn's legend and pilgrimage to the island. A cottage in south Anglesey has the curious name 'Virgin and Child' and is said to have been a hospice for pilgrims to St Dwyn's shrine. In the 14th century the church was one of the wealthiest on Anglesey, deriving most of its income from oblations to its saint. William Worcestre recorded that Dwynwen was buried in her chapel, two miles from Newborough and that there were only two cottages in the township. The parish itself was very poor, the soil produced little, being mainly sand from incursions of the sea, and the tithes came to less than a pound. An 18th-century manuscript stated that Dwynwen was said to have been martyred beside her well on Llanddwyn Island. A crucifix stood just before the church came into view, where pilgrims would place white stones which they had brought with them. A small building called Merddyn Main was associated with pilgrims (footings still survive), and Dafydd ap Gwilym recorded a practice of sleeping on Gwely Esyth (Esyth's bed), reputed to cure aches in the bones and stitches, and also the cutting of names into the turf. Gwely Esyth was the name given to the westerly rock on which the lighthouse stands.

St Winifred – a reliquary casket

A number of relics and reliquaries, now vanished, were recorded by antiquaries who travelled round Wales in the 17th century and later. Edward Lhuyd described and had a drawing made of the reliquary casket in Gwytherin church, Denbighshire, containing relics of St Winifred (*c.* 1699). The saint lived in Gwytherin and a small mound to the south of the church marks the site of a grave chapel. The style of metal-work on the shrine is similar to Anglo-Saxon work of the 8th–9th centuries and may give a clue to its date. A fragment of this reliquary did survive. In 1844 Friar John Wynne, a Jesuit priest, obtained a wood fragment from the sexton at the church. It was rediscovered in 1991 and later identified as one of

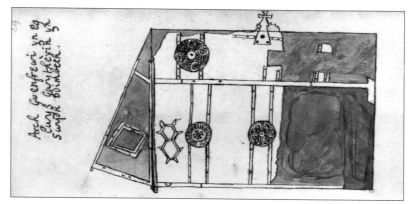

St Winifred's
reliquary casket,
sketch for
Edward Lhuyd

the gable ends of the reliquary drawn for Edward Lhuyd. Portions of a finger relic of St Winifred presented to the English College in Rome in the early 18th century are preserved in St Winifred's church in Holywell and the Catholic cathedral, Shrewsbury.

Cathedrals of the saints

The Norman cathedrals of Wales were built on sites of settlements and churches founded by the early saints and were on important land routes. Bangor and St Asaph were situated along the main route across north Wales and Llandaf was part of a nucleus of important early monastic sites, close to Bristol and the Channel, known as Severnsea, and also at the head of the road west to St Davids. St Davids was at a junction of sea routes between Ireland and the continent, well used by Irish pilgrims.

Llandaf

The riches taken from Llandaf Cathedral at the Reformation reflect the popularity of its shrine and saintly tombs, visited by pilgrims for centuries. Urban, first Bishop of Llandaf 1107–34, born in Glamorgan around 1076, was young and energetic when appointed to the see and intent on raising its profile. Important in the consecration of the new cathedral, begun in 1120, were the relics of major saints. St Euddogwy, an early bishop in south-east Wales and St Teilo were entombed in the cathedral. There may have been difficulties with St Teilo, whose body had miraculously triplicated itself after death, one body going to Penally and the 'real' one probably being buried at Llandeilo Fawr where the saint had died. Llandaf's sanctity was to be increased by the body of St Dyfrig who had cult centres in south Wales. The saint had ended his days on Ynys Enlli, whither Bishop Urban and his clerks went in early 1120. The translation of the relics was agreed to by the king and bishop and the remains of St Dyfrig and a relic of Elgar the hermit of Bardsey were exhumed. Bishop Urban returned in procession to Llandaf preceded by a relic-filled cross which included Elgar's hand. Accompanied by amazing miracles,

Stepsau Teilo, St Teilo's steps, with Ogmore Castle in the background

the bones were reverently washed and on 19 May 1120, the translation took place with great ceremony. Medieval 'Lives' of St Dyfrig and Elgar were written to accompany those of Saints Teilo and Euddogwy to further boost the sanctity and status of the new cathedral. At the Reformation the highly ornamented and valuable shrine with images of the three saints and their personal relics – including silver gilt, head and arm reliquaries with their mitres in silver and double gilt, 'Seynt Teilos shoes silver beyd with stones', his comb and the golden bell of St Euddogwy with 4–5,000 ounces of plate – were seized and taken to London, although jewels and plate were also secretly removed by the canons.

Llandaf Cathedral had a number of images of St Teilo and the devotion to the saint left other traces in, around and generally connected with the cathedral. The north door was called St Teilo's door and although unproven, a suggestion has been made that the northern entrance to cathedrals was possibly also a pilgrim entrance.[3] Pilgrims enter sacred places through doors designated for that purpose. In Christian tradition it is a symbolic act, based on St John's Gospel (Chapter 10, verse 7): 'Jesus said . . . I am the door of the sheep', marking the passage from sin to grace. It was also necessary to have a defined route around a shrine, in particular when a large, excitable and devotionally charged body of people was moving through a fairly limited space especially on festivals and saints' days.

[3] To mark the millenium, the Pope broke the seal on the Sacred Door of St Peter's Basilica. The door is normally bricked up and has only been opened 27 times since 1423, marking the start of holy years. The ceremony was repeated in Catholic dioceses throughout the world. In London the Rt Rev. Vincent Nichols opened the Pilgrim's Door to Westminster Cathedral, first knocking three times.
Press report by Bruce Johnston and Victoria Combe, 24.12.99

The 12th-century tombs of St Dyfrig and St Teilo survive and Teilo's holy well is tucked under the wall on the old road from the east end of the cathedral to the old bishop's palace: it continued to draw pilgrims up to the 20th century. There is a local tradition that 'Black Hall' in Heol Fair, associated with the Black Friars, was a pilgrim hospice. The building has two surviving medieval windows. Pilgrims on their way to Llandaf might have crossed the River Ogmore using the now vanished Stepsau Teilo, St Teilo's stepping stones near the church of Merthyr Mawr. The saint's feast day, Dilo Fair/Ffair Ŵyl Deilo, was celebrated in Llandaf and Llandeilo Fawr on 9 February.

Bangor

St Deiniol, founder saint of Bangor, was buried on Ynys Enlli. There is no record of a tomb in the cathedral but his picture, once painted on the north wall near the high altar, must have attracted pilgrim devotion: Bishop Skevington's (1509–33) heart was buried before it. St Dwynwen was also venerated at the cathedral. At the Reformation, in the August of 1538, Richard Ingworth, Bishop of Dover sent Thomas Cromwell 'the holiest relic in all north Wales' taken from the friars of Bangor with the following comment: '. . . there may no man kiss that but he must kneel as soon as he sees it, and he must kiss every stone, for in each is great pardon. After that he hath kissed it, he must pay a "meed" of corn, or a cheese or a groat, or fourpence for it. It was worth to the friars in Bangor, with another image which I have closed up, twenty marks by the year in corn, cheese, cattle and money.'

St Asaph

St Asaph's relics were preserved in his cathedral. One of these would have been the Gospel book known as Eugglethen (from *evangelium*). It was probably written in the 8th century and is comparable to Llyfr Teilo, The Book of Teilo, now known as The Lichfield Gospels. After the destruction of St Asaph's cathedral by the English in 1282, Eugglethen was taken in procession around the diocese, and in three years had attracted offerings of £95 towards the rebuilding of the cathedral. The pattern of pilgrimage to St Asaph can be seen in the granting of indulgences on the feast day of its saint and other major festivals of the church's year: '1344. Relaxation of a year and forty days of enjoyned penances was granted to penitents who visited the Church of St Asaph on the feast of that Saint.' In the year 1395, 'Relaxation of seven years and seven quadragenae to penitents who on the principal feasts of the year, those of the dedication, Holy Trinity, Saints Philip and James, the Octaves of certain of them and the six days of Whitsun-week; and of a hundred days to those who, during the said octaves and six days, visit and give alms to the fabric of the church of St Asaph.'

St Asaph was damaged again, this time by Owain Glyndŵr who burned the cathedral in 1402. The dependence on pilgrimage for the maintenance and repair of the building and its shrine is manifested in the granting of indulgences to those who visited the cathedral and gave alms for its repair in 1426: 'To all faithful. Relaxation during 10 years, of three years and three quarantines of enjoined penance to penitents who on the principal feasts of the year and that of St Asaph, the octaves of certain of them and the six days of Whitsun week, and of a hundred days to those who during the said octaves and days visit and give alms for the repair of the Church of St Asaph, which on account of wars and other calamities, has been burned and despoiled of its books, chalices, vestments and other ornaments and of manors and habitations belonging to the bishop and the episcopal mensa and whose costly repair has been begun by Bishop Robert.'

Images

> *He that adores an image adores in it the person depicted thereby*
>
> *Second Council of Nicea, AD 787*

> *. . . Images serve for none other purpose but as to be books of unlearned men that cannot know letters*
>
> H. Bettenson, *Documents of the Christian Church*, 2nd ed. 1963

> *Antique Gargels of ydolatry*
>
> Bishop William Barlow of St Davids,
> letters relating to the suppression of monasteries

From the 12th century there developed throughout Europe a devotion to sacred images carved in wood, stone or metal and often brightly painted. At first these were of Jesus and Mary, depicting and stressing their human and compassionate nature, an aspect of devotion inspired by the teachings of the monastic orders particularly the Cistercians. The sufferings of Jesus on the Cross and the desolation of his mother Mary, were depicted on the crosses or roods that appeared in churches, towns, villages and countryside. The devotion to images extended to saints – native, continental and apostolic – and continued up to the Reformation. Many niches once containing statues can be observed standing empty in churches and cathedrals. In St Davids Cathedral the nave altar niches remained empty until the early 20th century when they were filled by modern statues, and some niches bear scars where the crowbars of reformers have prised out the medieval images.

Images, wall paintings and the rich hues of stained glass gave colour and life to churches, conveying the teaching of the Bible and the lives of the saints with direct emotional appeal, seeking to teach the heart through the eye. Images of saints, the Virgin and Christ were imbued with the potency of relics. Realism could be taken to extremes: some appeared to weep, others moved by means of concealed mechanical devices. In Wales, images of Our Lady were sometimes called *Delw Fyw* or living image as in Mold and Rhiw (Llŷn). It is not known whether these were indeed moving images or simply very lifelike.

Spectacular and renowned beyond the borders of Wales was Derfel Gardarn, Derfel the mighty. Ynys Enlli claimed the body of this 6th-century warrior saint

St Derfel's horse, or deer, with pole for carrying

who was said to have been one of the few survivors of the Battle of Camlan. The footings of a pilgrim chapel dedicated to him can still be made out 300 metres up the slopes of Mynydd Maen, on the pilgrim track from Llantarnam to Penrhys. The chapel preserved a relic of the saint and its value at the supression of the monasteries was one-third that of Penrhys, but the famous image that attracted thousands of pilgrims was at Llandderfel, Montgomeryshire. People made offerings of cattle, horses and money to this image of a mounted and armed man. In 1538, the commissary for the diocese of St Asaph, Elis Price informed his master Thomas Cromwell that between five and six hundred people had gathered to pay tribute to the image of Derfel Gadarn on his feast day, 5 April. Cromwell's order that it should be confiscated and brought to London elicited an angry response from priest and parishioners who offered £40 to redeem Derfel and set out for London to secure his return. This was to no avail: it had been prophesied that the image would set a whole forest afire. How this came about is revealed in a contemporary account. 'A huge and great image was brought to the gallows ... brought out of Wales, and of Welshmen much sought and worshipped'. Friar Forest of Greenwich was burned to death in the flames that consumed the image of Derfel Gadarn. The following verse, giving accusation and sentence was displayed on the gallows:

David Darvell Gatheren
As saith the Welshmen
Fetched outlawes out of hell.
Now he is come with spere and shilde
In harnes to burn in Smithfelde,
For in Wales he may not dwell.
And Forest the frier
That obstinate lyer,
That wilfully shall be dead,
In his contumacie
The Gospell doth deny
The kyng to be supreme head

John Forest, one-time Chaplain to Queen Katherine of Aragon, was suspended in chains from a pair of gallows with the wooden image of Derfel set beneath him; the image was kindled and the martyr suffered a lingering death in the flames.

Queen of Heaven, Star of the Sea, Golden Sister

Lliw ynod a llawenydd
Yr holl saint eraill sydd

All the colour and joy of the rest of the saints that exist

Dafydd Epynt

The devotion given to the Blessed Virgin Mary ultimately surpassed every other saint in Wales and throughout the country, numerous churches, shrines and holy wells were dedicated to her. Statues and paintings that most powerfully drew the pilgrim were those of the Virgin. Her cult permeated all life. Such was the reverence accorded to her that her Welsh name 'Mair' was never used as a girl's name as it is today, only a diminutive, 'Mari'. Numerous wild flowers were called after her and have been exquisitely illustrated in the Frank Roper reredos in the Lady Chapel, Llandaf Cathedral:

Miaren Mair	Mary's Briar	Briar Rose
Clustog Mair	Mary's Pillow	Sea Thrift
Gwniadur Mair	Mary's Thimble	Foxglove
Gwlydd Melyn Mair Fair	Mary's Yellow Stem	Yellow Pimpernel
Mantell Mair	Mary's Mantle	Ground Ivy
Esgid Mair	Mary's Slipper	Monkshood
'Gold' Mair	Mary's Gold	Marigold
Llysiau'r Forwen	The Virgin's Herbs	Meadow Sweet
Ysgol Mair	Mary's Ladder	St John's Wort
Briallu Mair	Mary's Primrose	Cowslip
Chwys Mair	Mary's Sweat	Buttercup
Tapr Mair	Mary's Taper	Snowdrop

Some of the famous shrines and images dedicated to her which have disappeared are listed below:

Tintern Abbey – '1414, March 3. Grant of indulgence of 7 years and 7 quarantines to those who on numerous named major feast days visit the chapel without the west door of the church of the Cistercian monastery of St Mary the Virgin, Tintern . . . and give alms for the repair and decoration of its buildings and ornaments, in which chapel an image of St Mary the Virgin has been fairly and honourably and devoutly placed, and although the attempt has been made, has been unable to be placed elsewhere, on account of which miracle, and because mass is said daily by the monks at the altar of the said chapel, a very great multitude resorts to the chapel'.

Mold – Delw Fyw, a 'living' image which moved. In 1662, John Ray reported that in the church there was a 'stone pedestal and a canopy, where they say stood a living or quick image'. It appears to have been discovered in taking down the old tower in 1768, near the foundation, and ordered by the then vicar to be demolished as a 'popish relic'.

Gresford – miracle-working statue

Beddgelert – shrine to the Blessed Virgin of Snowdon

Haverfordwest – Our Lady of the Taper

Cardigan – Our Lady of the Taper

Penrhys – image and holy well

Llŷn – Rhiw, Delw Fyw, a 'living' image

Llŷn – Llanystumdwy, Our Lady of the Throne

The Welsh poets were lavish in their praise of her, and the conception of Christ in her womb was compared to the passage of the sun's rays through glass. A carol preserved in Cardiganshire – a rare survival – described her as *Dlos lili y dyffryn, wiw rosyn y nef*, 'fair lily of the valley, meet rose of heaven'. Another survival has been adapted for use at Penrhys; this protective prayer was still used in north Wales at the end of the 19th century.

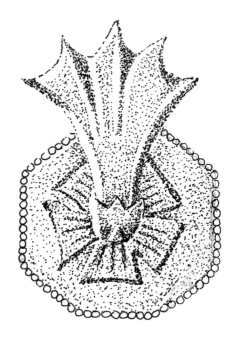

Lily and Rose pilgrim badge from Walsingham, representing the Blessed Virgin Mary

MARY'S DREAM

Blessed Mother Mary, art thou sleeping?
Yes my dear Son I am dreaming.
Blessed Mother, what dost thou see in thy dream?
I see thee pursued, followed, taken
And placed upon the cross;
Thy hands and thy feet nailed
And a dark blind horseman, deceived by the evil one
With the point of his spear piercing thee.

A sore but good dream is this, said Christ
He who recites this dream three times
Before he lays him down to rest
Will not by evil dreams be harried
Nor tread the land of Hell,
But reach the City of the Blest.

Traditional

Mair o Aberteifi (Mary of Cardigan)

The shrine of Our Lady of Cardigan is today the National Catholic Shrine of Wales. The modern statue holds her son upon her lap and a taper in her hand as the medieval statue once did. The Teifi river crossing, where the church of St Mary stands, had been a site of miracles and pilgrimages from the time of Gerald of Wales and although he makes no mention of the Virgin and taper, the church dates from 1158, thirty years before his visit. A commemorative chapel was built where Archbishop Baldwin stood to preach the third crusade. The chapel was probably on the Pembrokeshire side of the Teifi river, just upstream from the old bridge. A 'twmp' or mound and Capel Sidan once marked the spot. 'Later on crowds of sick people thronged to the spot from all parts of the country and many miracles were performed there', wrote Gerald, adding dismissively that he did not have the time to tell the reader about them.

The legend of Our Lady of the Taper, preserved in the correspondence of Bishop William Barlow *c.* 1538, recounted that the image was found standing by the river Teifi. It was taken to Christ church, later known as Holy Trinity, but repeatedly found its way back to the riverside 'Where now is buylded the church of our Lady'. The taper burned continuously for nine years until a man perjured himself on it, after which it never burned again. A chantry at the east end of St Mary's church was built to house the statue and a mass in honour of the Virgin was celebrated daily.

An account of the latter days of the taper was left by Thomas Hore, Prior of Cardigan. The taper's appearance was said to have dated back to the priory's foundation in the 12th century. Bishop Barlow's informant had never seen the taper itself but wrote that 'it was enclosed and taken for a greate relyque, and so worshipped and kyssed of pylgremes, and used often to sweare by in dificill and harde matters'; according to a previous prior, John Frodsam, people had taken wax away and a wooden container remained. To the reformers, people were apparently 'worshippinge . . . a pece of old rotten tymber'.

At the Reformation, *c.* 1538, it was ominously noted that the shrine 'ys used for a greate pilgrimage to this presente day'. It also supplied the Abbot of Chertsey of which Cardigan priory was a daughter house, with an income of 20 nobles a year. Its fate was sealed. The iconoclast Bishop Barlow of St Davids condemned it as an instance of 'develysh delusyon' and it was destroyed.

Mair o Fynyw (Mary of Menevia)
The devotion to the Virgin developed over the centuries to be another of St Davids' attractions. The building of a Lady Chapel is probably connected with the foundation of a daily mass in honour of the Blessed Virgin Mary by Bishop Anselm around 1248, though the present chapel was built by Bishop Martyn, 1290–1328. The veneration of the Virgin Mary appeared to flourish in the 14th century. The wills of two bishops directed that they should be buried in the Lady Chapel; Bishop Fastolfe, d. 1361, 'on the right hand of the image of the Blessed Mary in her chapel'. At the same period Dafydd ap Gwilym described her as 'Holy Mother of all happiness robed in purple/who lives between Mynyw and the sea'. St Mary's College of Priests was established in 1382 and the water from St Mary's Well, near the east end of the cathedral, ran through the crypt of the college chapel. The well was closed by Sir Gilbert Scott and the water drained into the river: its site is not known. South of the cathedral 'Merrivale' may be derived from Mary Vale. Bishop Benedict Nicholls, d. 1433, directed his body to be buried 'in St Mary of Menevia's chapel before her image'. In the 15th century Hywel Swrdwal, *fl.* 1430–60, celebrated 'Mair o Fynyw'. Pilgrims were drawn by a detailed representation of the Holy Family and of Mary's parents, St Anne and Joachim mentioned in the will of Bishop Vaughan, 1509–20. An extract from the local *Telegraph* dated 5 June 1901, reported that during the restoration of the Lady Chapel, 'a very ancient carving was found in the floor, which was preserved by Mr John Morgan. It represented the Mother of Our Lord recumbent in a stall with one hand raised to the Child in the manger and Joseph standing near Mary's feet. It was placed in Bishop Vaughan's Chapel with a number of ancient crosses . . .'. Cathedral architect W. D. Caroe described it as a relief representing the birth of the Virgin but the presence of a staff held by the standing figure is characteristic of St Joseph. These fragments were eventually set into the altar of Holy Trinity chapel and a closer inspection of the Nativity scene, although badly damaged, reveals some fine carving.[4]

---

[4] I have found this style of portrayal in two 13th-century depictions of the Nativity with Mary recumbent, Joseph at the foot of her couch and the Infant Christ in his manger, raised above the couch of the Virgin as appears in the Ingeburg Psalter (Musee de Conde, Chantilly, 1210) and in a Franco Flemish Annunciation and Nativity (British Museum Add. MS 287343, f2, late 13th century).

Mair o Gydweli (Mary of Kidwelly)

In three places, traditions survived of the Virgin Mary paying a visit to Wales: at Llanfair in Meirioneth, Ffynnon Fair near Aberdaron and at Kidwelly where pilgrimages were made to Ffynnon Fair (Mary's Well) on Lady Day (the Feast of the Annunciation, 25 March) and pins offered until recent times. Kidwelly is fortunate in preserving a medieval alabaster statue of the Virgin. Originally in the porch, it was curtsied to by women coming to church until the 19th century. A vicar of the time strongly disapproved of this behaviour and buried the statue in the churchyard. This once full-length image was disinterred in 1875 and has been reinstated in the church.

Mair o Cydweli, Mary of Kidwelly, medieval alabaster image

Chapter 9

Four pilgrim shrines

MYNYW – ST DAVIDS

Fair smooth paradise of Wales

OVER eight hundred years ago, on a barren windswept peninsula, a small, heavily built Norman cathedral crouched in a stony valley, beside a 'muddy and unproductive stream'. A feature of note was a large slab of marble spanning the stream, polished by the passage of many feet: its name was Llech Lafar, the talking stone. It is to Gerald of Wales, writing in 1188, that we owe this brief and earliest picture of St Davids, or Mynyw as it was then known. Two hundred years after Gerald had penned his disparaging, almost dismissive description of the place, it had become a major pilgrimage centre. St Davids or Menevia was also the largest and most controversial of the four Welsh medieval dioceses, asserting its perceived right to be independent of Canterbury. Welsh princes and magnates who strove to protect their inheritance and Norman and Angevin kings who would hold Wales in subjection, paid pilgrim visits to St Davids, mixing piety with their politics. On the

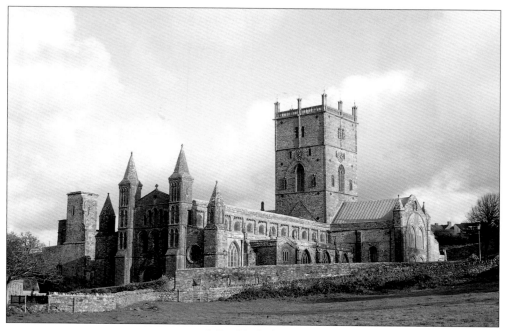

St Davids Cathedral

extremity of a western peninsula, the place was reached by roads which were extremely difficult. Gerald knew this well; he had travelled them often. Sea-going was easy by comparison: ships came to and from St Davids using the inlet or *ria* of Porth Clais, the small harbour of Porth Stinan (St Justinian's), or the wide beach of Porth Mawr (Whitesands).

By the closing years of the 14th century, the medieval city spread graciously within its high perimeter wall. Of the Cathedral, in its sheltered valley surrounded by the houses and gardens of dignitaries, the resplendent Bishop's Palace and St Mary's College of Priests with its chapel and cloistered calm, we have only one contemporary word-picture. The ageing Welsh poet, Iolo Goch, had his soul's salvation in mind when he wrote of his longing to go to Menevia. Caught by Iolo's pen, St Davids shines out like a rich painting from a medieval *Book of Hours*: an eternal summer of olive trees and vines. The poem speaks most eloquently for itself.

I Ddewi Sant

Dymuno da i'm enaid,
Heneiddio'r wyf, hyn oedd rhaid,
Myned i'r lle croged Crist
Cyd boed y ddeudroed ddudrist
Mewn trygyff yma'n trigaw,
Ni myn y traed myned draw.
Cystal ymofal im yw
Fyned deirgwaith i Fynyw
a myned, cymyrred cain,
Yr hafoedd hyd yn Rhufain.
Gwyddwn lle mynnwn fy mod,
Ys deddfol yw'r eisteddfod,
Ym maenol Ddewi Mynyw,
Mangre gain, myn y grog, yw;
Yng Nglyn Rhosyn mae'r iesin,
Ac olewydd a gwydd gwin
Ac edmig musig a moes
A gwrle gwyr ac orloes
A chytgerdd hoyw, loyw lewych,
Rhwng organ achlan a chlych,
A thrwblwm aur trwm tramawr
Yn bwrw sens i beri sawr.
Nef nefoedd yn gyhoedd gain,
Ys da dref ystad Rufain,
Paradwys Gymru lwys lefn,
Por dewistref p'radwystrefn.

To St David

Doing good to my soul,
I am getting old, this was necessary
to go to the place where Christ was crucified
although my two sad black feet
are stuck here in fetters,
the feet do not wish to go there.
It is just as beneficial to me
to go three times to Menevia
as to go, fine dignity
in the summers as far as Rome.
I knew where I would wish to be,
it is a virtuous residence,
in the manor of David of Menevia,
it is a fine spot, by the Cross;
in Glyn Rhosyn is the beautiful (place),
and olive trees and vines
and excellence of music and manner
and the sound of men and a clock
and lively harmony, shining brilliance,
between an entire organ and bells,
and a great heavy golden thuribulum
emitting incense to give a sweet odour.
Fine heaven of heavens open to all,
it's a good town after the fashion of Rome,
fair smooth paradise of Wales
choice sovereign town laid out like paradise.

Iolo Goch, 1320–98   translated by Dafydd Johnson

Seek St Davids twice . . .

The development of St Davids into a major pilgrim centre took place over the centuries that led up to and beyond the Norman Conquest. St David's Dark Age monastic foundation, Cille Muine, church of the grove, was reorganised under the first Norman bishop, Bernard. It was Latinised to Menevia and recognised by Pope Calixtus II as the church of St Andrew and St David.

A sequence of events that began with William the Conqueror's visit in 1081 and reached a high point two hundred years later, helped to place St Davids firmly on the map of medieval pilgrimage. Shortly after William's visit, a biography of St David was written by Rhygyfarch, the son of Bishop Sulien of St Davids. In the veneration of saints, martyrs and confessors, a saint's 'Life' was important in the development of pilgrimage. Readings from it would be used on the saint's patronal festival and the book itself would have had the status of a relic. Miracles attributable to the saint's intervention on behalf of humankind were also essential in the promotion of pilgrimage. A collection of St David's miracles has survived, probably compiled in the early 15th century and once in the possession of William Worcestre. It is small by comparison with other collections but gives a flavour of the atmosphere of excitable, credulous and emotional crowds gathering to celebrate major feast days. In the episcopate of Bishop Gower, 1328–47, the 'largest assemblage of the people' gathered on St David's Day, Whitsuntide and the Nativity of St John the Baptist, 24 June[1] and it was at a Whitsun, or Pentecost

---

[1] Crowds of pilgrims also gathered at Slebech on this feast day.

Pilgrims as they might have been. Members of the White Company assemble outside the west door of St Davids Cathedral

gathering when a miracle happened with which parents of any century could empathise. It probably took place in the nave. 'In the year of the Lord 1231, on a Monday, the day following Pentecost, while people were coming on pilgrimage from various regions to Saint David's church at Menevia, as is customary, there came a little boy about eight years old named David ab Gwrgeneu. Climbing up the highest stairs of the church, he played with the other boys. And as God the all-powerful, looking down from on high, aroused the devotion of the people towards Himself and His glorious confessor David, the little boy fell from the heights down to the ground, a distance of twenty cubits and more (35–40 feet). Yet, behold he got up happy, safe and without harm, and coming back through the church, he ran off as though he had never fallen. When they saw this, the clergy and people praised God, who works through his saints.'

The 12th century saw an expansion of the cult of St David. Bishop Bernard visited Pope Calixtus II in Rome in 1123 and a papal letter of the same date confirmed the privileges and possessions of the church of St Andrew the Apostle and St David: *Sancti Andreae apostoli et Sancti David ecclesiam.* From this emerged the official acceptance of David's sainthood as a matter of immemorial record. The St Davids 'indulgence', or privilege (two pilgrimages to St Davids equal one to Rome) has always been ascribed to Pope Calixtus II. In the words of the contemporary writer William of Malmesbury (?1080–?1143) the Pope 'encouraged English pilgrims to go to St Davids rather than Rome because of the length of the journey; those who went twice to St Davids should have the same privileges as those who went once to Rome': *adeo ut Anglos peregrines magis ad Sanctum David quam Romam pergere ammoneret pro uiae longitudine: ad illum locum bis euntibus idem benedictionis refundendum commodum quod haberent qui semel Romam irent.* He is said to have conferred similar benefits on Santiago de Compostela and Ynys Enlli (the latter required three pilgrimages). This privilege was written into the chronicles and is still quoted today. It was to be found at the end of the 9th lesson for the Feast of St David at Exeter Cathedral in a lectionary, a series of special readings brought out by Bishop Grandisson of Exeter *c.* 1340, in the form of a declaration that all British pilgrims who went to the shrine of holy David twice would be granted the same blessings and indulgences had they gone once to Rome. A miracle from an early 15th-century collection, said to have occurred in the time of Bishop Iorwerth (1215–29) claimed that 'the fame of St David had spread over the world' and directly attributed this to Pope Calixtus, adding 'as can be read in the chronicles'. Another reference is attributed to Archbishop Pecham when he visited in 1283 and discovered in an old chronicle there the following 'monkish verses':

> *Meneviam pete bis, Romam adire si vis*
> *Aequa mercestibi, redditur hic et ibi;*
> *Roma semel quantum dat bis Menevia tantum.*
>
>   G. Owen's MSS[2]

---

[2] The same wording is also used in the late 16th-century manuscript quoted by Browne Willis, *Memoirs Relating to the Cathedral Church of Saint David's.*

Translated, it runs thus:

> Seek St Davids twice if you wish to visit Rome,
> Equal merit will be given to you here and there;
> Rome gives once as much as St Davids gives double

The Welsh version was also a close translation:

> *Dos i Rufain unwaith ac i Fynyw ddwywaith,*
> *A'r un elw cryno a gei di yma ag yno.*

Rhymes and jingles like the above, extolling the benefits to pilgrims offered by various shrines, were typical of 'advertising' techniques that developed during the 12th century. Sometimes they appeared in pamphlets or were written on a wooden board or *tabula*, with details of indulgences and displayed near the shrine. It was celebrated in *Cywydd Dewi Sant* by Lewis Glyn Cothi and by Iolo Goch, whose recollection was somewhat vague. It has also been suggested that this was a papal attempt to ease pilgrim pressure on Rome.[3] However, although belief in this 'indulgence' was widely held, remembered long after the Reformation and often quoted right up to the present day, its precise meaning has been lost.

The growth of ideas and flowering of faith and devotion in the 12th century must have reached St Davids. In spite of the struggles and difficulties that colour the pages of the contemporary annals, two cathedrals were built in the space of 50 years (1131 and 1181) on the site of the old church and monastery of St David. At the end of that century St Davids had been visited twice by Henry II. Rhygyfarch's late-11th-century *Life* of the saint included local colour, places in west Wales associated with St David which would stimulate pilgrim interest. By the end of the 13th century, the status of St Davids was evidently sufficient for it to appear with Conway and Caernarfon – with their recently-built Edwardian castles – as one of only three settlements in Wales marked on the Mappa Mundi. This magnificent map, made in the late 13th century by Richard of Holdingham and taken to Hereford where it has been ever since, contained contemporary information on trade and pilgrimage routes.[4]

In the mid-13th century, the long sought grave of St David was rediscovered. A new shrine was constructed in 1275 and was followed soon after by the visit of Edward I and Queen Eleanor during the episcopate of Thomas Bek. The bishops must have had accommodation available to them suitable to entertain these crowned heads, though in 1171 Henry II declined to burden Bishop David Fitzgerald's

---

[3] In the holy year of 1300 for which figures are available, there were 200,000 pilgrims in Rome on any one day; according to Dante, a strict foot-traffic system was in force on the Ponte Sant Angelo.

[4] A number of these world maps were produced between the 12th and 14th centuries; the detail could only be seen clearly at close quarters and as they were in Norman French, they could only be read by a literate élite. Delos, originally the centre of the known world was replaced in 1100 by Jerusalem. On Hereford's map, Britain is on an outer rim, at the edge of which is Wales.

evidently limited resources with his entire entourage; however, the palace of Bishop Gower was yet to be built. Substantial funding would have been needed for such an enterprise and although Henry Gower's resources are not precisely known, presumably the processing of the relics throughout the diocese and the offerings of pilgrims played a part. The cult of St David would have been further enhanced during the 14th century by a translation into Welsh of Rhygyfarch's Latin *Life* of the saint. In its glorious finished state, the palace was sumptuously equipped to house the bishop and his retinue and to entertain important guests, but its zenith was to be short-lived. The Black Death in 1348 and its subsequent recurrences in the latter part of the 14th century were to decimate and restructure society in Wales as elsewhere: in the year 1349–50 an unprecedented number of priests were ordained from the diocese of St Davids indicating the replacement of large numbers of the clergy who succumbed to the disease. Towards the end of the 14th century pilgrimage either revived or never really ceased. In 1382 Bishop Adam Houghton established St Mary's College of Priests, training men and boys to sing the services and in 1385 decreed a safe conduct for pilgrims in the city and church of St Davids. In 1398, the year of Guy Mone's consecration, a celebration of the feast of St David with nine lessons was decreed by Archbishop Roger Walden and in 1401, safe conduct extended to pilgrims from the boundary of Pebidiog. Despite the disruption of the wars of Owain Glyndŵr at the beginning of the 15th century the veneration of St David continued to thrive: Henry Chichele, briefly Bishop of St Davids later to become Archbishop of Canterbury decreed a full choral setting for the saint's feast and the privilege of the 'two pilgrimages' became widely known and publicised. A

Medieval ruins of St Non's chapel, St Davids

Ruins of Bishop Gower's 14th-century palace, St Davids

praise poem by Ieuan ap Rhydderch linked the cathedral with the three great shrines of Christendom: Jerusalem, Rome and '*Sens a mwg ail Sain Siam yw*' ('here is incense and smoke of another Santiago'). He wrote of relics, vestments, images, lamps, stained glass, the wonderful choir and the organ. There is an unusual reference to a female pilgrim in the writings of Lewis Glyn Cothi: Edudful ferch Gadwgan who went first to St Non's church, where she placed candles on the altar, then visited the well before going to the cathedral where she kissed either the saint's image or his relics and left an offering. Verse and translation are given on page 212.

As the century progressed the palace at St Davids was much less used by its bishops but ruin was not yet imminent: in 1493 the office of keeper of the palace was established and its continued upkeep suggests that it was used to accommodate pilgrims to the shrine of St David. But by the mid-16th century decline and decay were advancing and although total destruction of the palace was threatened it never came about. Today, its majestic ruins whisper of the world once captured by the pen of Iolo Goch.

Royal Pilgrims

> 1081 *William the Bastard, King of the Saxons and the French and the Welsh came for prayer on a pilgrimage to Mynyw.*
> *y deuth Gwilim Bastard, brenhin y Saesson a'r Freinc a'r Brytanyeit, wrth wediaw drwy bererindawt y Vynyw.*
>
> Brut y Tywysogyon

> *William the Bastard came on a pilgrimage to Wales, and bestowed gifts upon the churches, the Bishops, priests, the monasteries and the monks, and went as far as Menevia.*
> *y daeth William Fastard i Cymru um mhererindawd, ac a ddug roddion i'r eglwysi, a'r Escyb, offeiriaid, ac i'r monachlogydd a'r mynaich, a myned hyd ym Mynyw.*
>
> Brut Gwent

Norman kings showed an early interest in St Davids. William the Conqueror, with shrewd acquisitiveness, would have assessed its strategic and political importance. In 1081 he came to Wales on pilgrimage as far as Menevia and its charismatic saint. What rumours of the conqueror had run before him when he rode with his entourage into that valley with its church and monastery that time has hidden from us, and what impression did William leave on St Davids? He is said to have made his encampment alongside Ffos y Myneich – Monks' Ditch[5], an ancient boundary that once marked sanctuary land, bisecting the peninsula. The small settlement north-east of St Davids, Rhodiad y Brenin (the king's highway), may owe its name to this visit but in local folklore other claimants to that title were king Arthur and

---

[5] Archdeacon Payne gives the plural form – Ffos y Myneich – Monks' Ditch.

Henry II. However, in 1815 it was noted that the section of the Ffos forming the boundary between the farms of Trelerwr and Llandrudion bore the name Ffordd Brenin Wiliam, or King William's Way which suggests an approach along the southern coast of the peninsula.

> 1171 *Henry II, king of England, came to visit St Davids from England and thence he entered Ireland.*
>
> Annales Cambriae

> *vynet y brenhin y Vynyw y pererinha. Ac offrymaw a wnaeth y brenhin y Mynyw deu cappan cor o bali ar veder cantoryeit y wassanaethu Duw a Dewi'. Ac offrymaw heuyt a oruc dyrneit o arant, am gyfyl y dec swllt.*
>
> Brut y Tywysogyon

The latter account claims that King Henry left gifts of two choral copes of brocaded silk for the use of cantors which would have been worn on major feasts during the singing of the Divine Office, and a 'handful' of silver, about ten shillings, a reasonably generous offering. Henry dined with Bishop David Fitzgerald then rode through heavy rain to Pembroke where he sailed for Ireland. He returned to St Davids the Easter of the following year.

> 1172, 17th April, *Henry II King of England, returning from Ireland, came to St David for the sake of praying.*
>
> Annales Cambriae

Gerald of Wales gave a colourful account of Henry's second visit. It was a particularly sensitive time for Henry who was not officially pardoned for his part in the murder of the primate Thomas Becket in 1170, until May 1172, a month after his visit to St Davids. The king landed at St Justinians and, dressed as a pilgrim, on foot and leaning on a staff, he made his way to the cathedral. He entered the Close by the White Gate, a site now vanished under brambles and remembered in the name Pen Porth Gwyn, where he was met by a procession of canons. Henry approached the cathedral, reaching the River Alun, spanned at that time by Llech Lafar, the talking stone, so called because it cried out when a corpse was carried over it. There he was accosted by a Welsh woman making a complaint about the bishop which could not be addressed at the time and thus thwarted she cursed him with Merlin's prophecy of death to the king who set foot on *Llech Lafar.* Apparently Henry knew the

Site of Porth Gwyn, the White Gate, St Davids

prophecy and entered into the spirit, challenging the Welsh enchanter and crossing unscathed before entering the cathedral for mass.

> 1284 On the morning of the feast day of St Catherine, 25 November, King Edward and Queen Eleanor visited the shrine of St David. The bishop was Thomas Bek.
>
> Annales Cambriae

Bishop Bek was no stranger to an event of this nature: a former archdeacon of Lincoln, the day of his consecration to St Davids was marked by the translation of the relics of St Hugh to the Angel Choir of Lincoln Cathedral. The ceremonial and festivities were paid for by the new bishop of St Davids, even making two conduits run with wine for the benefit of the poor, and the event was attended by King Edward and Queen Eleanor. Not long after Bishop Bek's installation at St Davids (1282), the king and queen paid their visit. It resulted apparently in generous donations by the king to the cathedral fabric and for the adornment of the new shrine (1275) of St David. It was common practice for distinguished visitors to shrines to be given relics: an arm bone of St David was found in the king's effects after his death and in 1285 he paraded the head of St David through London. The popularity of the shrine from this time is suggested by numbers of Edwardian coins that have been found in and around St Davids and are still occasionally found.

> 1394, September 18–19 Richard II visited St Davids
>
> N. Saul

No bishops' records for this period have survived. Evidence for the visit comes from details of a journey the king made to Ireland when he stayed at Llawhaden, St Davids and Haverfordwest before setting sail from Milford Haven. Bishop Guy Mone of St Davids was a loyal supporter of the king when storm clouds gathered towards the end of his reign, leading to Richard's deposition, imprisonment and in 1399, his untimely death.

Cathedral, pilgrimage and Santiago de Compostela

All over Europe, the 11th–13th centuries saw a great spiritual outpouring. On the continent, leading and charismatic figures such as St Bernard of Clairvaux, Peter Abelard and St Thomas Aquinas attracted large and enthusiastic followings. The crusades gave an added impetus to pilgrimage to the Holy Land and an interest in its sacred sites. Various important relics such as fragments of the True Cross found their way back to Britain. It was also the era of cathedral building, supported by the movement of vast numbers of pilgrims across the continent. The income brought by pilgrims could be of considerable financial benefit and it was important to attract and accommodate them. The building of shrines to house sacred relics influenced the way certain churches and cathedrals were constructed.

It was during this great ferment of ideas and spiritual aspiration all over Europe that the first Norman cathedral in St Davids was built in 1131. According to

St James, patron saint of pilgrims, 14th-century relief carving, St Davids Cathedral

records, Peter de Leia took down this building in 1181 and rebuilt the cathedral: his building stands today. We do not know precisely why this major and costly step was taken, but it is likely that it was in part motivated by contemporary church and cathedral building and rebuilding taking place all over Europe, mediated by the influential monastery of Cluny whose church in 1131–32 was the largest in Europe (555 feet), and the translation of sacred relics to new, costlier and more magnificent shrines. In particular the building of the new cathedral may have taken account of the style of church architecture that developed along the pilgrim routes to the great Galician shrine of St James, Santiago de Compostela, which involved an organisation of space designed to facilitate the movement of pilgrims around the shrines. These churches were built on a grand scale, with long-aisled naves, large transepts, walled-in choirs with fine acoustics and ambulatory-style east ends. They served as models for the design of many smaller churches. Borrowings from this 'pilgrim formula' can be seen in much 12th-century church architecture. Although Peter de Leia's 1181 cathedral in St Davids ended at the high altar, it was not long before it was extended to include an ambulatory around what is now Holy Trinity chapel, but previously may have been the site of the tomb of St David. The Lady Chapel was built east of this in the 13th century, reflecting the veneration of the Blessed Virgin Mary and her increasing popularity in St Davids.

Conveniently situated between Ireland and the continent, St Davids was visited by Irish pilgrims and may have been a gathering point for those travelling along the ancient sea routes. The many small medieval chapels on the shores of Pembroke-shire, where prayers for a safe voyage would be said and offerings made in thanksgiving for a safe landing, testify to a vigorous sea traffic. The evidence in St Davids for a firm link with Compostela is slender: there is a possible connection, through a similarity of architectural style to the churches en route to the shrine of St James, and the cathedral chapter has always met on the Thursday after St James's Day, 25 July. According to Archdeacon Payne (c. 1815) the opening of the cathedral chapter was celebrated on the saint's day 'according to ancient custom' with entertainments, a supper and a dance in the 18th and early 19th centuries: such festivities bear a strong resemblance to other similar saints' day survivals throughout Wales and suggest that St James's Day had a particular significance for the cathedral. A 14th-century stone reredos in the Holy Trinity chapel has a carving of St James (not its original site) and in recent years, two pilgrim ampullae in the shape of the scallop shell emblem of St James have been found in the vicinity of St Davids, although the scallop became universally accepted as the emblem of pilgrimage.

Rather more evidence has emerged from Spain itself. 1971 was a Holy Year, when special privileges are offered and celebrations held. To mark this year, Spain issued a series of stamps paying tribute to the countless thousands of pilgrims from other countries who came to make their devotions at the shrine of St James. The 50-cts stamp portrayed a medieval map of the routes taken to Santiago. Churches connected with the European routes are shown on stamps from the set. One of these is a 3-ptas stamp depicting St Davids Cathedral with the scallop shell of St James over crossed pilgrim staves in the right-hand corner.

Spanish stamps, Holy Year 1971, depicting St Davids Cathedral and the medieval routes to Santiago de Compostela

HOLYWELL

The well house at Holywell

Less than five miles from Flint, and close to the English border, lies Holywell, which has been a place of pilgrimage since the 7th century. Many regarded it as the greatest well shrine in the British Isles and its miracles were numerous. It was visited by the lowly and the great alike and, on several occasions, by the monarch of the day; like Penrhys, far to the south, it provided an inspiration for generations of Welsh poets.

Such was its fame and so valuable were the offerings left there annually that, even at the height of the Reformation, the well and its chapel were not destroyed, but were leased out by the crown. In spite of official disapproval, visitors insisted on bathing in the waters and its reputation as a place of healing continued undimmed; it remains today as much a centre of pilgrimage as it was centuries ago.

The drops of her blood (from a *cywydd* in praise of St Winifred by Tudur Aled[6])

The origins of the well are enveloped in legend. During the 7th century St Beuno, one of the early Celtic saints, obtained from a Welsh chieftain named Tewyth some land, on which he built a small church. He was also given permission to instruct Tewyth's daughter, Winifred, in the Christian religion. One day, whilst her parents were at mass, Caradoc, the son of a neighbouring king, visited Winifred – Gwenfrewi in Welsh – at home. Caradoc had been out hunting and asked her for a drink to quench his thirst. Realising that she was alone, Caradoc attempted to seduce her. Winifred fled towards the church, but was caught by the prince, who hacked off her head. Her blood spattered onto some nearby stones, staining them forever, and also dyed the surrounding moss, which became renowned for the sweet scent of frankincense or violets that it gave off. A spring of water burst forth at the spot where her head touched the ground; the head rolled on and came to rest inside the church door.

St Beuno, emerging from the church, took up the head and, with prayers that Winifred might be restored to life, rejoined it to the body. His pleas were answered, for the young girl recovered, though afterwards a thin scar encircled her neck, a visible sign of her martyrdom. St Beuno then cursed Caradoc, who was swallowed up when the earth opened beneath his feet.

Several years later, St Beuno left the area, but before his departure he took Winifred to her spring and told her that in future those who asked for her help should receive it, at the second or third time of asking, if not the first. He also made her promise him that she would each year weave him a cloak that, when placed in the stream, would miraculously be carried to him wherever he was. Winifred did this each May Day: her gift never failed to reach him and was never soaked by the water, so that St Beuno became known as Beuno of the Dry Cloak.

---

[6] A *cywydd* is a poem in strict metre consisting of rhymed seven-syllable couplets. The cywydd written by Tudur Aled in praise of St Winifride's Well is regarded as one of the greatest examples of its type in the Welsh language. See page 108 for a partial translation.

> Arogl o nef ir glyn yw
> Ag ar gwynt oi gro a gaid
> Fal y gwynt o fel gynthaid
> Main gwiw arogl mewn gweryd
> Mwsc a ban y mysc y byd
>
> Band y gwayd bendigedig
> Dagrau fel kafod egroes
> Defni Crist o fanau kroes.

Winifred is said to have established a convent at Holywell, though she later went to live at Gwytherin, where she became abbess of another nunnery and where she eventually died.

A breath of Heaven   (Tudur Aled)

In 1093 the Countess Adeliza had granted the well and adjoining chapel to the monks of Chester. She did so, it has been suggested, in order to advance the authority of the earldom of Chester in Wales over that of the Welsh princes. More than twenty years later her son, Earl Richard, was attacked by the Welsh whilst on a pilgrimage to Holywell and was forced to take refuge at Basingwerk. Despite the fact that King Henry II built a castle at Basingwerk and a Templars' hostel to protect pilgrims to the well, the Welsh eventually recovered most of the surrounding area. In 1240 Prince Dafydd ap Llywelyn gave the shrine to the monastery of Basingwerk, in whose possession it remained until 1537.

In 1138, Winifred's relics were acquired by the monks of Shrewsbury Abbey, who translated them from their burial place at Gwytherin to the abbey. Shrewsbury, in addition to Holywell, became a focus of pilgrimage. At first, Winifred's fame seems to have been local to north Wales and the Marches but in 1398, Roger Walden, Archbishop of Canterbury, ordered her feast to be kept throughout the province of Canterbury. In 1415, Archbishop Chichele, who had previously been Bishop of St Davids, instructed that her feast, together with those of St David and St Chad, should be observed throughout his province. As a result of these proclamations, pilgrimage to St Winifred's Well and shrine increased dramatically.

Visitors came to Holywell and Shrewsbury from all over Britain. Some, travelling from the north, went first to Chester to pray before the famous Rood of St John's church. Others, as we shall see, followed a track that ran from Holywell via the monastery at Ystrad Fflur (Strata Florida) to St Davids. Yet more pilgrims came from London and the West Country, passing through Ludlow where a special hostel was built to house them, before going on by way of the border country to Shrewsbury.

In 1427, Pope Martin V allowed the monks of Basingwerk to sell indulgences to all who 'should visit and give alms to the Chapel of St Winifred called Haliwell in the diocese of St Asaph, the buildings of which are now collapsed'. The influx of pilgrims was so great that, in the words of the poet Gutun Owain, the Abbot of Basingwerk was able to give away 'twice the treasure of a King in wine'.

Both King Henry V and King Edward IV visited Holywell and presumably added to its treasures. Henry is said to have gone 'in great reverence' on foot from Shrewsbury to Holywell, and it is possible that Edward, coming in 1461, hoped to secure the favour of Winifred during what was to prove a crucial year in the conflict between the Yorkists and Lancastrians. In any event, he is said to have placed in his crown some soil gathered from the vicinity of the well.

Richard III provided the Abbot of Basingwerk with an annual grant of 10 marks for the maintenance of a priest at Holywell, whose duty it was to minister to pilgrims. Not long afterwards, according to legend, Richard's great rival for the crown, Henry Tudor, came to the neighbourhood to confer with his allies, the Mostyn family, and had to leap through a window to avoid capture.

Towards the end of the 15th century the well chapel at Holywell underwent considerable rebuilding and refurbishment. This has traditionally been regarded as due to the generosity of Lady Margaret Beaufort, the mother of King Henry VII, who is also said to have encouraged William Caxton to print a life of St Winifred. No specific evidence exists to prove that she influenced Caxton to publish his work and it has recently been suggested that Lady Margaret was not a benefactor of Holywell. There is no record of her having made donations to the shrine and a carving high in the chapel roof which was thought to depict profiles of Lady Margaret and her fourth husband, Lord Stanley, may in fact represent a kinsman, Sir William Stanley, and his wife. Many of the badges decorating the chapel depict emblems from the coats-of-arms of the Stanley family and their relatives. Lady Margaret's emblems do not appear. It is possible that after Sir William's execution for treason in 1495, his link with the chapel was conveniently ignored and the story of Lady Margaret's generosity grew up. King Henry certainly promoted the cult of St Winifred, for when he died a statue of Winifred was placed in his chapel in Westminster Abbey.

The fame of the well was widespread. It was signposted from as far away as Walsingham and from the sacred well at Jesmond Dene in Northumberland. Many contemporary poems refer to it. One of the most famous of these, the *cywydd* by Tudur Aled, who wrote at the close of the fifteenth and the beginning of the

This corbel at Holywell is said to represent a pilgrim carrying another upon his back

sixteenth centuries, compares the well to the dew of the Holy Ghost and to the waters of Baptism:

> It is a breath of Heaven in the vale
> And the breeze which comes from it
> Is as the honey-bees first swarming,
> A sweet dour over the turf
> Of musk or balm in the midst of the world . . .
>
> The drops of her blood are as the red shower
> Of the berries of the wild rose
> The tears of Christ from the height of the cross

The wonted welles and places of superstition

(extract from a letter written in 1590)

During the Reformation, Holywell did not suffer the fate of Penrhys and other shrines: it is said that the offerings made there were too valuable a source of income. As soon as Basingwerk Abbey was dissolved, the chapel was appropriated by the servants of Henry VIII, who leased it to a Mr William Holcroft. It was Mr Holcroft's duty to collect up all the offerings made at the chapel and forward them to the king. This proved to be no easy task, for the ex-monks of the abbey did not relinquish their hold on the well without a fight. On several occasions the former Abbot, Nicholas Pennant, accompanied by his brothers John and David and three others, took away tithe corn valued at eight marks. Even worse, on St Winifred's Day, they marched into the crowded chapel carrying boxes and shouted, 'Such money as you offer into the common stock shall never be a remedy for your souls, for there stands one of the King's servants who will soon take it forth.' The congregation must have agreed with them, for when they left, their boxes contained £5 13 4d. They had also been given an ox valued at 23 shillings and 4 pence.

During the reign of Queen Mary I, a Catholic bishop, Thomas Goldwell, was installed at St Asaph and it was he who obtained a renewal of the ancient papal indulgences for pilgrims to Holywell. This reversion to the ancient rites of Catholicism lasted for only a short time. Following the accession of Elizabeth I, there came the establishment of the Protestant faith as the state religion and pilgrimage was again discouraged.

Catholics across England and Wales were now forced to practise their religion in great secrecy and this was certainly the case at Holywell. For several decades, a number of Catholic priests, protected by powerful local families, worked clandestinely from the shrine to preserve their religion. One of the first of these was John Bennet, who arrived in 1574. His presence became known and in 1582 he was caught and was tried in the chapel itself. Condemned to death, he was reprieved and imprisoned for three years before being banished. He returned to Holywell in great secrecy in 1587 and continued to work there until his death in 1625.

Another who celebrated mass in the vicinity of Holywell at this time was

Edward Hughes, who was tutor to the family of Sir John Throgmorton. Mass had been held at the home of John Edwards, the Squire of Plas Newydd, near Chirk, in the presence of Lady Throgmorton and numerous others. Eventually, news of these clandestine meetings came to the Court of the Council of Wales, which immediately sent a Commission of Oyer and Terminer to deal with the problem. During their investigations, the commission discovered that John Edwards' wife, Anne, had been travelling at night to Holywell to hear mass on every feast of Saint Winifred. In 1579, perhaps as a result of these and similar events, Queen Elizabeth instructed the Council of the Marches to 'discover all Papist activities and recommend measures for oppressing them and to pay particular attention to the pilgrimages to St Winifred's Well and in view of the claim that the water is medicinal to appoint two men to test its properties; if not medicinal the Well should be destroyed…'.

In 1593, John Gerard, another priest whom the authorities had been pursuing for some time, came to Holywell and later recorded his visit in his autobiography.

> Once I was there on 3 November, St Winefride's Feast … there was a hard frost at the time and though the ice in the stream had been broken by people crossing it the previous night, I still found it difficult to cross with my horse the next morning. But frost or no frost I went down into the well like a good pilgrim. For a quarter of an hour I lay down in the water and prayed. When I came out my shirt was dripping, but I kept it on and pulled my clothes over it and was none the worse for my bathe.

Despite the close watch kept by the authorities, the pilgrimages and the miracles continued. In 1574, William Shone was impious enough to wash his dirty shoes in the well and was paralysed as a result. He was restored to full health only by returning to the well twice a day. In 1602 a woman recovered from a stroke after visiting the well and in 1605 another woman was miraculously given back her sight.

In the same year, another secret pilgrimage took place to Holywell. About thirty people were involved, including, again, Father Gerard and several other priests, two ladies named Anne and Eliza Vaux, Sir Everard Digby and his wife and a fellow who, because of his small stature, was known as Little John. In reality his name was Nicholas Owen and his particular skill was in constructing secret hiding places within the walls of Catholic houses where hunted priests might take refuge. For years he had been travelling the length and breadth of England, carrying out his work in difficult and dangerous circumstances. He used the pilgrimage as an opportunity to build new hiding places and repair old ones in the houses at which the party stopped. The authorities eventually captured him and he endured the most agonising tortures without ever divulging the location of any of the hiding places.

As the group approached Holywell, the ladies went barefoot. Once their devotions were over, they began the long return journey. At Gayhurst, the Digby's home in Buckinghamshire, Anne Vaux voiced her concern over the number of horses she had seen collected in the stables of the houses through which she had passed. She feared some sort of plot and did not realise that what she had witnessed were preparations for the Gunpowder Plot. Within months, Sir Everard Digby and several others who had visited Holywell were executed for their part in the conspiracy.

As the numbers of pilgrims continued to increase, so the authorities became more concerned. A report handed to the local Justices of the Peace in 1629 noted that fifteen hundred people had visited the well on 3 November, St Winifred's Day; these included 'Lord William Howard, Sir Thomas Gerard, Sir William Norris, Sir Cuthbert Clifton, Mr Preston of the Manor ... Mr Lathom of Mosborough and his five brothers who are all priests ... the lady Falkland and with her Mr Everard, Priest ... and divers other knights, ladies, gentelmen, to the number of 14 or 1500 and the general estimation about 150 more priests'.

In an attempt to reduce the numbers of pilgrims, in 1636 'all unnecessary alehouses' in the town were closed down and innkeepers were required to hand in a list of all who lodged at their premises. In the following year, harsher measures were undertaken: all the inns except two were closed, the iron railings around the pool in which pilgrims bathed were removed and the statue of St Winifred was whitewashed. Divine vengeance followed, or so the faithful believed. The magistrate who had ordered this desecration died less than a year later, and of the churchwardens involved, one suffered a stroke and the other lost his house in a fire.

Not long after, one of the inns in Holywell was bought by George Petrie, who hoped to turn it into a hospice for pilgrims, but this met with such opposition in the town that the plan was abandoned.

In 1674 there occurred one of the most remarkable of all the miracles seen at Holywell. A young man named Cornelius Nichol, who lived near Cardigan, had suffered a 'malignant disease', which left him unable to use his knees and ankles. So serious was his illness that he was incapable of moving from one position. For over six months various remedies were tried but there was no improvement. At last he resolved to implore the assistance of St Winifred. He and his friends were too poor to pay the costs of the journey and so, with the help of charitable people, he was passed on from house to house in a cart until he reached Holywell. He arrived at the well at the hour of Vespers on 11 June and was helped into the waters. He immediately found himself able to stand and walk without support. All signs of his former lameness and disability had vanished and within a few days he was able to begin his homeward journey. As so many people had witnessed his former state, the miraculous cure could be well attested and news of it spread rapidly.

A royal baby

During the Civil Wars, the fury of the iconoclasts was turned upon the chapel, which was seriously damaged; the statue of the saint was destroyed. So bad was the state of the building that following the visit of King James II and Queen Mary in 1686, the queen gave £30 for the upkeep of the fabric. A legal battle ensued over the ownership of the chapel. Judgement was given in the king's favour and he duly presented the building to the queen. Restoration work was carried out over the next twelve months and this prevented further deterioration.

The king and queen had visited the shrine to 'crave the prayers of St Winefride that they might be blessed with a son'. James gave to the chapel a portion of the dress worn by Mary, Queen of Scots at her execution. Less than a year later, the queen gave birth to a healthy boy, and it was said that St Winifred's intercession had been successful.

During the 18th century the chapel became a day school, though visitors continued to bathe in the waters. In 1840, seven crutches and two hand-barrows were noted at the well, left no doubt by pilgrims. Thirty years later, a new hospice was opened in the town and in 1851 and 1887 papal indulgences were granted to pilgrims visiting the well.

Holywell remains today a centre of pilgrimage, much as it has been for over a thousand years, fulfilling the words of William Byrsinsa, a 17th-century poet:

> A well in a much loved dwelling
> I know that on high, it belongs to Winefride.

PENRHYS

The Maid, Mary the Virgin, with a crown!
At Penrhys is this Virgin.
Here is her image where there is plaintive crying,
There, verily, is the image from Heaven!
An angel in the Decalogue
Would never with his hands make the image of Mary.
An honour, they say, that when it was obtained,
A miracle was discovered of yore in the woods:
Up from her shrine of oak trunk,
She, gentle maid, would not be borne.
The mountain's brow is the place where most frequently
Great Mary's miracles are precious.

When, in the first half of the 16th century, Lewys Morgannwg wrote the above lines in praise of the shrine of the Virgin Mary at Penrhys, he was describing one of the most famous sanctuaries in Wales. Situated on a hillside in the valleys roughly twenty miles to the north-west of Cardiff, the well and chapel of St Mary attracted pilgrims from all over Wales and beyond. The well, a natural spring which bubbled out of the ground, was enclosed in a small well house. Pilgrims entered the building through a low doorway and, whilst preparing to bathe, sat upon a stone bench which ran along three of the walls. A small cistern in one corner received the spring

The well house at Penrhys photographed in recent years

water which was then conveyed by means of a pipe into a much larger cistern in the opposite corner, in which the faithful washed themselves.

A short distance away was the chapel, which housed a statue of the Virgin Mary holding the Holy Infant. The fame of this image was widespread and it has been described in a large number of poems surviving from the medieval period. It was tall, with red cheeks and was painted and gilded; a precious stone was set into the bosom. Its head was slightly bent, as if to kiss the Infant Jesus, who had His hand upon her arm. The chapel was filled with offerings left by the faithful and the statue itself was often decorated with further gifts.

The site also included a hostelry where pilgrims might stay, a barn, stables, a bake house, a brew-house and a malt-house; there may even have been a mill. An area nearby was called Y Fynwent, the churchyard, whilst other areas were known as Cae'r Eglwys, the church field, Cae Tyla Capel, the field of the chapel ascent and Erw Porth, the acre of the gate. These names were preserved as field names well into the 20th century.

This modern statue of the Virgin stands on the site of the altar of the vanished chapel at Penrhys

When he wrote his poem, Lewys Morgannwg could not have known that Penrhys would shortly be swept away. Within a few years the chapel had been despoiled, the famous statue of the Virgin had been burned, a long tradition of prayer and healing was ended and an important influence on medieval Welsh literature had ceased to exist. Today all that remains of one of the greatest of Welsh shrines is the much restored well house and a section of the chapel wall incorporated into a modern boundary wall; the rest of the site is covered by a modern road and a housing estate.

Origins

The origins of the shrine are mysterious. The well may have been the focus of worship during the Iron Age and subsequently was regarded as a healing well by Christians. Small chapels were often built close to such wells and it is possible that one was erected at Penrhys and was later enlarged to accommodate the increasing numbers of pilgrims visiting the site.

There are several legends that describe the founding of the shrine. According to an ancient tale well known in the medieval period, a swineherd, or in other versions a huntsman, found an image of the Virgin Mary within the branches of an oak tree.[7] When news of this remarkable find was relayed to Llantarnam Abbey, which owned the land, a team of men and a cart drawn by eight oxen was sent to bring the statue to the safety of the abbey. Despite all their efforts, the Virgin could not be moved and this led to the building of a chapel at the spot.

Iolo Morgannwg, writing in the 18th century, claimed that the name Penrhys commemorated the beheading of Rhys ap Tewdwr, Prince of South Wales by a rival, Iestyn ap Gwrgant. Rhys' grandson, Robert of Gloucester, later founded a Franciscan friary at the spot in memory of his ancestor. Owain Glyndŵr is said to have held an eisteddfod at the friary, which was subsequently suppressed for its support of him during his rebellion, leaving only the chapel containing the statue.

These details are probably fictional. What is certain is that Robert of Gloucester founded an abbey at Margam, which received from certain Welsh lords grants of land at *Pendar*, where a daughter house might be created. The location of Pendar is uncertain, but it may well have been at the head of the Dare valley, and the lands there were handed over to Llantarnam Abbey in 1204 as part of a boundary agreement with Margam Abbey. In the centuries that followed, Llantarnam suffered several disasters: there were the social and economic effects of the Black Death and, in 1398, the Abbey was seriously damaged by fire. In the early years of the 15th century Llantarnam supported Owain Glyndŵr in his war against the English and suffered reprisals because of it.

It is possible that at this time tenants of the abbey's lands at Penrhys, fearing punishment, hid their valuables, including a statue of the Virgin, which was later discovered intact in an oak tree. Lacking either the means or the time to remove the effigy to the abbey, the local people perhaps came to believe that the Virgin did not wish to be moved and this in turn gave rise to the legend of the swineherd. There is also the possibility that the monks of Llantarnam deliberately publicised the story in order to restore some of the wealth lost as a result of the Glyndŵr rebellion.

The number of thy miracles (Lewys Morgannwg)

If the monks of Llantarnam did spread rumours of the miraculous powers of the statue, they were remarkably successful; by the end of the 15th century, pilgrims

---

[7] There is another possible explanation for the presence of this statue. The well and its oak, as already noted, may have been the focus of pagan worship. Christian priests sometimes re-dedicated such trees by putting statues of the Virgin amongst the branches.

were flocking to the shrine in great numbers. According to the 15th-century poet Rhisiart ap Rhys, 'Her parlour was to numbers of invalids like a hostelry.' Gwilym Tew, writing at about the same time, states that Penrhys was frequently visited by labourers, 'where…there is ever a host of them'. Lewys Morgannwg, in the poem quoted at the beginning of this chapter, goes on to say that sailors who 'are driven afar, Mary will bring them from sea to land'. These two statements may indicate that the shrine was a focus for mariners and ordinary folk rather than the richer pilgrims who could afford to make journeys further afield.

Penrhys' curative powers were famous. According to Lewys Morgannwg's poem, the waters of the well healed cripples, the blind and the deaf and even restored the dead to life. In particular, illnesses such as rheumatism, skin and eye ailments were cured and the usual custom was to throw a pin into the water. If it became discoloured it was a sign that the cure would be effective; as recently as the 19th century, the well was half full of pins offered by the faithful.

The appointed time for a pilgrim (Gwilym Tew)

Gwilym Tew, in a long poem of praise for the shrine at Penrhys, mentions that he will attend 'at the appointed time for a pilgrim'. This suggests that there were certain times of the year at which pilgrims came to the shrine in greater numbers than was usual. These were probably the great church festivals held in honour of

The chapel at Penrhys as it may have appeared in the medieval period

events in the Virgin's life, such as Candlemas on 2 February, the Salutation, celebrated on 25 June in the medieval period, or the feast of the Assumption on 14 August. Rhisiart ap Rhys says that 'the diseases of the multitude who wait upon thee, after their weeping, are healed on the second night', indicating that such a visit involved a stay of two days or more.

If so, then pilgrims would have arrived at Penrhys on the evening before the festival. They would have attended the vigils held during the night, as well as all the services on the following day. The sick would have bathed in the well during the feast day, amidst great excitement if a cure was effected. On the last day further services were held before the pilgrims set out on their journey home.

Most pilgrims brought offerings to the shrine. Wealthier visitors donated articles of clothing and one lady, it is said, gave 'rare and heavy gold,' as well as 'the weight of two hundred in posts of wax'. The gift of a candle was quite common, especially amongst the poorer members of society and people purchased the biggest and most expensive one they could afford. Gwilym Tew took a candle 'a fathom long'. The medieval fathom was based on the average height of a man, or the measurement from finger tip to finger tip of his outstretched arms. It is likely that many such candles were to be seen within the chapel at Penrhys.

Our great Sibyl (Hugh Latimer)

In 1537, as part of the suppression of the monasteries, Llantarnam Abbey was surrendered to the crown. During the following year the abbey, together with some of its lands, including Penrhys, was granted to John Parker of the Royal Stables, but the statue remained within the chapel. So potent was the reputation of several of the shrines dedicated to St Mary that Hugh Latimer, Bishop of Worcester, wrote to Thomas Cromwell describing the Virgin as 'our grett sibyll…She hath byn the Devyll's instrument to bryng many…to eternal fyre; now she heresyllf, with her old syster of Walsyngham, her younger syster of Ipswych, with ther other two systers of Dongcaster and Penrysse, would make a jolly muster at Smythfield. They wold nott be all day in burnynge.'

On 23 August Cromwell in turn wrote to William Herbert instructing him to remove the statue at Penrhys 'as secretly as might be' for fear of local unrest. On 26th September, under cover of night, the statue and its apparel were taken away and were later burned with a number of other effigies in London. The shrine, having lost its focus, fell into disrepair, though the healing reputation of the well continued for many years. During the 19th century local farmers came every summer for water to use in making butter pats after the churning was over.

YNYS ENLLI / BARDSEY ISLAND

Capel Mair, St Mary's chapel, Aberdaron, with Ynys Enlli in background,
Thomas Pennant's Tours, 1773

The origins of human settlement on Ynys Enlli fade into myth and legend. Its Welsh name is probably a contraction of *Ynys yn y lli* (island in the flood) but folklore has attributed it to Benlli Gawr, a wicked and tyrannical king of mythical origins. The name Bardsey is probably derived from Old Norse, meaning the island of Bardr, perhaps a personal name, 'Bardr's Ey'. One legend claims that Merlin retired there with the thirteen treasures of the Isle of Britain, Arthur's favourite ship *Gwennan* foundered in its straits once known as Gorffrydau Caswennan (the tide rips of Caswennan) and the early saints of Wales established a monastic community earning it the title of the Isle of Saints. As an outlier of mainland Wales, it is inevitably drawn into the rich Atlantean folklore of the Welsh coast, the fabled Cantre'r Gwaelod, the drowned hundred of Cardigan Bay. Two islands, Ynys Dewi (Ramsey) in the south and Ynys Enlli in the north were said to mark its limits. A curious and persistent tradition surfacing in the 17th and 19th centuries, claimed that Enlli was part of Pembrokeshire to which it paid its taxes. Myth and folklore have been handed down over the generations, in later years in-mixed with historical fact and antiquarian interpretation. Bardic poetry and material compiled and disseminated in the Middle Ages celebrated Ynys Enlli as a pilgrim destination. A number of islands around the Welsh coast were home to early religious communities and desired places of burial where stories of native saints were preserved with accretions of colourful local folklore: Ynys Cybi (Holy Island),

Barry Island (St Barruc), Ynys Bŷr (Caldey), Ynys Dewi/Ynys Tyfanog (Ramsey), Ynys Lannog/Ynys Seiriol (Puffin Island/Priestholm) and Ynys Enlli (Bardsey), the last perhaps the most well endowed.

According to medieval tradition Cadfan, the first abbot, came from a forgotten place in Britain called Llydaw at some time in the 5th century, bringing many followers. His cult centre is Tywyn where there are several dedications, but no trace of any on or near Enlli, unlike the second abbot, Lleuddad, whose name occurs a number of times in the topography of the area: Gerddi Lleuddad (Lleuddad's gardens) is a field name on the island. Another field, Cae'r Faglau (the field of staffs) is also connected with Lleuddad who, as proof of his fitness for abbacy, joined the staffs or crosiers of the bishops together and then separated them, though in Lleuddad's medieval *Life* this took place on Bryn y Baglau (hill of staffs). According to medieval tradition, St Dyfrig ended his days there. At the Synod of Brefi, Llanddewi Brefi (mid-6th century) St David's sermon could be heard on Enlli and after the Synod, on the advice of St Cybi, many holy men went there. The Battle of Chester in 613/615 served to enhance further the island's reputation as a sacred refuge. The event was called the 'Massacre of the Saints' and recorded in the Anglo-Saxon Chronicle. The agressor, Aethelfrith of Northumbria and his army killed 900 of the 2,400 monks of Bangor Iscoed, Clwyd, as they prayed for their embattled countrymen which, Aethelfrith maintained, was tantamount to fighting against him. The survivors fled to Enlli, creating a route later to be followed by thousands of medieval pilgrims. The traditions of the entire Llŷn peninsula reinforce the impression of a considerable pilgrim presence.

The much quoted tradition of the island being the burial ground of 20,000 saints is first documented in medieval writings; it was recorded in the late 15th century by William Worcestre in his *Itineraries*: *'miliare ibi sunt sancti 20,000 sanctorum'*, 'there are 20,000 saints there'. Although this number may be a convention for 'very many', thousands of burials are not unlikely. Two 5/6th century inscribed stones from Anelog on the mainland, now in St Hywyn's church, Aberdaron, commemorate priests Veracius and Senacus 'with a multitude of Brethren', indicating substantial early settlement within a short sail of Enlli.

According to the 12th-century *Book of Llandaf*, Ynys Enlli acquired a privilege attributed to Pope Calixtus II, of three pilgrimages to the island equalling one to Rome which probably dates from the early 1120s. In 1123 the remains of St Dyfrig and a hand and possibly some teeth of Elgar the hermit[8] were translated from Enlli to Llandaf by Bishop Urban. Gerald came as close as Nefyn and described it as a small island occupied by devout monks, where the air is so pure that they die only from old age. He continues, 'in Welsh the place is called Ynys Enlli and in the Saxon tongue Bardsey Island. The bodies of a vast number of holy men are buried there, or so they say, among them that of Daniel, Bishop of Bangor.' Abaty Santes

---

8 Magister Caratocus, mentioned in the Life of Elgar the hermit (Book of Llandaf) went to Ynys Enlli in the early 12th century to ascertain if Elgar the hermit still lived and wrote from this an account of his life. This may have been the St Caradog who is buried in St Davids Cathedral.

13th-century ruins of Abaty Santes Fair, St Mary's Abbey

Fair, the Augustinian abbey of St Mary on the island, dated from 1195. The abbey had a library, six excellent bells, vaults and cellars. Fifteenth-century poets Hywel ap Dafydd ap Ieuan ap Rhys and Thomas Celli extolled the 20,000 saints and wrote of relics, pilgrims, pardons, the abbey's five elegant windows, images and costly chandeliers. There were two burial grounds, one for the 'saints' and the other for common people; it was said that the ground was as thick with graves as the cells in a honeycomb. It was important enough for Edward I to land and stay there in his progress on the Llŷn peninsula, from 30 July to 2 August of 1284. A detailed list of indulgences and privileges of Enlli, calling on the intercession of saints Cybi, Dewi, Cadfan, Deiniol, Seiriol, Beuno, Cawrdaf 'to the honour of God and of the Blessed Virgin Mary and the twenty thousand saints of the monastery of Enlli', followed by a list of pardons granted by the church, is known as the Rhyl manuscript. It is dated 1547 and apparently was at one time in the collection of William of Bodwrda.

The problems of getting to Enlli across an invariably rough Swnt, the Bardsey Sound, were compensated for by the following: 'by reason of ye hardness of saylinge and passage to the Isle' if any of the pilgrims 'should die by the waye they should not be damned'. When they reached the abbey there was a designated route rewarded by what appears to be a considerable indulgence: 'for every tyme ye pilgrimes shall goe about the churchyard of the xxtie thousand sainctes, & ther in eu'y wyndowe shall say o'r Lordes prayer they shall obteine of o'r Lord mercifully a thousand and fyve hundreth yeeres'. The indulgence goes on to claim that 'when the feste of James thap'le & the feste of Sancte Laudatus [Lleuddad] the Abbate are celebrated vpon one & the selfsame Sondaye then ... that yeere is cofirmed a Jubliee by the Apostolical aucthoritie in the same Ilande'. The meaning of this is obscure. One of the later abbots, John Conway of Mellteyrn made a pilgrimage to Rome in company with a large group of Welsh pilgrims, many from the diocese of Bangor, being signed into the English Hospice by the guestmaster on 28 March 1507.[9]

At the Reformation, pilgrimage to the island was in decline. In 1535 the abbey's annual income was £46 1s 4d. By 1539, the church, its spire and the monastery had been defaced and despoiled of all their lead, iron and glass. Presumably its once excellent library of manuscripts was dispersed or destroyed. Thomas Pennant in 1773 described the abbot's house as a long arched building with an 'insulated stone altar near the east end', occupied by island residents. In 1814 the abbot's house was still lived in but by 1846, only the ruined tower remained. Medieval finds were recorded on the island of 45 gold coins of c.1434–35 and a hand and forearm modelled in silver which could have been either a votive offering or a reliquary: unfortunately their whereabouts is unknown. In 1876, part of a bishop's silver crozier, an Edward III noble in mint condition and a key which seemed to incorporate both a ring and a seal were recorded.

Aberdaron

In the centuries after the Reformation, Aberdaron left its busy medieval past behind, becoming a quiet fishing village but retaining memories of the pilgrim traffic in traditions and place-names. Y Gegin Fawr (the big kitchen), which in its present state is 17th century, was reputedly a gathering point for pilgrims to Enlli, once offering them a free meal. They departed from Porth Meudwy (hermit's harbour), and Cwrt, at the head of this deep valley, provided bed and board for pilgrims to Enlli in lieu of tithes. The church is dedicated to St Hywyn, a follower of St Cadfan; a second aisle was added in the 15th century to accommodate pilgrims. Pilgrims sought the protection of Mair, Morwyn y Môr (Mary, Virgin of the sea) and would have made their devotions at Capel Anelog, Ffynnon Saint, Capel Mair and climbing down the steep Grisiau Mair or Ysgol Fair (Mary's steps/ladder) to Ffynnon Fair, drink its pure, yet tide-washed, water and sit in Mary's seat[10]. They would place a hand on the ledge where the Virgin was said to have placed hers as she rose from the rock, 'wearied with her burden of sorrow'. Traditionally, contact with the abbey would be made by lighting a beacon on

---

9 'Mar 28, Dns: Johannes Conwey abbas monast(er)ii Ste: Virginis in insula de bassey bangoriensis dioces.' Lloyd, D. T. Welsh Pilgrims at Rome 1471–1738 Trivium vi 7 1971.

10 Francis Jones recorded another tradition based on folklore, which involved carrying water, climbing up the cliff and walking round the chapel without losing a drop: the usual way is to take a mouthful. The tradition is still current and was passed on to me by Mr Gareth Jones of Cwrt Farm, Aberdaron; it is quite possible to do, but requires some concentration. A similar ritual was practised on St Cybi's Day at Ffynnon Lochwyd near Holyhead, down a similar steep cliff where sand and water had to be carried back without spilling either.

Y Gegin Fawr, Aberdaron

20th century pilgrim at Ffynnon Fair, St Mary's Well, Aberdaron, Llŷn

Y Cafn, the harbour on Ynys Enlli, with sleeping seals

Mynydd Gwyddel just south of Capel Mair. Delays in sailing, still a risk even in today's high-powered crafts, were a probability in earlier times. Ynys Enlli is surrounded by ferocious tide races. A crossing from Porth Meudwy to Y Cafn, Enlli's harbour, a distance of about 3 miles, took two hours to row under good conditions. Thomas Pennant in the 18th century recorded that it was still the practice of mariners to row a little way out and there 'they made a full stop, pulled off their hats and offered a short prayer'. The return journey was equally uncertain and might land an unfortunate pilgrim anywhere between Caernarfon and Cardigan.

On these furthest western shores, beyond the wild tide race, Ynys Enlli lies bathed in the light of setting suns and the words of the 12th-century poet, Gwalchmai ap Meilyr, find a resonance today when he writes of 'a wilderness of unperishing glory ... Island of radiant Mary, holy island of the saints'.

> ... dydryf didraul ei bri
> ... Ynys Fair firain, ynys glân y glain.

The place of burial was the end of life's pilgrimage. To rest finally at Ynys Enlli in the presence of the blessed Virgin Mary, among that great company of Welsh saints and to rise with them in glory on the last day was a reassurance greatly desired. The thin soil of Enlli barely covers the bones of that multitude of saints and pilgrims.

Ynys Enlli

Chapter 10

Healing Waters: Holy Wells

A MONGST the most popular healing sites resorted to by pilgrims were holy wells, examples of which were to be found in every parish in Britain. Many of these wells were of great antiquity and rich in legend.[1] This folklore frequently had its roots in the religion of the pagan Celts, when wells were regarded as entrances to the supernatural world and were inhabited by gods or guardian spirits. Human heads were occasionally left at these sites as an offering to the presiding deity, which may explain why some wells later became associated with legends of the beheading of a Christian saint. St Justinian, for example, was decapitated on Ramsey Island and a spring of water gushed from the ground to mark the spot. This later became famous for its healing properties. John of Tynemouth, writing in the 14th century, records that its waters 'quaffed by sick folk, conveys health of body to all'.

Other springs came into being through the stroke of a saint's staff, hand or foot, or because the saint had been born nearby or had performed a miracle in the immediate vicinity. Ffynnon Dewi, located inside a cottage in the parish of Llanddewi Brefi, marked the spot where St David raised a youth from the dead. A delightful legend explains the creation of St Deiniol's Well, next to St Deiniol's (Daniel's) church outside Pembroke. St Deiniol had been on a long pilgrimage to Jerusalem and when he returned to his hermitage on the hill overlooking Pembroke, he brought with him a vessel containing water from the River Jordan. There were no wells or springs in the vicinity at that time, a lack that St Deiniol immediately remedied. He invoked the name of Christ and thrust his wooden staff into the ground and poured the Jordan water around it. The staff straightaway grew into a beautiful tree. A well of pure water bubbled from the ground, which became a focal point of local pilgrimage. It was famous for curing a variety of illnesses, but was unfortunately destroyed at the close of the 16th century.

The most famous well in Wales was probably St Winifred's at Holywell which, together with Ffynnon Fair at Penrhys, is discussed at greater length elsewhere. This came into being when Winifred (Gwenfrewi) was beheaded by Prince Caradoc, whose advances she had refused. According to legend, the severed head rolled in through the door of the nearby church and St Beuno, who was inside, emerged to fasten the head back onto the body, at the same time breathing air into her mouth and nostrils and praying until life was restored. St Beuno later

---

[1] These legends are amply described in Francis Jones' magnificent book *The Holy Wells of Wales*, from which much of the information in this chapter was gleaned.

prophesied that all who sought Winifred's help at the well should obtain their wish. This promise drew pilgrims to Holywell from all over Britain, as it still does today.

The itch and the stitch

Some wells, like those mentioned above, were effective against a wide range of illnesses. The nine wells of Trellech in Monmouthshire, fed by several different springs, were known to heal scurvy, the colic and 'other distempers'. The Marcross well in Glamorgan was reputed to cure baldness, amongst other ailments; such was its fame that it inspired the following verse:

> For the itch and the stitch,
> Rheumatic and the gout,
> If the devil isn't in you
> The well will take them out.

Other wells could only be used for specific ailments. Skin diseases such as scrofula, sores, erysipelas and rashes could be healed provided the correct well was visited. Paralysis might be cured by drinking the waters of Ffynnon Gwyddfaen in Llandyfaen parish, Carmarthenshire, where the water was scooped up and drunk from a human skull. The reputed skull of St Teilo was the receptacle at Ffynnon Deilo in Pembrokeshire, whilst at other wells special cups were used. At Ffynnon Aaron (Pembrokeshire) the water had to be taken from the palm of the hand and at St Govan's Well, in the same county, a limpet shell was used.

The Virtuous Well, one of the nine wells of Trellech

St Govan's Well as it appears today

Diseases of the eyes could be treated at numerous sites. St Leonard's Well, on the north-east slope of the Iron Age hillfort at Crundale in Pembrokeshire, was especially good for sore eyes. At the Eye Well, Llandrindod, a definite ritual had to be carried out if a cure was to succeed. The pilgrim had to walk towards the well taking a certain number of steps. An incantation was uttered in a low voice, after which the fingers of the right hand were dipped into the well and the water was applied to one eye. The fingers of the other hand were then used to bathe the remaining eye. Following this, the eyes were not wiped and if they smarted and tears formed the cure was more likely to succeed.

Ritual

Rituals similar to the one enacted at Llandrindod took place at most wells and were carefully enacted, no matter how bizarre they might seem. Pilgrims to Ffynnon Barruc on Barry Island took care not to bathe in the well. Instead, they threw into the water a bent pin or a brass buckle. A silent prayer was then offered, followed by a wish, after which the supplicant travelled home in silence until spoken to by a complete stranger. At Ffynnon Gybi on the Llŷn peninsula, the patient had to drink equal quantities of well water and seawater every morning and afternoon for 7–10 days. It was also necessary to bathe in the waters of the well. After each immersion the patient was taken via the east side of the building enclosing the pool to a bedchamber in an adjoining cottage. There, whilst resting, the sick person was given

St Leonard's Well, near Crundale, the waters of which cured eye complaints

a concoction consisting of well water mixed with the tips from a broom plant and valerian or wood soot. If the patient grew warm beneath the blankets, the cure was working.

To ensure a cure at St Dwynwen's Well on Anglesey, sick pilgrims carried a candle during their visits. A single strand of hair was tossed into the depths of Ffynnon Ddegfel in Pembrokeshire in the hope that a cure for warts and eye complaints would miraculously occur. By the 17th century, a complex ceremony was taking place at Ffynnon Degla (Denbighshire), which probably had its origins in medieval religious ritual, if not in paganism. Anyone suffering from epilepsy had to visit the well after sunset on a Friday. Hands and feet were washed in the waters and the afflicted person then walked around the well three times chanting the Lord's Prayer thrice and carrying a cock in a basket. The unfortunate bird was then jabbed with a pin, which was thrown into the well. A groat was given to the parish clerk, and the visitor then walked three times round Llandegla church, again repeating the Lord's Prayer thrice. After entering the church and placing a groat in the Poor Box, the sick person lay under the Communion Table with the Church Bible as a pillow and, covered with a carpet, remained until dawn. The supplicant then placed the head of the cock into the mouth and blew hard before releasing the bird; this was supposed to transfer the epilepsy. A silver coin was dropped into the Poor Box and the pilgrim exited the church, leaving behind a very bewildered bird. A last visit to the well was made, where the walk around the building and the recitation of the Lord's Prayer were both repeated three times. If the cock died the cure had been successful.

Gifts and offerings

It was usual to leave some sort of gift at a holy well to ensure a blessing or a cure. Money was frequently offered, either to the priest in charge of a nearby chapel, or the coins would be placed next to the well or tossed into the water. The total income for the year could be considerable. The image of St Dyfnog and his holy well at Llanrhaeadr, not far from Holywell, attracted large crowds of visitors during the medieval period and there were once quite substantial buildings at the site, which may have been associated with the pilgrim trade. It has also been suggested that the magnificent Jesse Window inside the church may have been paid for by pilgrim offerings.[2]

Clothes, rags, buttons or flowers, even food, might also be left at the site. White or quartz stones were also considered to be suitable offerings. This is another custom, widespread in the Middle Ages, which probably has pagan origins; similar stones are frequently discovered in Neolithic or Bronze Age burial mounds as well

---

[2] The survival of the Jesse Window is in itself remarkable. According to tradition the glass was taken down from the window during the Civil Wars of the mid-17th century and was buried in an oak chest in the woods to the west of the church. With the Restoration, the window was restored to its rightful place.

The magnificent Jesse Window at Llanrhaeadr

The healing waters of Gumfreston, into which pilgrims threw bent pins

Gumfreston church, Pembrokeshire

as in early Celtic Christian churches. Perhaps the pure colouring of the stones was believed to impart magical qualities to their surroundings. A white pebble thrown into St Anthony's Well near Llansteffan, Carmarthenshire, was thought to ensure the granting of any wish.

As we have already seen, the throwing of pins, sometimes deliberately bent, into the water was also common. The custom of offering iron, in the form of pins or coins, may date back to the pagan Celtic era, when iron was a valuable metal, one of the greatest gifts that could be offered to a presiding spirit. At Gumfreston near Tenby, pilgrims arrived on Easter Day and threw bent pins into the water, a custom known as 'throwing Lent away'. At Ffynnon Fair on Cefn Bryn on the Gower, pins already in the water would rise up to greet new pins, provided they were offered in true faith. At Ffynnon Chwerthin in Caernarfonshire, the custom was still so prevalent during the 18th and 19th centuries that thousands of pins were to be found in the well and many corks with pins pushed into them bobbed on the surface.

The seasons of the year

Well water was believed to be most potent during the spring and summer months. Accordingly, people would flock to them from Easter onwards. Easter Monday was also a popular visitation day, as was Ascension Day. At Ffynnon Gybi in Cardiganshire, the sick were washed in the water on Ascension Eve and were then placed under Llech Gybi, a cromlech 'an arrows flight from ye well'. If the sick person slept, a cure had been effected; if not, death was the result. Baglan Well in Glamorgan, was resorted to on the first three Thursdays in May, one of which was Ascension Day, when children suffering from rickets might be cured.

Any well named Trinity Well could be visited on Trinity Sunday. In Montgomeryshire people sat around the Trinity Well in Guilsfield Without parish and sang hymns. As late as 1910 water from this well was still drunk, sweetened with brown sugar and at two more wells in the same county, sugared water was also drunk on Trinity Sunday.

St Govan's Well in Pembrokeshire was at its most potent in July; Ffynnon Dewi, Cardiganshire, was best visited on Midsummer Eve, whilst Ffynnon Geler in Carmarthenshire was visited from 21 June to the feast of St Peter. There was also a belief that water taken from wells between 11 and 12 o'clock at night on New Year's Eve would turn into wine. So strong was the belief in the powers of water collected at this time that in later centuries it would be carefully carried into houses, where sprigs of evergreen were used to sprinkle it over the contents and the people within to bring good luck.

Some wells could be visited at any time of the year, their healing powers being equally great in any month. Others were at their most effective on the saint's day to which they were dedicated. Certain days of the week were more popular than others. Sundays were favoured, whilst Thursdays in May and any Friday saw an increase in the number of visits. The hour of the day was important, too. The hours after sunset, especially midnight were deemed to be best, whilst mornings, in particular the dawn, before the rising sun had evaporated the dew, were also important.

Signs and portents

Wells were also used to foretell the future and their authority in this respect was as varied as their healing powers. Some wells could warn of future national disasters, whilst others predicted an individual's marriage prospects, identified thieves or prophesied illnesses and their cure.

The methods by which the future was interpreted varied from well to well. The rise and fall of the water level, the spread of ripples across the surface or the rush of bubbles from the depths were all carefully studied. At Ffynnon Elwoc in Denbighshire pilgrims offered a pin to the waters on Easter Monday: if bubbles appeared the pilgrim would live for another twelve months, but the lack of them was sinister in the extreme. Similarly, at Ffynnon Aelhaiarn (Caernarfonshire), a visitor would only bathe in the waters after bubbles had appeared. At a number of sites across Wales, a sick person's clothing, once placed in the water, gave an indication of the patient's future prospects: if the garment floated, recovery was sure, but if it sank death would follow. The nine wells of Trellech gave an indication of the success or failure of a wish by the number of bubbles which followed the dropping of a pebble into the waters; if there were many bubbles, success was assured, if a moderate amount there would be a delay in granting the wish, but if there were none the wish would not be granted.

Eels and fish lived in the depths of many wells and gave an indication that the water was pure. Their movements were believed to foretell the future, and their appearance whilst a patient was bathing was regarded as lucky. The sick who bathed in the waters of Ffynnon Beris hoped for the appearance of the well's two trout; non-appearance was regarded as a bad omen. At Ffynnon Elath on Anglesey, the movements of the resident eel were interpreted and the future forecast by a local inhabitant, a practice that continued into the 18th century.

The eel that dwelt in the depths of Ffynnon Gybi on the Llŷn peninsula healed patients by coiling round their legs, though when it was stolen, the well lost its power. Another story told about this well was that it had once contained a sacred fish, which was caught daily by monks from a nearby monastery. The fish was cooked and eaten and all the bones were carefully collected. They were then secretly returned at night to the well where, next morning, the miraculously restored fish waited to be caught again.

Wells today

During the last decades of the 16th century, harsh measures were taken by the authorities against suspected Catholics and those who were described as 'slow and cold in the true service of God ... supporters and bearers of superstition and idolatry.'[3]

In particular, well-visiting and vigils at chapels were discouraged. In July 1592, the Privy Council issued an order specifically targeting one of the most famous shrines in Wales: a company of men was to proceed to the well at Capel Meugan in Pembrokeshire and pull it down stone by stone. They were to forbid any access to it 'by night or day ... in superstitious manner'. St Deiniol's Well overlooking Pembroke is thought to have been destroyed in the same purge.

Many more wells were wrecked or abandoned as a result of similar orders, their stone canopies torn down, their stone tanks filled in. Some were put to agricultural use and the comings and goings of pilgrims were replaced by the daily gatherings of cattle for water. Wells, which in their day were locally or even nationally famous, became completely lost, whilst others, in more modern times, have become wishing wells into which tourists, half-jokingly and half in earnest, throw their pennies.

There are now only a few rare survivals, such as St Non's Well or St Winifred's Well, to remind us of how important the well cult once was.

---

[3] Bishop Richard Davies of St Davids in an episcopal report on his diocese written in 1570.

PART III

Pilgrim Roads

Chapter 11

Wales, an overview

Ym mryn, yn nhyno
Yn ynysedd môr
Ymhob ffordd ydd eler
Rhag Crist gwyn nid oes ynialedd.

On hills, in valleys on the islands of the sea,
Wherever you may go,
Because of holy Christ there is no desert place.

Black Book of Carmarthen, 13th century

THE reconstruction of the medieval road system in Wales has to be largely conjectural and only a general view is possible. The early map-making of Britain was rudimentary. The Antonine Itinerary, probably produced in the early 3rd century but with later additions, charted south-coast and north-coast routes to Carmarthen and Caernarfon respectively and an inland route along the border linking Chester (Deva) with Caerleon (Isca). The central massif of Wales, although mountainous and inhospitable, was traversed by ancient road systems and the mysteriously named Sarn Helen linked military establishments between Caernarfon and the south. After the departure of the legions in AD 410 the sophisticated road network, manned at intervals by Roman stations in Wales, was neglected but did not cease to exist and was complemented by numerous tracks leading between farms and settlements. The medieval Welsh laws specified legal requirements governing highways and byways and the King's Highway itself had to be maintained at a width of 12 feet. By the time of the Norman Conquest there was a complex of roads created and maintained by the needs of whose who travelled distances such as traders, tax-collectors, officials both ecclesiastical and secular and pilgrims, though it was the old Roman roads along which the Conquest would be conducted.

After conquest, Welsh land tenure retreated to higher ground, while the Anglo-Normans settled the low-lying and valley areas where land cultivation and settlement became typically English. William Rees's study of the road systems of south Wales in the 14th century is based on contemporary records which begin to reveal a pattern of settlement and land use when the old ways were still evident and the process of change, later to accelerate, had only just begun. River crossings, by bridge, ford or ferry help to identify the course of these roads. The upland areas remained Welsh where the system of mountain roads crossing from east to west and indicated by names such as Henffordd (old road) or Cefn Ffordd (ridge road), continued to survive. Parts of these can still be traced, such as the Flemish Way which branches off from the Roman roads north of Carmarthen towards St Davids via the Teifi Valley and the ridgeway of Preseli. There seems to have been an extensive system of mountain roads and bridle paths. Another network crossed the central massif of mid-Wales from east to west and linked up with other ancient road systems.[1] Bulk transport relied more on rivers and coastal trading vessels as the roads, besides being often inadequate for the purpose, could often be neglected and were also the territory of thieves and murderous villains.

---

[1] According to Geoffrey of Monmouth (*History of the Kings of Britain* 93, Penguin Classics, 1988) a road constructed by the legendary Beli Mawr who also appears in the *Mabinogi,* ran from St Davids to Southampton. The road along the south coast to Bristol is known to be of ancient origin and a direct route to the south coast likely, but its mythic origins must be handled with care. St Davids is used as a measuring point for the country by other writers: William Worcestre (late 15th century) gives its width from St Davids to Canterbury as 300 miles. *A Cronicle of Yeres* (1550–51) states 'the bredeth from Saynt Davys in Wales unto Dover is thre hundreth myles'. (William Worcestre *Itineraries* 325–27 and n.1 326. J. H. Harvey, ed. Oxford 1969)

Using these systems, pilgrims travelled country-wide: roads led to Glastonbury in the south, Oswestry and Shrewsbury in mid-Wales and Chester in the north. The pilgrim track to St Davids was apparently known in the High Wycombe area. Unusually, there is documentary evidence from Norfolk dated April 1481: Nicholas Markaunt the elder, aged 44 and more, says that he went on pilgrimage to St Davids, '*iter peregrinationis arripuit versus Meneviam*'. In October of the same year, in the same county William Gatisend, aged 60 and more, began a pilgrimage to St Davids in Wales. St Patrick's Purgatory, *Purdan Padrig*, on the shores of Lough Derg in Ireland was popular. In John Heywood's play *The Four PP*, written on the eve of Reformation in the early 1530s, the palmer lists his extensive journeyings to English and continental shrines including two Welsh shrines of an obviously comparable importance: 'Saynt Wynefrydes well in Walles' and 'Saynt Davys'.

> To these with other many one,
> Devoutly have I prayed and gone,
> Prayeng to them to pray for me
> Unto the blessed Trynyte.

Gerald of Wales and Archbishop Baldwin travelled the length and breadth of Wales in 1188, at the height of the pilgrim era and their route was probably well used by pilgrims then and in years to come. The movements of Norman and Angevin kings around Wales indicate that the road system was adequate for their purposes. Edward I travelled extensively in Wales and his journeys reveal an energetic coverage especially of north Wales where he was encountering major insurrection led by Prince Llywelyn ap Iorwerth. One of the few 'constructed' roads in Wales of this period was Edward's 30-mile highway from Chester to the River Conwy, passing through Flint and Rhuddlan. He ordered that woodland on either side of the road was to be cleared to a width of one bowshot, as set down in the Statute of Winton (1285) which specified a clearance of 200 feet on either side of the King's Highway to deprive the lawless of hiding places. The 'Roman steps' east of Harlech are currently believed to have been created by Edward as an access route to Harlech Castle. Kings and bishops used the road from Carmarthen via Llawhaden and Haverfordwest to St Davids throughout the medieval period although its precise track is far from clear. The relics of St David were carried from his cathedral as far north as Llanbadarn Fawr and as far east as Ewyas Harold on the border with England. The poets and bards whose profession required them to attend their patrons who were usually heads of the great houses, churches and monasteries, would have had a specific knowledge of the main pilgrim centres, the patronal feast days and the best routes to travel.

In the aftermath of the Black Death of 1348–49 and the depletion of manpower caused by the Wars of the Roses and the Glyndŵr rebellion, the little road maintenance there was became non-existent. The exception to this was in the area of the monastic houses, in particular the isolated Cistercian abbeys whose lands covered many acres and one of whose important duties was the accommodation of visitors and pilgrims. The distribution of monastic and hospitaller houses follows coastal routes, river valleys and mountain passes and gives an indication of the spread of pilgrim travel. Unlike Chaucer's pilgrims on the flat or gently rolling countryside of middle England, pilgrims in Wales faced a very different terrain: hostile, bleak and dangerous and their mode of transport uncomfortable at best. Those who travelled as penitents, barefoot with irons round their legs, the crippled and the sick must have undergone sufferings unimaginable today. Only a well-heeled fortunate like Archdeacon Gerald could afford to compliment the abbey of St Dogmaels on the comfort it offered the traveller, especially as one of the party happened to be the Archbishop of Canterbury. Gerald is dismissive in his attitude to the hardships of the journey but nevertheless his pack horse, carrying vestments and precious books nearly drowned in the treacherous quicksands of Neath. The mountainous country of Merionydd and Gwynedd beyond the Dyfi estuary he described as 'the wildest and most terrifying region in all Wales, for its mountains are very high and inaccessible, with crags as sharply pointed as the defences of a fortress'.

Some stretches have retained their tradition as pilgrim roads, such as Goodwick to Llanwnda, Llantarnam to Llandderfel, Holgan (*Heol y gân*), near Llawhaden and a paved road that once led from Clynnog Fawr to Aberdaron. Stepping stones facilitated river crossings: Stepsau Teilo (St Teilo's Steps) once crossed the River Ogmore near Merthyr Mawr. The name Bwlch y Groes (pass of the Cross), occurs in Cardiganshire, Breconshire, Denbighshire and between Bala and Machynlleth. This last, at 1790 feet, is the highest road pass in Wales and the medieval cross which marked the summit apparently survived until the Civil War (1640–60).

A few other features survive: Ffynnon y Groes (Well of the Cross), in Llangrannog parish was where pilgrims quenched their thirst. Creed Stones, Meini Cred, were way-markers and spiritual protectors of the pilgrim as too were road-side calvaries. Some buildings, ruins or simply sites have the name *ysbytty* or its derivatives *spite* (in Pembrokeshire an old pronunciation was 'Spit' which was changed to 'Spite' because it was deemed unattractive), *spital* (Spittal, Pembrokeshire) and *spytty*, from the Latin *hospitium*, meaning hospice. This has been questioned by scholars and although etymology has to be handled with caution, these names do occur with considerable frequency along the roads of Cardiganshire and Pembrokeshire – a major section of the route used by pilgrims travelling between Ynys Enlli, St Davids and Holywell – and most of those mentioned have associated pilgrim traditions. Land could be set aside for use by pilgrims. On the Llŷn peninsula the name Cae Eisteddfa (field of the sitting or waiting place), is found at Abererch, Pistyll and Llangwnadl, all traditional pilgrim stopping places; the field so named in Llangwnadl, not far from Aberdaron, is next to the churchyard, where pilgrims would wait for favourable tide and weather for the crossing to Ynys Enlli. Near St Davids some stretches of land were known as '*tir pererinion*', pilgrims' land. Another obscure reference dated 1924, refers to some roads in the St Davids area as being known as 'St Patrick's roads', perhaps preserving a memory of the Irish pilgrims who were known to pass through St Davids.

White stones at a
medieval chapel
site, 1993

In Wales, pilgrims offered white stones at shrines and holy wells. The clearest evidence for this comes from north Wales. On Llanddwyn Island, Anglesey, there was a 'spot near the roadside on a hillock just before the church comes into view where the crucifix stood and marked now by a heap of pilgrims' stones'. They were described as 'round white stones of the size of a potato, which the pilgrims carried all the way, and dropped at the end of their pilgrimage, at the foot of the crucifix'. Apparently the same was done at the shrine of St Beuno at Clynnog Fawr[2] and two white stones were offered at St Gwenfaen's Well. It might also explain the quantities of white quartz stones of a similar size found on the excavation of the altar areas of the chapels of Saints Patrick and Justinian in Pembrokeshire. Although no explanation has ever been given for the Pembrokeshire stones, both chapels are situated on the coast at known harbours and were frequented by pilgrims: their offerings at St Justinian's chapel were recorded in the *Liber Communis* in the 15th century.

The journey was through a sanctified landscape. Each monastery had some relic or marvel to amaze the pilgrim. As the centuries advanced so too did the adornment of churches and the proliferation of shrines and images. Indulgences were offered at major abbeys and churches and at lesser shrines on patronal feast days as the Middle Ages drew to a close. The earliest-known example of a printed sheet relating to Wales and preserved at the National Library of Wales is a Latin indulgence offered for sale at Strata Marcella Abbey, *c* 1528–29. Ynys Enlli offered

---

[2] The practice of leaving pilgrim stones continues today. In the Spanish mountains of Leon near the borders of Galicia on the road to Santiago de Compostela, stones brought by pilgrims from their homes, some with prayers written on them, are left before the *Cruz de hiero,* an iron cross placed at the highest point on the route, creating a large cairn.

The significance of white stones in folklore and archaeology is discussed by A. D. Rees, 'Notes on the significance of white stones in Celtic archaeology and folk-lore with reference to recent excavations at Ffynnon Degla, Denbighshire', 87–90 *BBCS* vol. 8, part I, 1935.

a variety of pardons and a copy of a Latin manuscript made in the hand of William of Bodwrda, 1593–1660, of the pardons and privileges of the abbey preserved the form of absolution. Abundant pardons were available from St John's priory at Slebech; Abbot Dafydd ab Owain provided the same facility at Valle Crucis Abbey, and St Davids Cathedral was roundly castigated by Bishop Barlow for its traffic in pardons. However steep the mountain pass and trackless the waste of estuary and moorland, the pilgrims travelled on in the hope of healing, forgiveness and soul's salvation.

Strata Marcella, printed indulgence, National Library of Wales

The following chapters outline pilgrim routes through Wales but make no claim to be comprehensive or definitive. The complexities of the road systems and the wandering nature of pilgrimage, make it unrealistic to present a neatly interlinked network. Wales's extensive coastline offers many landfalls and therefore numerous starting points for pilgrimage. The sections on Anglesey, Straits and Estuaries and Strata Florida gather information from a number of sources concerning routes. The more defined sequences belong to the major shrines discussed in Chapter 9. In Pembrokeshire where routes converge, the division between northern and southern routes lies along the Landsker, an ancient land division bisecting the county and marked by a line of Norman castles.

Chapter 12

The Northern Routes

Anglesey to the south

HOLYHEAD'S proximity to Ireland and accessibility to major seaways has made it a landfall for travellers for centuries. The Romans established a sea fort and St Cybi, whose medieval 'Life' indicates that he had close links with Ireland, made his settlement within the abandoned Roman fort. Holyhead's Welsh name is Caergybi, the fort of Cybi, while Holy Island is also called Ynys Cybi. The cult of St Cybi flourished here in the Middle Ages. Two of Ireland's major saints are culted on north Anglesey: St Patrick at Llanbadrig and St Bride of Kildare. The chapel of St Ffraid at Treaddur Bay, where St Bride and her maidens landed after crossing from Ireland on green turfs on their way to Llansantffraid (Glanconwy) must have

Capel St Ffraid, Trearddur Bay, 1776

Site of Capel St Ffraid today

been an attraction for Irish pilgrims and at one time pilgrims came here from France. It was on the 'Monks' Path' from St Cybi's monastery to Rhoscolyn. The chapel stood on a mound containing numerous graves. The walls were standing in 1780 but all traces of the chapel were destroyed in a storm in 1913: only the mound remains.

Many of Anglesey's churches and holy wells drew pilgrims who travelled across and round the island to celebrate the festivals of individual saints such as Cybi, Seiriol, Eilian, Pabo, Gredifael and Nidan. The Virgin Mary was venerated at various holy wells, and particularly at her chapel at Rhosfair which was later combined with the church of St Peter and the name changed to Rhosyr. It is not far from Newborough and pilgrims on their way to Llanddwyn would have venerated the famous image of St Peter in the church, celebrated in verse by Lewis Daron.

Details of road systems on Anglesey do not become evident until the map-makers and travel-writers of the 17th–19th centuries. The roads they used would have been well established and give some guide to earlier systems. W. Wynn Williams attempted to trace the Sarn (a raised ditch) said to be the Roman road leading from Tal y Foel opposite Caernarfon, to Holyhead. The road from Holyhead to the north Wales coast passed through Llangefni and Beaumaris with a link road to Bangor via Porthaethwy (Menai Bridge) as it was not always possible to cross the Lavan Sands. On the west coast, in 1751 Richard Pococke landed at South Crook and went to Holyhead via Newborough and Aberffraw 'mostly over strands'. The crossing to Holy Island was probably near today's Four Mile Bridge at Pont Rhyd Bont.

Six ferries plied the treacherous waters of the Menai Straits in the Middle Ages between Beaumaris and South Crook, opposite Abermenai point, the only links with the mainland until Telford built his suspension bridge (1819–26). The first reference to the South Crook-Abermenai crossing is 1296 and by 1302 it became the most frequented. At one time Maen Beuno, a creed stone, stood at Bryn Seiont, Caernarfon, where the old highway crossed the river the incised cross was made by two strokes of St Beuno's thumb. It was moved to Aberglaslyn Hall and finally to Capel y Bedd, Clynnog Fawr. The crossing at Llanidan should also be mentioned. In existence in 1296, it led from Pant yr Ysgraphie, the inlet of the ferry boats, just below Llanidan, to Llanfair-is-Gaer. The prior of Beddgelert owned land at Llanidan, also the churches and rectories of Llanfair-is-Gaer and Llanbeblig, en route for the monastery and hospice of Beddgelert.

Maen Beuno, St Beuno's Stone,
Clynnog Fawr church

Straits and estuaries: the pilgrimage of Morfudd

Dafydd ap Gwilym, Wales's great 14th-century poet of love and nature and early contemporary of Geoffrey Chaucer, lamented his rejection by Morfudd, a lady who features in much of his poetry. One poem describes her journey from Anglesey to St Davids – Môn to Mynwy to do penance for 'words that killed her angry lover', probably a literary conceit but giving us a possible pilgrim track along the shores of west Wales. She followed a similar route to that taken by Gerald and Archbishop Baldwin from St Davids to north Wales in 1188 some 150 years previously (though they were not pilgrims). Gerald had the protection of company and the advantage of an organised, pre-planned journey. Unconstrained, he was free to convey gossip and observe curiosities and did so with the eye and ear of a journalist. The landscape he saw and recorded was much the same as that which Morfudd travelled but missing two notable features which are very much part of the landscape today, the Norman castles of Harlech (1283) and Aberystwyth (1277). The major challenges were, as ever, the river estuaries. Although Gerald was ferried across and his passage was uneventful, he begins many of his chapters with the words 'How we crossed the river . . .'. His observations are pragmatic and topographical; Dafydd's are lyrical and his solutions impractical!

We attempt to follow a north–south route from Anglesey to St Davids. Dafydd begs 'kind straits of Menai let her through' but we are not told where Morfudd made her crossing and we can only pick up a possible trail in the region of

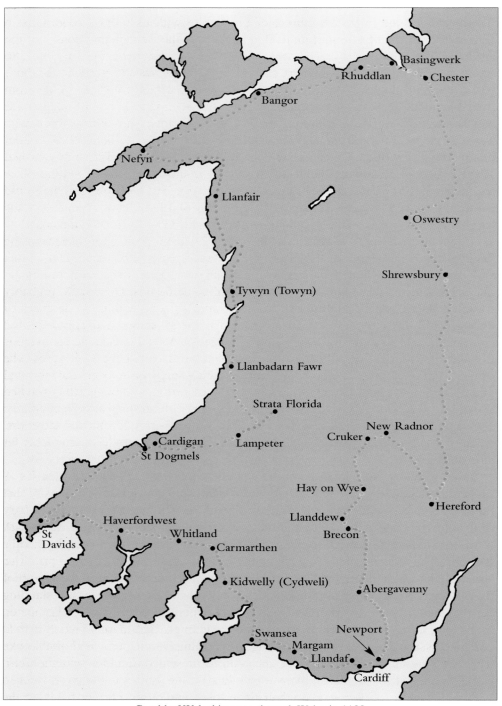

Gerald of Wales' journey through Wales in 1188

Caernarfon. A Roman road led from the outskirts of the town from the fort of Segontium and the important church of Llanbeblig with its famous rood, Crist o Gaernarfon, Christ of Caernarfon, to Beddgelert and the Benedictine house 'of the valley of the Blessed Mary of Snowdon'. The priory's Edwardian charter of 1286 described it as a 'resort for the poor, and for English and Welsh travellers, for those passing from England and West Wales to North Wales, and for those going from Ireland and North Wales into England'. It was thus at an intersection of many roads and had a shrine and hospice to accommodate pilgrims, particularly those who came to celebrate the feasts of St Nidan and St Cawrdaf (Abererch) to whom indulgences were offered, granted by Pope Boniface IX *c.* 1399. The long-vanished Augustinian priory appears to have retained the tradition of being a resting place for Irish pilgrims till the 20th century. Beyond Beddgelert lay Aberglaslyn; an old name for the parish was Llan Ybor, a corruption of Llan y Porth, church of the harbour. The waters were navigable from this point to Cardigan Bay, the coastline opening out into Traeth Mawr, great beach, and Traeth Bach, little beach, in the angle of the Llŷn peninsula, comprising an extensive stretch of tidal water, marsh and sandbank. Gerald briefly described them as two tracts of sea sand, one large, one small and remarked on two 'recently built' stone castles, Deudraeth, probably Castell Aber Ia near Portmeirion and Carn Fadryn situated within the defences of an early hillfort above Dinas. Saxton's map of 1575 shows a deeply indented coastline here. The area was reclaimed in 1811 by W. A. Maddocks, the eponymous founder of Porthmadoc who built the enclosing wall called the Cob across the estuary, thus radically changing it. Two churches may have been the spiritual guardians of these particularly dangerous sands: Llanfrothen in the north is situated on the edge of Traeth Mawr and on the southern shore, Llanfihangel y Traethau, the church of St Michael of the sands, a church associated with pilgrims and travellers, stood on what was once a tidal island at the mouth of the Dwyryd estuary on the far side of Traeth Bach.

In his poem to Morfudd, Dafydd named and described all the river estuaries as far as Cardigan in compressed and elegant verse. Both he and Gerald observed that the Dovey, rising in the 'snow-clad mountains of Snowdonia' marked the boundary of the diocese of Menevia. Dafydd implored the 'Deep Dovey with your wine-dark flood and shivering waters, let nine waves carry (Morfudd) to sweet St David's country'. The river Ystwyth reached the sea 'below Aberystwyth castle', a primitive structure built by Gilbert FitzRichard of Clare in 1110 on a site near the mouth of the Ystwyth, about one and a half miles south of the Edwardian castle standing today. Gerald was northward-bound and detoured at Cardigan to Lampeter, Llanddewi Brefi and Strata Florida before reaching Llanbadarn Fawr. Morfudd continued south along the coast, crossing the 'Boiling Aeron, noisy and nimble like a lover'. The last river estuary that appeared to present difficulties was the Teifi. Gerald stayed at St Dogmael's Abbey and thought the Teifi a noble river, stocked with fine salmon; he digressed on their finer points and on the curious habits of the river's other denizens. Cardigan Castle had already celebrated Wales's first recorded 'eisteddfod' in 1176, although the word is not used in contemporary chronicles, when Gerald passed that way. The old crossing of the Teifi was upstream of the castle, probably between the church of St Mary and the Angel Hotel, the latter originally a Knights' Hospitaller establishment and in later times described as St John's Hould. The Teifi was Morfudd's last challenge: 'springing golden water . . . carry her strongly to the river's mouth, so let her come to the end of her journey'.

Cywydd i Ferch o Fôn oedd myned i Offrwm i Fynyw, am ladd y bardd a'i thraserch

Gwawr ddyhuddiant y cantref
Lleiau aeth er llu o nef,
Ac er Non, calon a'i cel,
Ac er Dewi, eigr dawel;
O Fon deg, boed rhwydd rhegddi
I Fynyw dir, f'enaid i!
I geisiaw blodeuaw'r blaid,
Maddeuant am a ddywaid,
Am ladd ei gwas dulas dig,
Penydiwr cul poenedig;
O alanas gwas gwawdferw,
Yr aeth oer hiraeth ar herw;
Greddf ffoes gruddiau ffuon,
Gadewis fy newis Fon.
Crist arglwydd! boed rhwydd y trae
Cas, a chymynas Menai;
Y Traeth Mawr, goludfawr glod,
Treia, gad fyned trwod.
Y Bychan Draeth, gaeth gerynt,
Gad im'dyn gwyn hyn o hynt;
Darfu'r gweddiau dirfawr,
Digyffro fo Ertro fawr!
Talwnfferm porth Abermaw

Ar don drae, er ei dwyn draw;
Gydne gwin, gad naw gwaneg,
Dysyni i dir Dewi deg;
A dwfn yw tonau Dyfi,
Dwfr rhyn yn ei herbyn hi;
Theidiol, gad er d'anrhydedd,
Heol i fun hael o fedd;
Ystwyth, ymhwyth, gad im'hon,
Drais dew-ddwfr; dros dy ddwyfron;
Aeron, ferw hyson hoywserch,
Gad trwod fy eurglod ferch;
Teifi, dw'r tyfiad eurwawn,
Gad i'r dyn gadeirio dawn;
Durfing drwy'r afon derfyn,
Yr el ac y del y dyn.
Mam hirffawd, mae ymhorffor,
Os byw, rhwng Mynyw a'r mor;
Os hi a'm lladdodd, oes hir;
Herw hylithr, hwyr yr holir,
Maddeued Mair, neddair nawdd,
I'm lleddf wylan a'm lladdawdd,
Diau mae im a'i dihaur,
Minau a'i maddau i'm haur.

Dafydd ap Gwilym

A day of promise dawns for the whole neighbourhood: Morfudd the Nun (my dear love) is going from Mona on her pilgrimage to Mynyw to seek forgiveness through the heavenly hosts, through St Non and St David for the words that killed her angry lover. A thin tormented penitent, she seeks forgiveness with offerings of flowers from the guilt of this young man whose boiling song is dead; so now she goes in grief and longing on her journey. Morfudd's heart is secret, her lips silent: let this journey be safe and easy for her.

When you leave my lovely isle of Mona it is as if the colour drained from ruddy cheeks; Lord Jesus let her have an easy crossing! Kind straits of Menai let her through; Traeth Mawr beach, let your tide ebb and let her pass; Traeth Mawr and Traeth Bach, you estuaries joined like lovers, let my dear pass on her journey. I can make no greater prayer than this: be calm for her, great Arthro; I would give the price of a farm for an ebb wave to carry her across the estuary at Barmouth.

And now, deep Dovey with your wine-dark flood and shivering waters, let nine waves carry her to sweet St David's country. Rheidol, for your honour's sake give passage to her: Ystwyth grant this to me, a crossing of fair water between your two banks. Boiling Aeron, noisy and nimble like a lover, let through my golden love. Teifi, springing golden water, let her pass beyond your spreading grace, carry her strongly to the river's mouth, so let her come to the end of her journey.

Holy Mother of all happiness robed in purple, who lives between Mynyw and the sea, though my love has killed me, let her long escape, and let it be long till she is called to reckoning. May Mary with her hand of charity forgive my gentle seabird who has killed me. Though I am the one who should defend myself, freely I forgive her for the harm she did me.

Translation by Nigel Heseltine

Strata Florida

The first abbey was founded in 1164, beside the Afon Fflur from which it derived its name. The site lies south-east of the present abbey ruins, near the old abbey farm. The monks moved in 1201 so Gerald and Archbishop Baldwin (1188) would have stayed in the earlier building. The new Abbey became one of the most magnificent buildings in medieval west Wales. A combination of saintly attractions, good husbandry and monastic marketing skills ensured that crowds gathered at Ffair Rhos (SN742680) for the great fairs held on St James's Day, the Feast of the Assumption and Holy Rood Day. The abbey was associated with a relic which achieved fame in the 19th and 20th centuries, the Nanteos Cup, believed to have been carved from a fragment of the True Cross and the find of a pilgrim bottle has been recorded. The great yew tree in the abbey precincts is reputed to mark the grave of Dafydd ap Gwilym.

Like Beddgelert and Lampeter, Strata Florida was situated at an intersection of ancient tracks and close to the coastal route, attracting hundreds of pilgrims in its time. A pilgrim track led from Ponterwyd to Devil's Bridge: the lowest of the three bridges was said to have been built for pilgrims by the monks of Strata Florida. The crossing of the Rheidol was at Llanbadarn. The place name, or prefix 'ysbyty' with its various derivatives proliferates in this area: a farm name, Rhyd y Pererinion (pilgrims' ford), on the way to Pontrhydygroes bears witness to pilgrim traffic and possibly the farm of Palmon (palmer?) (SN569722). A short distance from the abbey the word 'cleifion' features in a number of place names: Cae Cleifion identified with *territorium leprosorum*, Hafod y Cleifion (SN712672) and Tir-llety y cleifion – former name of Tre Isaf farm. *Cleifion* is the plural of *claf*, meaning the sick and is often associated with lepers. The name is also found at Pistyll on the Llŷn peninsula, Pont y Cleifion in Cardigan (in full 'Pont Nant tir Cleifion', the bridge over the stream of sick men's land), and Dŵr Cleifion on the pilgrim road just east of St Davids and not far from the medieval hospitium at Llandrudion. It would indicate that some sort of quarantine for sick, leprous and infectious pilgrims would have been sensibly situated away from the main religious establishment.

Ystrad Fflur, Strata Florida Abbey ruins, 12th–16th centuries, Ceredigion

Pilgrim roads to Ynys Enlli – approaching from the north

The pilgrim roads to Enlli appear to be identifiably distinct from other pilgrim ways, separating out from the general north/south axis to follow the north-western coastal margins till they come together on the Llŷn peninsula and generally speaking, are marked by church dedications to saints connected with Enlli. These roads are taken separately and described from the northern and southern approaches.

The northern approach to Enlli is taken up at Bangor, where Nest Davies and Enid Pierce Roberts suggest that pilgrims would have taken the road over Mynydd Bangor, leading to Pont Caerhun through Pentir and skirting Caernarfon, *via* Llanbeblig church with its famous rood Crist o Gaernarfon, near the remains of the Roman fort at Segontium. Llanfaglan church with its holy well was a likely stopping place for pilgrims and dedicated to St Baglan, brother to Abbot Lleudad. From this point, the road taken by pilgrims is more discernable. Further along, Capel Bettws in the grounds of Glyn Llifon Park, was a mortuary chapel where bodies being taken for burial on Enlli would rest for the night: only footings remain. Nearby was a hospice, later converted to an inn and latterly a farmhouse. Plas Newydd was said to occupy the site of older buildings once known as 'Mynachdy', implying a grange belonging to a Cistercian monastery.

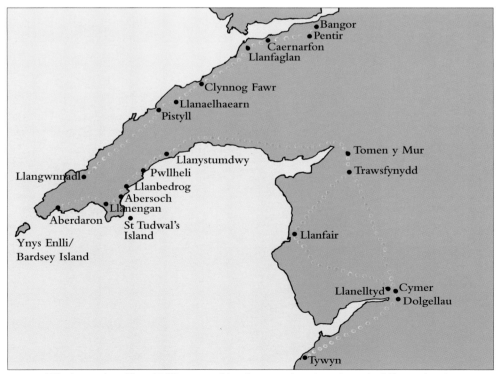

Pilgrim roads to Ynys Enlli, approaching from north and south on the Llŷn peninsula

Llanfaglan church, Caernarfonshire

Clynnog Fawr was the traditional gathering point for pilgrims to Enlli: a major early monastic settlement and later collegiate church, founded by St Beuno, preserving his remains and the centre of his cult. St Beuno could be called the patron saint of north Wales, feared, revered and loved in life and beyond. Abundant evidence of a once thriving veneration remains in the folklore and history of Clynnog. Pilgrims came to his well, lay for a cure on his tomb, took pillar-scrapings from his grave chapel and left white stones as a witness of their visit,

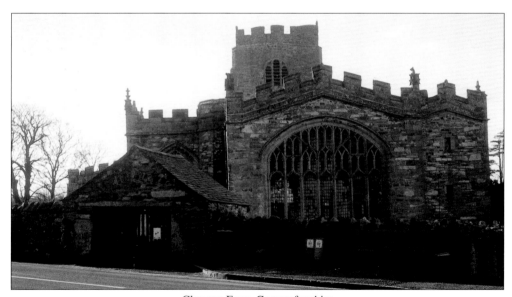

Clynnog Fawr, Caernarfonshire

though where is not known.[1] In 1847 there was 'a well-paved road, still to be traced across certain unenclosed lands and certain farms' down the Llŷn peninsula.

Some way beyond Clynnog the steep sides of Yr Eifl plunge seawards and a necessary detour would be made through Llanaelhaiarn. When the church was restored in 1892, pilgrim graffiti were found on the walls. Nearby is the healing well of St Aelhaiarn. At this point pilgrims turned towards the sea where a footpath crosses Bwlch yr Eifl. W. Williams Wynn noted a 'Monks' Path' in the area. On Yr Eifl above Nant Gwrtheyrn a dwelling, now a farmhouse was once held on a tenure agreement of assistance to pilgrims. Tenure on similar terms was also granted to Pistyll farm.

Pistyll church is dedicated to St Beuno and one of the saint's burial places is claimed to be beneath the altar. It is rich in pilgrim tradition: a hospice stood on Cefnedd Hill nearby, the field name is Cae Hospice, and a separate area was set aside for lepers. A variety of medicinal herbs have been identified in the vicinity, still re-seeding, and the holy well is in a field nearby. Four cross-inscribed stones, now hard to find, marked a path to Nefyn, Llŷn's most important and thriving medieval town. It is said that metal pilgrim tokens of some sort were manufactured here which could be offered on Enlli and the small priory would have provided food and shelter.

Pistyll church, Llŷn

---

[1] The prescribed form of 'sin offering' was found in an old Welsh manuscript in Beuno's Chest: 'Here I offer to God four pence for my private sins, on which account the Almighty is now punishing me, to be given for the same service that the Blessed Saints used to offer, in the name of the Father, the Son and the Holy Ghost. Amen. (Evans, J. *Beauties of England and Wales*)

The next church where a pilgrim tradition survives is Llangwnadl. It has two side-aisles added in the 15th century to cater for pilgrims. North of the altar a 15th-century inscription on the pillar in Gothic script marks the grave of the church's founder St Gwynhoedl, *c*. 7th century. Adjoining the churchyard is a field named Cae Eisteddfa (field of the waiting place), where pilgrims gathered to wait for a crossing to Ynys Enlli. In the area were a number of small medieval churches and chapels, now ruined or vanished and known by name only.

Pillar with inscription in 15th-century Gothic script, marking the grave of St Gwynhoedl, Llangwnadl church, Llŷn

Ynys Enlli, approaches from the north and south

Vessels carrying pilgrims to Enlli probably took advantage of the tidal streams running across Cardigan Bay departing from Fishguard and Cardigan. Churches are sited at crucial river and sea crossings where risk was greatest and divine assistance most necessary. Lleuddad, second abbot of Enlli and his brothers Tygwy and Tyfriog have churches dedicated to them near the Teifi river mouth, Cenarth, Cilgerran, Llandygwy and Llandyfriog. The small, simple, beautiful churches of Mwnt (Ceredigion) and Llandanwg (Meirionnydd), virtually on the sea shore, have a tradition of being mortuary chapels for bodies awaiting transport to their last resting place on Enlli. Mwnt, church of the Holy Cross was a station on the pilgrim road and a cross is said to have crowned the nearby hill. Gerald of Wales's stopping places indicate settlements that would have been equipped to cater for pilgrims, offering attractions of their own.

The Enlli land route approaching from the south appears to start at Tywyn and the church of St Cadfan, described in the 12th century by Llywelyn Fardd as *'Uchel-lan Gadfan ger glân glas fôr'* (the high church of Cadfan by the clear blue sea), at a time when the tidal waters reached the cemetery. A stone bearing a plain, incised cross has been built into the wall of the church tower at the south-west

Church of the Holy Cross, Mwnt, Ceredigion

Llandanwg church, Meirionnydd.

angle. It originally stood at Bryn Paderau, a hill near Tywyn which gave pilgrims to St Cadfan's shrine their first sight of his church. The name and association suggests that pilgrims marked this station by tracing the cross with a finger and reciting the Lord's Prayer, a common practice all over Wales. One of the church's three medieval altars was dedicated to Cadfan and his holy well was a little below the church. In 1894 the well chamber, proving no longer profitable, was filled in and converted to a coach house and stables. A slender inscribed stone once known as Cadfan's stone stood in the churchyard. Now inside the church it preserves much weathered memorials in the earliest written Welsh (*c.* 750).

Llanfair, further up the coast was a centre of veneration of the Virgin Mary as the name suggests. It is one of only three places in Wales where, according to legend, she came ashore and delightful stories were told of how she bathed in a certain spring with her maidens and left her footprint on a rock.

In the wild and open moorland of eastern Merioneth there is sporadic evidence that pilgrims used the inland route, following stretches of Roman road named in sections as Sarn Helen, from Tomen y Mur to Dolgellau. Trawsfynydd church, just south of Tomen y Mur was founded by two women pilgrims to Enlli at an early period. Madrun, daughter of Gwrthefyr Fendigaid, accompanied by her maid sought shelter in a thicket for the night and both had the same dream that here they must build a church. Dolgellau, on a river crossing at the head of the Barmouth estuary, was a meeting point of many roads including the Roman road from the north. Here was preserved the skull of Gruffudd ab Adda ap Dafydd, *fl.* 1340–70, a poet and contemporary of Dafydd ap Gwilym. Gruffudd was killed in Dolgellau by a kinsman with a single sword-blow to the head and lamented in verse by Dafydd – 'Lord of May's lovely bows'. His skull was kept in Dolgellau as a famous relic and for centuries, people came to drink from it to cure whooping cough and other ailments. David Jones, parson of Llanfair Dyffryn Clwyd, wrote (*c.* 1580–90) that he had seen this skull which bore the mark of a blow.[2] North of Dolgellau on the bank of the Mawddach is the Cistercian abbey, Cymer, established 1198–99, and on the other bank is Llanelltud. The abbey would have catered for travellers and pilgrims at this important intersection of mountain and coastal roads. Inside Llanelltud church at the west end of the nave is a stone bearing the imprint of a foot said to have been made when Cynwric set out as hostage to the king of England, although this has been interpreted as a pilgrim's footprint.

Pilgrims who followed the southern route to Aberdaron, however they crossed the sands of the Deudraeth, would still have difficult tidal marshes to negotiate. Ynys Cynhaearn church[3] was on an island in Llyn (Lake) Ystumllyn, reached by a causeway and established by Cynhaiarn, a pupil of St Beuno. Llanystumdwy had a famous image of the Virgin and Abererch was an important pilgrim centre with a

---

[2] Not to be confused with Gruffudd ab Adda 'the Crying Knight' a sheriff whose tomb is in St Cadfan's church, Tywyn, and who died *c.* 1331 in his 70th year. His right eye is worn away with centuries of weeping (ref. church leaflet).

[3] 'Dafydd y Garreg Wen' the harper after whom the lovely Welsh song is named and who is supposed to have sung it on his deathbed, is buried in the churchyard.

mortuary tradition. Pwllheli was surrounded by an area of extensive marshland reclaimed in the 19th century and beyond the town was Penyberth, a loyal Catholic house after the Reformation (*c.* 1599) where pilgrims could find a resting place. A pilgrim in the reign of Elizabeth I was given detailed instructions of the route to be followed and urged to call on Sion Wynne of Penyberth who would row him across the Sound. No trace of the old farmhouse is left: 20th-century vandalism caused its destruction replacing it with a bombing school in the mid-1930s. Further on Llanbedrog preserved the spear of the warrior saint Pedrog. Off Abersoch, the small Benedictine cell on St Tudwal's Island must have played a part in pilgrim care, especially of the storm-bound. The relatively safe haven of St Tudwal's roads offered shelter in a notoriously dangerous area. Lewis Morris (1748) reckoned it to be one of the best roads in Britain. Llanengan became a popular pilgrim haunt towards the end of the 15th century: John Leland (*c.* 1536–39) in his *Itinerary* recorded a 'late great pilgrimage' to the shrine of St Engan, *Fanum Niniani Reguli*. The screen, a chest and 6 bells, three of which remain, are believed to have come from Ynys Enlli after the dissolution of the monasteries. Beyond the wide bay and treacherous waters of Porth Neigwl lay Rhiw. Its 12th-century church was dedicated to St Aelrhiw, with a nearby holy well and widely famed Delw Fyw (living image) of the Virgin Mary, though where the last was is not known. Beyond Rhiw was Aberdaron, the final gathering point before setting sail for Ynys Enlli.

Chapter 13

Holywell to St Davids

ST Winifred first established her community at Gwytherin, where she was buried and her relics kept before they were translated to Shrewsbury. A pilgrim track led from Gwytherin to Holywell through Nantglyn, Henllan and Bodfari and was said to have been lined with yew trees. Holywell and St Davids were apparently visited as part of the same pilgrimage.

Although there had been early maps of Britain, detailed maps of Wales do not appear until the late 16th-century Saxton map. Late 17th-century additions and improvements to this map included roads for the first time. In 1675, John Ogilby, Cosmographer to Charles II produced a 'ribbon' map, running in strips down the page, detailing roads and the terrain over which they passed, giving distances in miles and furlongs. The full distance from Holywell to St Davids is given as 156.5 miles. In 1689, Philip Lea produced a map based on Saxton with roads added which called the route 'the Pilgrims' Way, St Winifrede's Well to St Davids' and went as far as Bala. Robert Morden's map of 1695 took the Holywell road as far as Aberystwyth and covered the same initial area as Philip Lea's map.

John Ogilby's route is the fullest and most detailed, but it is evident that the road used then differed considerably in detail from the roads in common use today and is given from north to south: Holywell, Ysceifiog, Ruthin, Clocaenog, Melin-y-Wig, Betws Gwerful Goch, Maerdy, Llanfor, Bala, Llangywer (on the shore of Llyn Tegid), Bwlch y Groes, Llanymawddwy, Aberangell, Machynlleth, Tal-y-bont, Llanbadarn Fawr, Llanrhystyd, Llanarth, Cardigan, Trefdraeth (Newport), Fishguard, Mathry, Llanrhian, Gwrhyd, St Davids.

The stretch of road from Clocaenog to Bala is characteristic of tracks linked by tradition to pilgrim traffic and long fallen into disuse, consisting of minor roads, green lanes or holloways and footpaths, in later centuries to become part of the network of drovers' roads.

At Clocaenog, a long, low white house aptly named 'Paradwys' (Paradise), was traditionally a 15th-century pilgrim's inn. Beyond Clocaenog the old road follows a green lane to the healing well Ffynnon Sara (St Saeran's Well); a clapper bridge survives close by. Connected with this pilgrim's well was Derwen ('upper Derwen chapel'), which appeared on Lea's 1689 map. St Saeran was an Irish saint buried at Llanynys 'to which place a branch of an ancient road led direct from this spot through Clocaenog and Gyffylliog'. The minor road from Clawdd Newydd via Ffynnon Sara to Betws Gwerful Goch is identified as the pilgrim route. Just north of it, above Pont Petryal on a creed stone on the slopes of Cefn Bannog were etched two crosses and 'HR 1630', apparently the initials of Hugh Reinallt of Hendre farmhouse which was held by tenants of the Salesbury family on condition

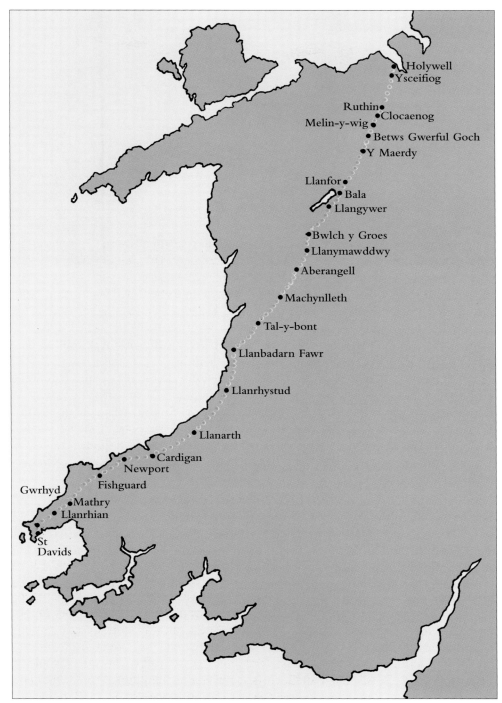

John Ogilby's route of 1675, Holywell to St Davids

Ffynnon Sara, St Saeran's Well, Denbighshire

that free lodging was given to 'travellers and pilgrims'. The narrow, steep and winding roads affording magnificent views of Clwydian scenery descend through lovely countryside to Betws Gwerful Goch 'the prayer-house of Gwerful the Red', traditionally founded for pilgrims by the 12th-century Princess Gwerful of Meirionnydd, the red-haired granddaughter of Owain Gwynedd, King of North Wales. A medieval pilgrim inn backed onto the churchyard. Behind the church altar are three carved panels from a 15th-century rood screen. They were recovered from 'a heap of rubbish' in 1840. The isolated village of Betws Gwerful Goch once ranked in importance as a halting place with Bala and Ruthin. Beyond it the original path crossed the moor traversing a kerb circle and ring cairn on Cefn Caer Enni, Meironeth, to Sarnau and on to Bala.

From there the road leads to Llyn Tegid, Bala Lake, and south to Machynlleth. The most difficult and dangerous stretch of the northern section of the road was from Bala to Machynllech over Bwlch y Groes, Pass of the Cross: the sight of it quelled even Gerald's dauntless spirit. More often than not it is covered by cloud and once had the name the 'Preachers' Road'.

William Rees's map of south Wales in the 14th century shows a similar track to that of Ogilby: the main route runs through Llanbadarn Fawr, once a major medieval monastery, to Llanrhystyd which lay close to a bog called Rhos y Miniog, sufficiently terrifying to travellers to have been cursed by a Cardiganshire bard.[1]

---

[1] *Os oes i m'elyn, boed ei ran,*   If I've a foe, may it be his fate
  (y felltith annrhugarog!)   (unmerciful is the curse!)
  Fyn'd wrth ei hun, ac wedi'r nos   To go by himself after night(fall)
  Dros gefn Rhos y Miniog.   Over the ridge of Miniog Bog!

H. T. Payne, *Collectanea Menevensia* Vol I cxxxv NLW 1815

Betws Gwerful Goch, former Pilgrim Inn

Pilgrim track across the Denbigh moors

The road rising from Llyn Tegid to Bwlch y Groes (Pass of the Cross), Denbighshire, at 1,790 feet the highest mountain pass in Wales

Also in the region the name Spytty Hal marked the site of three demolished cottages suggesting some sort of hospice, on land granted by Rhys ap Gruffudd to the Knights Hospitaller of the Slebech commandery who administered other properties in the nearby region of Strata Florida. Between Aberarth and Llansantffraid, Ogilby's map shows a path along the beach as well as the coastal route. A pilgrim track traditionally runs to and beyond St Ffraid's parish church. Llanon and Henfynyw had strong links with St David who was educated at Henfynyw, Old Menevia, and whose mother, St Non, is commemorated in Llanon, which also has a tradition of being a station on the road to St Davids. North of Cardigan, on the coastal route, Ffynnon y Groes in the parish of Llangranog was traditionally where pilgrims rested to quench their thirst and to make the sign of the cross. The medieval road follows the coast, entering Cardigan via Crug Mawr.

There is a confluence of roads at Lampeter, with one track undoubtedly used by pilgrims leading through Llanddewi Brefi and Strata Florida, through Yspytty Ystwyth to join with the roads heading north and west. Llanddewi Brefi was the site of St David's triumphant preaching. A huge ox's horn, Corn yr Ych, kept for centuries in the chancel, acquired the status of a relic. It was 17 inches in diameter at its base. A 12-inch fragment survives in the Museum of Welsh Life, St Fagans. The story goes that two giant, horned oxen, the *ychain bannog* of Llanddewi Brefi and sometimes known as St Davids Oxen, were used to carry stones to build the church. They were continually overloaded and one day, one of the pair died as it

Llanddewi Brefi church, Ceredigion

struggled to drag its burden. At this its companion bellowed nine times, causing Foelallt Hill to split open, levelling an easier path for the survivor to continue the work. Another folktale claimed that the horn belonged to a monstrous animal that plagued the surrounding countryside until destroyed by the prayers and miraculous powers of the patron saint. St David's staff was preserved in the church, but no longer exists, and the name is now given to a cross-inscribed stone in the church. In a nearby house is Ffynnon Dewi, near the site of the holy well which appeared where David raised a child from the dead who later became his disciple.[2]

Pilgrims travelling between St Davids, Ireland and Ynys Enlli, through Cardigan would have used the southern part of the route. Irish pilgrims could have come ashore at many points on the Welsh coast but there would have been a concentration of sea traffic in the Fishguard/Goodwick area. Vessels carrying pilgrims to Ynys Enlli probably took advantage of the tidal streams running across Cardigan Bay departing from Fishguard and Cardigan. Mwnt and Llandanwg were also departure points. A number of landfalls were possible on the south coast of Llŷn and land routes led along the peninsula to Aberdaron and Ynys Enlli. In the Cardigan Bay area, a picture builds up of a network of roads carrying local traffic and long-distance travellers alike; a situation which would have remained fairly static until the 20th century.

Cardigan to St Davids

At Teifi mouth as also at Newport and Fishguard, sea and land routes come together leading the medieval pilgrim towards St Davids. Apart from sites more characteristic of long-distance pilgrimages, numerous small chapels in the region of Cemais were used for solemn processions on Holy Days and were recognised as pilgrimage chapels. Many were left to fall into ruin after the Reformation and George Owen noted twenty of them in a dilapidated state at the end of the 16th century.

St Dogmael's Abbey must have received many pilgrims: Gerald of Wales wrote of being 'very comfortably lodged' there, and from this point south it is possible that a track followed a coast road via Moylegrove to Newport sands. Another medieval route to Nevern runs from St Dogmaels east of Monington through Bayvil to Nevern where there was probably a convergence of roads from other directions. Only the large church with its massive tower and the substantial remains of a motte-and-bailey castle suggest what a bustling medieval settlement it must have been. Pilgrim traditions are plentiful here, linking Nevern directly with the track from Llanddewi Brefi and reflected in a local folktale about St David and the Nevern Cross. The saint was making his way to Llanddewi Brefi carrying on his back a large and curiously carved stone cross, to be his own memorial, but was prevailed upon by his friend St Brynach to rest awhile in Nevern and leave his cross

---

[2] There are two houses opposite each other, one is 'Ffynnon Dewi' and the other, traditionally believed to be the site of the well itself is 'Dewi Well'.

Nevern church, Pembrokeshire.

Nevern Cross,
late 10th/early 11th centuries

Pilgrim Cross, Nevern

behind. Nevern was believed to be the final resting-place for pilgrims who were too close to death to make the remaining miles to St Davids. The pilgrim path crosses Pontgarreg, stone bridge, behind the church joining a path leading to the ancient relief cross in the cliff above the village, with a worn kneeling stone below it. Just to the north of the cross are hollows in the rock-face bearing small incised crosses, worn smooth by the feet of pilgrims from Llanddewi Brefi. The path stays north of the river – beside it was a wishing well, no longer visible but perhaps originally a healing well – and emerges at a former Knights' Hospitaller commandery at Berry Hill. At the estuary the river Nyfer was crossed by a bridge first mentioned in 1278; in the 16th century it was stone-built with six arches. Upstream stood the chapel and well of St Curig whose saint's day was celebrated with a 'greate fair' on 16 June: Newport's annual fair is still known as Ffair Gurig. The track is said to have

Hollow in rock with small incised cross

Interior of the old chapel, Dinas

followed Feidr Brenin to the main Fishguard road, at the junction of which stood Capel Dewi (SN043391). Both Capel Curig and Capel Dewi were named by George Owen as pilgrimage chapels.

A pilgrim tradition emerges at Dinas. Near the Old Rectory (now a caravan club house) was a small building, now converted to a cottage and known as the old chapel, sometimes called the Bell House. It was believed to have been a chapel where pilgrims from Llanddewi Brefi and Nevern stopped to pray before going on to St Davids. Inside this curious building there is what appears to be a solidly constructed Gothic-arched chamber with a hole in the ceiling for a bell rope. In a field below are the remains of a holy well (Ffynnonwen). About half a mile away, Bryn Henllan and nearby Tŷ Gwyn where graves have been found, mark earlier church and religious sites.

George Owen's 'Hilltop of Presely'

The Flemish Way, an important ridgeway of ancient origin, runs in the direction of Cwm Gwaun and Fishguard. It has been known by other names – the Golden Road, Robbers Road and the Pilgrims' Way, said to lead to St Davids, and is clearly marked just below the crest of the Preseli hills. George Owen wrote 'along the said hilltop of Presely from the begining to the end there is seen the track of an ancient way, now clean out of use, yet such has been the trade in ancient time that way that to this day the ancient track thereof is yet apparently to be seen'. Many early roads are now no more than footpaths and bridleways, joining with metalled roads for stretches and typical of this area. As the peninsula narrows, so a number of ancient roads coming in from all directions begin to converge. A suggested continuation of the way once it leaves the Preseli hilltops would be to cross Cwm Gwaun at Llanychaer.[3] At Puncheston near Martel Bridge were two wells where pilgrims were said to refresh themselves before the last lap to St Davids. There is an old tradition that the pilgrim road/Flemish Way passed through Letterston via Croesgoch to St Davids.

Llanstinan church, north Pembrokeshire, showing pre-Norman, circular churchyard enclosure

Fishguard was a major landfall for seafaring pilgrims. One track heads south from Lower Fishguard harbour to Llanstinan where more tracks meet. There was a medieval village here and the ancient church dedicated to St Stinan (Justinian), soulfriend of St David still stands. The only other 'Stinan' church dedication outside St Davids is at a tidal creek south of Haverfordwest at Freystrop. In the sacred territory of the patron saint, Stinan was important, famed for his miracles and interred in St David's church (now the cathedral); the distribution of 'Stinan' churches suggests pilgrim traffic coming by sea. A medieval road leads from Llanstinan, crossing the A420, over an ancient bridge at Dolau and on towards Mathry.

---

[3] A mile from the church (dedicated to St David) an old OS sheet shows old buildings beside the Aer river, one of which was known as 'Spite'. Information from Mr Richard Davies.

Ancient bridge at Dolau, north Pembrokeshire

At Goodwick, the pilgrim entered the territory of Pebidiog, later known as Cantref Dewi or St David's Land according to Camden, a land division that extended south and west to Newgale, and within this area the Statutes of Bishop Guy Mone, 1401, decreed that he had safe conduct 'during the natural day of his pilgrimage' to St Davids.[4] The traditional pilgrim route is indicated by a modern sign-post and climbs directly up Penrhiw towards Llanwnda church and holy well. A weathered, cross-marked stone is set into the hedge at the cross-roads near the church. Apparently three similar stones once marked entry points of the other roads and the track rounded Strumble Head passing Capel Degan and Llanwnwr. Harmony also has a pilgrim tradition: on the site of the old burial ground (in the area of the toilet block) was a hospitium for pilgrims[5] and a local tradition concerning an unidentified curved feature in the church of the Holy Martyrs at Mathry served as a sign that lepers could be left there and cared for.

A mile outside Croesgoch, there is a small settlement called Mesur y Dorth (measure of the loaf). The name appears to have been that of a stone bearing an encircled cross, set into the wall on the roadside. One tradition claims that pilgrims broke bread here for the last time before continuing to St Davids and another that in time of famine, St David, or in some accounts, the bishop of St Davids, decreed that loaves should be baked no bigger than the circle. Archdeacon Payne writing in 1815, commented 'this is only one of many, which, at intervals, have been remembered by the inhabitants as pointing out the avenue to St Davids, the Arabian Felix of the pious pilgrims, who, formerly in prodigious numbers resorted thither'.

The road passed through Llanrhian; Cwmwdig farm has the remains of a holy well, and medieval deeds described it as Eglwys Cwmwdig. As the road nears St Davids, field and place names suggest an ecclesiastical presence.[6] Archdeacon Payne gave the following information: 'It is said that certain portions of land, mostly of a triangular form, to distinguish them from other property, and which in documents even now existing are called Tir y pererinion or Pilgrims' land, were granted by pious christians for the accommodation of these religious, and other devout pilgrims and their horses, when they paid their visits to the holy shrine of David, and that they extended at various distances along the road. An aged person who is now deceased, informed me that in his youth, some of these long since fallen into the hands of the adjoining landowners, they had now lost their character, though, in some instances, they were still recognized by the traditions of the place'.

---

[4] Statutes of Guy Mone, 1401 'No secular Officer of the See shall be allowed to arrest or cause to be arrested, any Pilgrim visiting, or on his way to visit the threshold and reliques of St David, during the natural day of his pilgrimage, within the Lordship of Pybidiog, at the suit of the Lord, or of any other party.' Payne, H. T. *Collectanea Menevensia* Vol 1 p 121 NLW SD/CH/B/27i & 28ii

[5] The local story goes that a new chapel was built on the other side of the road using local stone and labour on a field named 'spite' given by a farmer. A neighbour had jeered at the farmer, asking if he was going to call the chapel 'Spite', to which he retorted that the chapel would be called Harmony.

[6] A number of farms are prefixed by 'Llan'; stone coffins have been found in the Penberi area: other names are Maen y Groes (cross stone), Waun Beddau (marsh of the graves), Parc Ysbytty (hospice field), Parc Treprior (field of the tref of the prior), Parc yr Hen Fynwent (field of the old cemetery, site of a vanished chapel).

Pilgrim track leading from Goodwick to Llanwnda

Strumble Head looking
towards St Davids

Mesur y Dorth, cross-inscribed stone,
7th–9th centuries

Ruins of Spite Cottage,
Dowrog Common, St Davids

Maen Dewi, St David's Stone,
Drws Gobaith, St Davids

To the east, names on the Dowrog suggest an association with pilgrimage: Spite Moor (north-east Dowrog) and the ruins of a cottage also called Spite. A standing stone in the area is called Maen Dewi, David's Stone and marks an intersection of land boundaries at Drws Gobaith, its original site, which according to local tradition was a gathering place for pilgrims on their way to St Davids. It could also have been a marker of sanctuary land.

There are two chapel sites along the approach road to St Davids from the north, one marked by the field name Hen Fynwent (old cemetery), opposite the entrance to Hendre Eynon farm and the other in a field alongside the road just north of Rhodiad: Capel y Gwrhyd (chapel of the fathom) was clearly marked on Ogilby's road map of 1675. It was described in 1715 as being 'where they show St Davids Fathom, [the length of his extended arms] upon an arch of the Chapel, which is about Three yards and half long. He is describ'd in the old Chronicles, to have been "a very tall Man".' The episcopal registers record that on 8 September 1398, Bishop Guy Mone 'happily visited the Cathedral Church of St Davids . . . for the grace of his installation and enthronement to be done, to wit walking from the chapel called Fethemchirch (Fathomchurch) after masses first heard and prayer poured forth as is the custom with bare feet as far as his City of St Davids' (about a mile).[7] A direct route from Gwrhyd to the cathedral did exist: a path known as Meidr y Saint, Saints' Lane, now called Feidr Dywyll, led from Gwrhyd to Pont Halawg or Halog (polluted bridge), and was that taken by clergy from Llanbadarn Fawr when they visited St Davids. It was also known as Ffordd y Pererinion, Pilgrim's Road. Following the example of Bishop Guy Mone, it is possible that pilgrims walked this last mile barefoot to Pont Halog now known as Pont y Penyd, the Bridge of Penance where, according to local tradition and following a common penitential practice, they would have washed their feet before proceeding to the cathedral. The grassy triangle beyond the bridge was known as Penitent's Lawn, traditionally the location of the stocks, but in 1894 the name given to this was Calvary after a calvary cross raised on three steps, where coffins were placed as they were brought for burial. There was another calvary on the hill by the deanery.[8]

Remarkably little has survived in the cathedral to give any indication of what happened to pilgrims when they got there and no pilgrim route has ever been identified. Bishop Barlow's efficiency in obliterating all trace of 'ungodly ymage service, abhomynable ydolaterye . . . Popish pilgremages, disceatefull pardons and feigned indulgences' had seen to that. Henry Evans in the 1923 *Tŵr y Felin Guide*

---

[7] Compare also the following account: in 1285, a list of miracles relating to St David recorded that a ship bound for Ireland from St Justinians got into difficulties and a Cistercian monk bound the company to a barefoot pilgrimage to the church of St David if they were saved from wherever the ship made landfall, as it happened she returned successfully to port and they fulfilled the vow. (M. J. Curley, University of Puget Sound *Eleven Miracles of St David* unpublished manuscript.)

[8] According to Richard Fenton there were a number of these crosses in and around St Davids. The only survivor is that on Cross Square. The Speed Map of 1610 marks a cross in the churchyard and there was an old tradition that one stood at the top of Quickwell Hill.

Pont y Penyd, Bridge of Penance

stated a traditionally held view that the doorway in the west wall of the north transept was the pilgrim entrance to the cathedral. At various times the cathedral possessed venerated images of St David and the Blessed Virgin Mary and important relics including those of St David and St Stinan, a tooth of St Andrew, the incorrupt body of St Caradog and a fragment of the Cross of Salvation or the True Cross. The medieval shrines of St David and St Caradog are on the north side of the cathedral. The site and nature of the tomb of St Stinan is unknown. The north transept was dedicated to St Andrew, and the chapel of St David was in the south transept where relics were kept.[9] The ambulatory at the east end was probably connected with a pilgrim route past an open area which may have contained the saint's tomb but is now Holy Trinity chapel. The elaborate recess in the west wall may have provided a view of an earlier shrine situated behind the high altar, the usual place for a shrine, and the arms of the central cross are rubbed smooth as if with frequent handling. To the east of the ambulatory, St Mary's chapel which contained her statue was a focus for the veneration of Mair o Fynyw, Mary of Menevia.[10]

Feidr Dywyll, the Dark Way, pilgrim track from the north to the cathedral

Medieval shrine of St Caradog

[9] The will of Archdeacon Thomas Sant of St Davids directs his body to be buried 'in ye south cross isle, by ye relicks'. 2 March 1511 PRO.

[10] Bishop Fastolf (d. 1361) and Bishop Nicholl (d. 1433) requested to be buried near the statue of the BVM in their wills. Menevia Sacra pp 370 and 381.

Recess with casket and reliquary containing
bones traditionally believed to have been those of
St David and St Stinan

Pilgrim graffiti, St Davids Cathedral

The westward slope of the nave floor is a traditional characteristic of pilgrim churches. The reason is practical: as a gathering place for large numbers of humanity, among them the sick and incontinent, it is easier to clean by sluicing down a gradient; however, before the present floor was put in, the surface was uneven and the slope less obvious. The popular practice of leaving graffiti to mark a pilgrim visit was complained about by Felix Fabri in the 15th century in the Holy Land when some came equipped with chisel and hammer for that purpose. In the region of Holy Trinity chapel, various crosses scratched on the stone work may mark the passage of pilgrims. Other etchings, including ships and inscriptions in the chapel are unlikely to be earlier than the 16th-century; however, David Powel, a Denbighshire cleric recorded late 16th-century pilgrimages to 'St David's church in Dyfed every year'. Small crosses can also be found chiselled on pillars in the nave. In 1873 it was said that 'very recently' there were stones remaining in the pavement to the back of the shrine which had been indented by the knees of a long succession of pilgrims. In front of the shrine, wear and tear on the 16th-century encaustic tiles around the shrine in the presbytery was noted by Jones and Freeman but this evidence was lost when the tiles were re-laid by Sir Gilbert Scott. Numbers of Edwardian coins found in and about St Davids suggest that the shrine attained great popularity in the 13th and 14th centuries. From a collection of rather nebulous fragments, it seems that

pilgrim practices at St Davids were typical of those at other shrines and still in use
in the Roman Catholic church.

The sanctity of St David's was
not confined to the limits of the
city, but the whole parish, called
emphatically, Plwyf Tŷ Ddewi,
the parish of the house of
David, was thick sown with
chapels, crosses and sainted
wells; and many of the latter are
to this day held in great repute.
At some distance without the
several gates there were crosses
corresponding, like the gates
nearly with the cardinal points
to give more awfulness to the
approach . . .

Richard Fenton, 1810.

A   ritual   landscape . . . the
persistence,   preservation   and
development of earlier sites into
the high middle ages in the St
Davids area must have been
partly   created   by   and   in
response to the demands of
pilgrims

Heather James

14th-century cross, Cross Square, St Davids

On this thinly populated peninsula which has seen relatively little change over the
centuries, the association of the founder saint and his followers with natural
features such as springs, stones, rocky outcrops, headlands and islands survives in
the local names – a characteristic of many other early Christian sites in Wales.
Three harbours on the peninsula, known to have been the main arrival and
departure points for those travelling by sea had chapels dedicated to the saints
venerated in the cathedral: at Porth Clais, Capel y Pistyll (vanished) marked the site
of St David's baptism and Porth Stinan (St Justinians) is called after St David's
confessor and friend, St Stinan where a chapel (now ruined) was dedicated to him.
It was first recorded by John of Tynemouth, d. 1350, in the saint's 'Life' which
associated him with Ramsey Island where a chapel and holy well were dedicated to
him. Stinan was decapitated by his followers 'and bearing the head between (his)
arms, went over to the creek called by his name; and in the place, where now stands
a church dedicated to his honour, falling on the ground, lay there, and at that spot

Penmaen Dewi/St Davids Head: summer sunset

Porth Clais, St Davids

Ramsey Island/Ynys Dewi, St Davids: winter sunset

he deserved to be buried'. The church was the site of many miracles, as too was his well on Ramsey Island. John of Tynemouth recorded that St David and his brethren 'carried the sacred body with hymns and chants to the Church of Mynyw and placed it honourably in a new sarcophagus'. The remains of St Patrick's chapel are covered by a mound at Whitesands/Porth Mawr. According to Rhygyfarch's *Life* of St David, St Patrick was David's forerunner and there are a number of sites dedicated to him in the area: a small rocky outcrop further inland is his 'seat' and the south-facing medieval gateway to the cathedral, Porth Padrig, is named after him. In the cathedral itself, the earliest description of St David's shrine is given in a late 16th-century manuscript and described as being 'between two Pillars of the Chancel, within a fair Arch of Timberwork painted. St David himself is painted in his pontificalibus and on each side of him is a Bishop Saint; one, by the inscription is known to be St Patrick; the other is somewhat defac'd.' This last may well have been St Stinan.[11] Medieval pilgrims arriving by sea would be left in no doubt that

---

[11] By the 18th century, the appearance of the shrine had changed. An account was given to Browne Willis by a correspondent from the St Davids area, reporting that the paintings had disappeared and the third saint was then understood to be St Denys of France: 'Formerly it was all of one flat stone, which is now broken into several pieces: Above it were anciently three images: St David's in the middle, St Patrick's on the right hand, and St Denys's on the left, as Tradition informs us' (Browne Willis p. 13). This could be a confusion with St Stinan who is also described as bishop and martyr in Richard Whitford's Martyrology of 1526. Both saints would have been depicted iconographically as bishops carrying their heads as emblems of martyrdom. The 16th-century account is confident and the writer is familiar with the layout and terminology of the cathedral; the later description is more confused and the shrine is called a 'tomb'. I am grateful to Tristan Gray Hulse for this suggestion which presents a reasonable solution to the puzzle 'Why St Denys?' He suggests that confusion may have arisen because St David and St Denys are linked in a popular late 16th-century text *The Champions of Christendom* reprinted in the 18th century.

St Justinians, St Davids

Capel Stinan, St Justinian's
chapel, St Davids, interior. The
'crop-marked' square may mark
the grave site of the saint

this was the sanctified territory of the great saints of Wales and Ireland. There were a number of chapels on the peninsula, remembered by tradition or marked on early OS maps, either on the roadside or coast. Some were associated with holy wells and all or most probably developed from early burial sites; the physical remains of only the chapels of St Non and St Stinan are visible today. In the late 16th century, the coastal chapels were described as 'commodiously seated to draw the devotions of pilgrims . . . All these Chapels are near the Sea-Side, and adjoining to the Places where those that came by Sea commonly landed. They were plac'd here to draw the Devotion of the Sea-Men and Passengers, when they first came Ashore; other Pilgrims us'd likewise to come to them. What was there offer'd was carry'd to the Cathedral, and divided every Saturday among the Canons and Priests. Some yet living, that belong to the Church, can remember since the Offering-Money was brought on Saturdays to the Chapter-House and there divided by Dishfuls, the Quantity not allowing them Leisure to tell it.' There were two well chapels on Ramsey Island, but its local reputation of being the burial ground of 20,000 saints is probably a translation of legend from Ynys Enlli. Although there are undoubtedly many early Christian burials, the island lacks the clear-cut bardic tradition which is so much a part of Enlli's history.

St Patrick's chapel mound in foreground, Porth Mawr/Whitesands, St Davids

Probably there were sequences of pilgrim stations ultimately leading to the cathedral, but slight evidence of only one survives between Nine Wells, St Nons and the cathedral. What is still striking about the peninsula is that a landscape with chapels, holy wells and sites connected with the early saints (David and his companions), its continuation into the Middle Ages and the era of pilgrimage, despite physical, political and religious turmoil and the immense passage of time, is still with us today.

Shrine of St David as it has appeared since the mid-19th century

1275 Shrine of St David in 1810, engraving by Charles Norris

Chapter 14

The Southern Routes

The Portway

PILGRIMS travelling to St Davids from their homes in southern and eastern
England, or the Midlands, could follow a network of roads criss-crossing the
countryside which led them past a multitude of wayside crosses, holy wells, shrines
and great cathedrals. Often these roads were no more than mud tracks and the
diversions involved in visiting other holy sites were considerable, but slowly the
pilgrims moved westwards until they came to the ports of the Bristol Channel or
the fortified towns of the Welsh borders. Now the various tracks became more
tightly enmeshed as they were channelled through the valleys of the Black
Mountains or the coastal plains of south Wales.

For those travellers departing from the harbours of the West Country, it was a
short voyage across to the opposite shore of the Bristol Channel. Once safely
arrived they could begin the last leg of the long trek westwards.

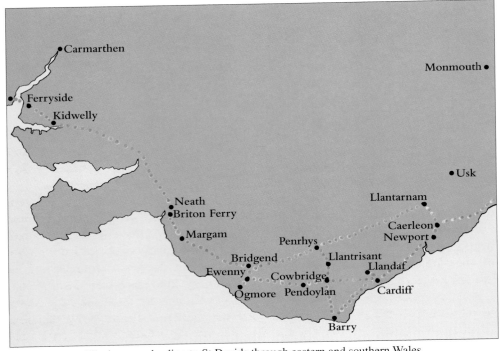

Pilgrim ways leading to St Davids through eastern and southern Wales

The road they now followed was known as the Portway. It was in origin the old Roman road that linked the coastal towns of south Wales and it began near the ancient fortress of Caerleon and led eventually to Carmarthen. Most of the old Roman roads in Wales had survived the passage of time and were still in use. The Portway, as well as carrying pilgrims, was a vital commercial link between the towns along its route and was always busy.

Caerleon was traditionally the site of the martyrdom of Saints Aaron and Julius. They were two townsmen who, during the reign of Emperor Diocletian, had been 'torn limb from limb and mangled with unheard of cruelty' for their faith. Gerald of Wales, who passed through the city with Archbishop Baldwin in 1188, mentions three churches, which had once stood there. One was named for St Julius, the second for St Aaron, whilst the third, according to Gerald, was the metropolitan church for the whole of Wales. No doubt many pilgrims would have halted at Caerleon to visit the sites of the martyrdom and burial of the two saints.

From Caerleon, the Portway ran on to Newport and from thence on to Cardiff and Llandaf Cathedral, rich in associations with St Teilo.

At Cardiff, pilgrims could turn south towards Barry to partake of the waters of St Barruc's Well. The healing powers of the well were varied, but close to it was St Barruc's chapel. This tiny building was visited by Gerald of Wales in 1188, who described it as 'ivy-clad'. The body of the saint lay in a shrine, which was the focus of much pilgrim worship. The chapel appears to have been a free chapel, not linked to a particular parish church or other religious establishment, and so great were the numbers of visitors to it that the officiating clergy drew their income solely from the offerings left there.

To the north of Cardiff lay another shrine, that of the Virgin Mary at Penrhys. A trackway led to it from Llandaf Cathedral via Llantrisant and Pendoylan, where it merged with other roads from Llanilltud Fawr and the Vale of Glamorgan. Other pilgrims may have wished to visit Llantarnam Abbey, which owned Penrhys and another track led from the abbey through the Ebbw and Rhymney valleys towards Caerphilly and Pontypridd.

From Cardiff, the Portway stretched on towards Swansea, passing along what is now the High Street of modern Cowbridge. The house known as the Ancient Druid at Eastgate was once a resting-place for pilgrims and still retains a medieval door and archway.

Beyond Cowbridge the road wound on through Bridgend, where a strong tradition exists of another hospice dedicated to St John, to Ewenny priory. The way was now punctuated by a series of river crossings that, if the weather was bad, would delay progress. At Ogmore Castle the Ewenny river is still forded by a line of stepping stones which, though of a more recent date, are reminders of the difficulties faced by medieval pilgrims as they struggled to reach their destination.

Margam Abbey, the next stop on the road, was famous for the hospitality offered to pilgrims and the poor. So liberal were the monks in their charity that food supplies sometimes ran low. On one occasion during a famine a vast crowd had gathered outside the gates of the monastery and it was clear that they could not be fed. A boat was hastily dispatched to Bristol to purchase extra corn, but its return was delayed by contrary winds. The monks and all those at their doors were facing starvation when a miracle occurred. A field of corn was found to have suddenly ripened and was ready for reaping a full month before the normal harvest-time.

Another tale concerned a young man who disputed the ownership of certain lands given to the abbey. He carried out various acts of violence in pursuit of his claim and at last, inspired by the Devil, set fire to one of the abbey barns piled high with corn. As a punishment he was stricken with madness and was chained up by his relatives. He eventually escaped and arrived at the abbey gates, baying like a dog and screaming that 'he was being burnt up inside'. Not long afterwards, still howling and screaming, he died.

No doubt these stories were eagerly relayed to visitors as they sat over their evening meal within the abbey walls, for the monks would have been anxious to demonstrate that Margam was under God's special protection. This idea, spread by pilgrims returning home, helped to ensure an increase in visitor numbers over the years.

Travelling on from Margam, pilgrims had to ford the River Afan, where Gerald of Wales had been delayed in 1188 by the slow ebbing of the waters. If the Afan was hazardous, the next crossing, of the River Neath, was doubly so. There were quicksands along the shores that would suck down anything, man or animal, that strayed upon them. Fording places were difficult to find, since they shifted with the tides and were impossible to locate when heavy rain had swollen the river. Most travellers crossed by boat in the vicinity of Briton Ferry. In the 15th century, William Worcestre recorded a ferry service between Llansawell (Briton Ferry) and Swansea. A chapel dedicated to St Giles was built near the crossing place at Neath for the benefit of pilgrims. It became known as Pilgrim's Gate. Its construction may have been paid for by one of the guilds that were formed in the medieval period to pay for the maintenance of roads and bridges. Local communities in Britain and across Europe were expected to provide shelter and protection for travellers and to plant trees near crossroads, under which travellers might seek rest. Shelter was provided for travellers at a hospice founded in Swansea in 1332 by Bishop Gower of St Davids.

The Pilgrims' church

Between Swansea and Kidwelly, the road crossed three more rivers, the Loughor, the Gwendraeth Fawr and the Gwendraeth Fach, although pilgrims could have used the ferry that plied between the Gower and Cydwelli. Cydwelli itself was an important stopping place on the way to St Davids because of its legendary associations with the Virgin Mary. It was also one of the landing places for passengers from ports in south–west England and from the continent. A trackway running to a crossing point on the Tywi estuary at Ferryside was known as the Ferry Way. A chapel dedicated to St Leonard stood in the vicinity and pilgrims crossed the River Tywi to Llansteffan using boats that, according to tradition, were maintained by the commandery of the Knights Hospitaller at Slebech.

At Llansteffan was St Anthony's Well, famous for its healing properties. It has been used within living memory as a wishing well into which a pin or a white quartz stone must be thrown for the wish to be granted.

The road now wended its way across the great triangle of land bounded by the Tywi and Taf rivers. On the eastern shore of the Taf lie two sites with strong pilgrim associations. The first of these is Llandeilo Abercywyn where, in an enclosure beyond the present farm, stands the ruined and overgrown church of St Teilo. This simple rectangular building dates from the 13th century and for countless generations it served as a focus of worship in the area before being abandoned at the close of the 19th century. It was in medieval times frequented by pilgrims, who would gather within its walls at the end of a day's journey from Llansteffan and who would assemble there again in the morning to ask for a blessing on the next stage of their travels. It is probable that on the day of departure they entered through the door in the south wall and left through the arched opening, now blocked, in the west wall. By doing so, they ensured that they kept to the oath they had sworn at the outset of their journey: never to retrace their steps until they had reached their final destination.

The ancient church of Llandeilo Abercywyn, frequented by generations of pilgrims

The ruined church at
Llanfihangel Abercywyn

On the opposite side of the farmyard from the church is a building known as
'The Pilgrim's Rest'. Although modernised, it dates to the 15th century: the upper
floor once consisted of a great hall extending the full length and width of the
building, supported on a row of three vaulted cellars. A flight of stone steps led up
to the first floor, above which there was a second storey, removed at the end of the
19th century. At the east end there exists a wheel-shaped window with curved
tracery. As its name suggests, the building may have been a hospice for travellers.

From the church of St Teilo, pilgrims made their way down to the banks of the
Cywyn stream, which acts as a boundary between two parishes and which here
flows into the broader waters of the Taf. Crossing the Cywyn by boat, the pilgrims
then made their way up through the water meadows to the church of Llanfihangel
Abercywyn.

The church of St Michael was probably founded in the late 12th century by the
owners of the nearby motte-and-bailey castle, the remains of which stand beyond
Trefenty farm. Like St Teilo's church, it served the needs of the local community
before being abandoned in favour of a newer parish church in 1848. Although much
of the north wall is gone, the other walls remain to roof height and the western
tower is almost complete. There are three entrances to the west into the tower porch
and to the north and south. The arrangement of the last two doors had a similar
purpose to that at St Teilo's: it allowed pilgrims to enter the south door on their way
up from the river crossing and, after prayers, to exit through the north door without
having to turn back on their pilgrimage.

The churchyard at Llanfihangel Abercywyn is now encircled with trees, with breathtaking views over the Taf estuary. In the midst of the long grass and sheltered by the branches of the trees lie six graves marked by medieval decorated slabs and headstones. They are thought to date from the late 12th or early 13th century. Of those furthest from the church, one depicts a small figure dressed in a long skirt, apparently standing at some sort of barrier. It may be the grave of a child. Another grave has a headstone upon which is carved a mounted knight with a lance in one hand. The three memorials nearest the church are also highly decorated. One depicts a female figure that covers half the slab, the other half being carved with a lattice pattern. Another, hog-backed in shape, has a cross at its head and includes rope-like mouldings. The third is perforated with a hole.

Three of the graves at Llanfihangel Abercywyn, traditionally known as the pilgrim graves

This gravestone may depict a child

Many legends have been woven around the pilgrim graves at Llanfihangel Abercywyn, including the belief that a rope-maker, a glazier and a mason lie beneath these stones

All six graves may well contain the remains of people who once lived close by in the motte-and-bailey castle. The fact that they were commemorated with costly, highly decorated grave slabs indicates that they were certainly wealthy and of some standing. Tradition insists that they were pilgrims who died during the journey to St Davids and for that reason Llanfihangel is often referred to as 'The Pilgrims' Church'.

The story most often told is that they had decided to make the journey on foot and by begging for food and shelter along the way. By the time they reached Llanfihangel Abercywyn they were dying of exhaustion and malnutrition and they took an oath amongst themselves to end their sufferings by killing one another. The last survivor buried the other five, then lay down in one of the graves prepared for them and attempted to pull the covering slab over himself. He lacked the strength to do this properly and the stone has been crooked ever since. The legend also explains that the stone perforated with a hole is the burial place of a mason, a glazier lies beneath the slab ornamented with a lattice pattern, whilst the rope-like mouldings indicate the resting-place of a rope-maker.

We shall probably never know how much of this story is true, but in 1838 the middle one of these last three graves was opened and was found to contain the skeleton of a slender youth or young female. Scattered around it were half a dozen cockleshells, indicating that at least one of the dead had been on pilgrimage. It is also said that the sanctity of the pilgrim graves keeps the parish of Llanfihangel free from serpents, toads and reptiles, except when the tombstones are overrun with weeds. Should this happen, the surrounding land will pass out of the hands of its owners.

The way to Whitland

The next stage of the road onwards from Llanfihangel is uncertain. Pilgrims may have continued on past what is now Trefenty farm and the adjacent motte-and-bailey castle, following the eastern bank of the Taf until they reached St Clears. A priory of the Cluniac order stood here, served by a tiny community of no more than three monks. It is possible that travellers were housed within the priory or its outbuildings, though all that remains now is the priory church, which serves the local parish. A stone bench in the garden of one of the nearby houses is said to have been a resting-place for weary pilgrims.

When G. Hartwell Jones published his *Celtic Britain and the Pilgrim Movement* in 1912, he included in the appendix a description of a possible alternative track from Llanfihangel. This began immediately to the south of Trefenty farm, where a ferry had once crossed the River Taf. Traces of the trackway still existed then, as did a local tradition of its existence. On the Laugharne side of the Taf, the track crossed the modern A4066 and continued on past the present-day farms of Cresswell and Maesgwrda and through Maeslan farm to the village of Llanddowror. Some of the field names along the way suggest an association with pilgrimage: Parc y Groes (field of the cross), Parc Ffynnon Saint (field of the saints' well).

These stones, known as the Pilgrim Stones,
stand in a field adjacent to Llanddowror church

At Llanddowror, it passes just west of the churchyard, bordering a field – now a sports ground – in which stand two stones carved with crosses. They date from the 9th or 10th centuries. On the high ground overlooking the village, the way then joins an ancient road leading to Tavernspite. This road, known locally as The Roman Road, or The Old Road, traverses the ridge in an almost straight line for over two miles, forming the boundary between the parishes of Cyffig to the north and Eglwys Cymyn to the south. About half way along its length, a trackway leads northwards to the farm of Great Pale where there was an ancient chapel. Also in this direction, at Llwyn Dewi, was a well to which St David was reputed to have sent sick people to be cured. The waters were especially good for sore eyes.

At Tavernspite, the road from Llanddowror merges with another well-used highway that links Tavernspite with Pendine and Laugharne (see map). It is possible that this is yet another pilgrim way, which would have enabled the faithful to visit a cluster of holy wells at Laugharne, before going on to Parc y Cerrig Sanctaidd and Eglwys Cymyn and, finally, Whitland.

Parc y Cerrig Sanctaidd, the field of the Holy Stones

Parc y Cerrig Sanctaidd, the field of the Holy Stones, is a stone-walled enclosure off the road between Llansadyrnin and Eglwys Cymyn. Within the enclosure are to be found two pillars of stone, one carved with a simple ring cross dating from the 7th to 9th centuries. The other has a hollowed-out depression on the upper surface that fills with water during rain. Pins were once dipped into this and were then used to prick warts in the hope of a cure. When, during the 18th and 19th centuries, funeral corteges passed by, the coffins would be unloaded from the carts and were rested on the stones for a short time before the journey was resumed. Traditions like this illustrate the belief in the power of such stones, developed over centuries of pilgrimage.

The church at Eglwys Cymyn was once surrounded by a grassy track known as the Pilgrim's Path

The church of Eglwys Cymyn stands in a circular enclosure, around which ran a grassy track known as The Pilgrim's Path. It left the churchyard on the western side, nearest Tavernspite, at a spot where a thorn tree grew. A spring bubbled up from the ground at the foot of the tree and its waters were said to have sacred properties. Pilgrims drank from it before setting off on the next leg of their journey. From Tavernspite, the way ran downhill to Whitland Abbey and a night's rest.

The Borders

For pilgrims approaching the Welsh Marches from the Gloucester, Hereford and Worcester area, there was a choice of several roads. One of these, the north–south road along the Welsh borders, passed Gresford. By the close of the 15th century this had become a major cult centre and there is an image of a pilgrim in the church porch. At Shrewsbury, the relics of St Gwenfrewi were housed in the abbey and at Oswestry (Album Monasterium), relics of Thomas Becket were venerated. Ludlow was the site of the hospital of St John, built to shelter pilgrims travelling in the border lands. The hospice was a property of the Knights Hospitaller, who also maintained a bridge across the River Teme. St Lawrence's church still contains the Palmer's Window. Welsh pilgrims were drawn in considerable numbers to the shrines of St Wulfstan at Worcester and St Thomas Cantilupe at Hereford. Other holy relics were enshrined at Monmouth and Chepstow.

Stretching eastwards into Wales were a number of ways marked by churches dedicated to major saints such as Beuno and David. Tradition relates that one pilgrim track led past Llanthony Abbey and the delightfully lop-sided church of St Martin in Cwmyoy. A medieval cross, discovered in 1871 at the adjacent farm and now within the church, may have marked the road. There was other pilgrim activity in the area around Partrishow, where the martyrdom of St Issui was marked by a holy well. A nearby stone slab is inscribed with a tiny stone cross. A grateful French pilgrim cured of leprosy left a sack of gold, which built the earliest church on the hill between 1056 and 1103.

Cwmyoy church, on the pilgrim way to Llanthony Abbey

A number of churches in the area are dedicated to St David: Llanthony, Llanddewi Skirrid, Llanddewi Rhydderch and Llanddewi Fach. The track is said to continue on over Bwlch Trewyn, where there is a medieval chapel site. Skirting the eastern approaches to Abergavenny, it then heads south to Usk. Although it does not run in an obvious direction for St Davids, it is fairly close to that taken by Gerald of Wales in 1188.

From Hereford to Whitland

One of the most popular shrines near the Welsh border was that of St Thomas Cantilupe at Hereford, where many miracles were reported. From Hereford, pilgrims could move on towards Hay-on-Wye, though a diversion to the north-west was also likely in order to visit Glascwm. Here was St David's church, the most important one in the region and reputedly founded by the saint himself. Glascwm housed a relic of great importance, a handbell called Bangu which had supposedly belonged to St David. A story well known at the time demonstrated its miraculous powers. A woman had taken the hand bell to the castle of Rhaeadr Gwy in an attempt to liberate her husband who was chained to the wall in one of the dungeons. The garrison refused to set the man free and drove the woman away, seizing the hand bell. That night the whole town was burned down, except the wall on which the hand bell was hanging.

Onwards from Hay

From Hay, the road wound on towards Brecon, allowing travellers the opportunity to sample the waters of St Nicholas' Well, famous for curing whooping cough and nausea. The water had to be carried to the patient without the container first touching the ground or the cure would fail.

Another famous Brecon shrine was that of St Eluned (Ailed) at Slwch, revered for its healing properties and for the wild religious dances performed by the crowds that flocked to it. The town also contained the rood of Brecon, *y grog yn Aberhonddu*, which was associated with the Virgin and was widely praised in the poetry of the day.

At Llanfaes, on the western outskirts of Brecon, the church of St David contained a stone that bore the marks of a miraculous punishment. A young boy had attempted to steal some young pigeons from their nesting place within the church and was punished for his impiety when his hand stuck fast to the stone against which he was leaning. For three days and nights he was unable to release himself. His parents and friends offered vigils, fasts and prayers until at last the saint relented and allowed the boy to go free. The stone was preserved amongst the relics in the church with the marks of the boy's fingers clearly visible on it. Perhaps because of this story, Llanfaes became a popular burial place for the local gentry.

From Brecon the road wound on through Llanspyddid (Llan ysptty), where the monks of Malvern priory founded a hospitium, towards Llandeilo, important to pilgrims as the place where St Teilo founded a monastery. A few miles away was Dryslwyn Castle. In 1287, it was besieged by English forces. One of these, Ralph le Butler, was struck beneath the eye by an arrow fired from the battlements. His friends called upon St Thomas Cantilupe for help and he was miraculously cured.

At Carmarthen, there were more holy wells to be visited, of which Job's Well cured scabs, ulcers and rickets. Upon leaving Carmarthen, pilgrims could travel south-west to Llansteffan and from thence to Llandeilo Abercywyn and Laugharne, or they could take the more direct road to Whitland via St Clears.

Whitland to St Davids

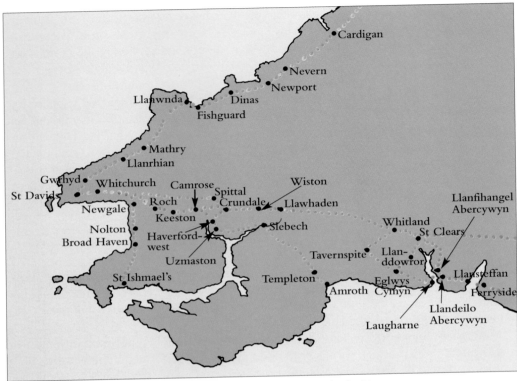

Pilgrim roads to St Davids through Pembrokeshire

The great Cistercian house of Whitland had been founded in 1140, though the monks moved to a new site in 1151. This lay to the north of the town in a secluded river valley. The abbey, which later became the mother house to several other abbeys scattered across Wales, was surrounded by fields, orchards and fishponds. Here the tired travellers might find a night's lodging within the almonry or the abbot's lodgings.

Beyond Whitland the way led towards Llawhaden, though it is likely that, shortly after leaving the abbey, pilgrims made a short northward diversion. St Canna's Well and Chair, in the modern parish of Llangan West, were visited each year by numerous pilgrims because of the reputed power of the water to heal all manner of ailments, especially the ague and intestinal complaints. A pin would first be offered at the well and the supplicant would bathe in and drink the water. A period of rest followed, the patient sitting on Canna's Chair, a boulder incised with the letters CANV. The healing process was more likely to be successful if the sick person fell asleep. If the treatment was not immediately successful, it would be repeated for up to fourteen days.

From St Canna's Chair, the pilgrims continued westwards until they came to Llawhaden. The church at Llawhaden owes its foundation to St Aidan: according to

Llawhaden church, on the way to St Davids, was visited by pilgrims because of its association with St Aidan legend, this saint, who lived 1,500 years ago, discovered a crossing place over the swiftly flowing waters of the eastern Cleddau. To mark this event, a cross was set up near the spot and subsequently the church was built. Because of its association with the saint, the church became a focal point on the pilgrimage to St Davids. As the tower came into view, so legend says, the travellers would burst into song. The place where this occurred became known as Heol y Gan, the road of song and is still called Holgan to this day.

Pilgrims often burst into song as they approached a holy place

After visiting the church, the pilgrims began the long ascent of the wooded hill to the village. No doubt they were tired and dusty after the march from Whitland, but the sight of the castle must have heartened them. Its towering walls and battlements were a reminder that they were at last under the guardianship of the saint in whose name they had travelled so far, for Llawhaden was one of the estates of the bishops of St Davids. At the end of the village street was the hostel built in 1287 by Bishop Bek.

The Haverfordwest area

From Llawhaden the road wound on through Wiston and Crundale, near Haverfordwest. To the north of Crundale lies Crundale Rath, a hilltop encircled by the banks and ditches of an Iron Age hillfort. During the medieval period, this was known as Simon's Castle and a Norman motte-and-bailey castle had been constructed within the ramparts. On the northern slopes of the fortification St Leonard's Well still exists on private land, though the chapel dedicated to him which stood nearby has long since disappeared. It had been granted during the medieval period to the commandery of Slebech.

The way then turned westwards towards Camrose, crossing the Cleddau via St Catherine's Bridge, where a chapel to the saint stood close by. Skirting the modern Robleston, Eweston and Rhyd y gele, the road finally joined other pilgrim routes heading for St Davids at Whitchurch. A second road passed through Spittal and Hayscastle, each the location of a hospice. The Spittal hospice was established by Bishop Bek, and stood in the vicinity of the church, though there is now no trace of it. A hoard of gold was discovered close to the site in the 16th century. A road near the church is still known as The Pilgrims' Lane.

Some pilgrims may have preferred to turn south at Crundale, heading for Haverfordwest, where there were a number of holy wells. Higgon's Well, on a riverside footpath about a mile south east of the town centre, still retains its vaulted covering within which can be seen the stone benches upon which sat the sick and ailing. About a mile away, on the banks of Merlin's Brook and not far from another hospice, was St Caradog's Well. Sanctified by the frequent visits of the saint, its reputation was such that in the early 19th century an Easter fair was still held at the spot. Unmarried women would offer three pins in the hope of seeing in the water the faces of their future husband.

At Haverfordwest there are tangible reminders of the pilgrims who once thronged the town. In St Mary's church is the battered effigy of a man wearing the traditional pilgrim's garb: a long, ankle-length tunic with a hood and a bag or scrip, embroidered with three shells, the symbol of pilgrimage. His identity is unknown. He is said to have been a Portuguese visitor who died either on the way to St Davids or on his way back from the shrine. He may have been a cleric, since an illustration that appears in *The Duke of Beaufort's Progress*, a book published in 1684, contains a contemporary drawing of the effigy. The figure is shown with thick, wavy hair, above which a tonsure is visible. A pilgrim staff was also included in the illustration, passing under the right elbow and down the right side, but the passage of time has destroyed many of these details.

This effigy of an unknown pilgrim can be seen in St Mary's church at Haverfordwest

Another pilgrim is commemorated at St Thomas' church, which contains the 14th-century tombstone of one who made the greatest journey of all, the long and difficult trek to Jerusalem, namely Brother Richard the Palmer, described in Chapter 6.

From Haverfordwest, pilgrims travelled north through Pelcombe to Keeston, where a pilgrim hospice stood,[1] and on to Summerhill. This farm was once a property of the Knights Hospitaller and just off the trackway near Hilton and Churchill are chapel sites. At Roch,[2] tradition records the existence of a pilgrim path leading northwards across the top of the valley leading down to Newgale. This may have enabled pilgrims to keep to the drier high ground during winter storms, whilst another path descended to Newgale where it joined a coastal road coming up from the south. This road, known as the Welsh Way, began at Monks' Haven, near the entrance to Milford Haven, where ships are said to have landed their passengers in the rocky inlet where a monastery once stood. The road then wound past the ancient church of St Ishmael's and on to Little Haven, Broad Haven and Nolton before reaching Newgale.

St Ishmael's church at the beginning of the pilgrim road known as the Welsh Way

---

[1] The Pembrokeshire Archaeological Survey gives a fascinating description of the hospice's appearance at the close of the 19th century. There were three buildings clustered together. The largest was very long and narrow, measuring some 20 feet wide by 120 feet long. It was entered by 'a curious semi-circular porch'. The ruins stood in the grounds of The Manse until the early 1960s, when they were demolished as being unsafe.

[2] The church at Roch is dedicated to the Virgin and not far off is the Lady Well. The street, named 'Pilgrims' Way', though it does not necessarily follow the original route, at least preserves the tradition of an ancient track passing through Roch towards St Davids.

At Newgale the chapel of St Caradog was situated. This now vanished building was erected to commemorate a miraculous occurrence; following the death of St Caradog in 1124, his body was taken to St Davids Cathedral for burial. As the cortege passed through Newgale there was a tremendous rainstorm. When the mourners emerged from shelter they found that the coffin, covered by a silken pall, was completely dry, whilst the surrounding area was running with water.

To the north of Newgale an ancient track, now a minor road, led past Rickeston Hall to Ffynnon Dewi. This well was said to have risen where the tears of the saint had fallen and it was frequented by many pilgrims.[3] A pilgrim ampulla was found in the vicinity of Rickeston.[4] The track merged with the road coming up from Camrose and, passing Clyn Yspytty, the site of yet another hospice, went on to Middle Mill and Whitchurch (Tregroes).

Routes from south Pembrokeshire

Most of the ports and beaches of south Pembrokeshire were landing places for pilgrims. Numerous pilgrim badges have been discovered beneath the shingle and sand at Amroth, Wiseman's Bridge and Tenby. A hospice is said to have existed at Templeton, and stood approximately where the present church is today. The farmhouse at Westerton farm, not far from the village, is believed to be a converted pilgrim shelter.[5] A few miles to the north–west, on private land near Minwear, a vast complex of buildings lies shrouded in the undergrowth overlooking the upper reaches of the Cleddau. Known as the Sisters' House, the remains include a walled garden, a fishpond, a great barn, a mill, a well, several 'tower houses' and a large barrel-vaulted cellar beneath a building once called the chapel. These ruins are reputed to have been a resting-place for female pilgrims: the name Sisters' House was once *Systerne* or *Sistern*, the plural of the Old English word *sweoster* or sister.

Across the river from the Sisters' House, at Slebech, stood a commandery of the Knights Hospitaller. Although that building has long since vanished, the adjacent church of St John remains, roofless and in ruins, on private land next to Slebech hall. From Slebech, travellers could make their way along the roads leading through Wiston towards St Davids, or they could follow an ancient way that led through the village of Uzmaston into Haverfordwest.

---

[3] This well was visited in the 1990s, in connection with this book; it is a small, stone-lined structure on uncultivated land and is hard to find. It was used by Ffynnonddewi farm for water.

[4] This ampulla, shaped as a cockle shell, was kindly donated to St Davids Cathedral Library, where it is on display.

[5] Local information.

The Sisters' House at Minwear, a complex of buildings said to have been a resting-place
for female pilgrims

Approaching St Davids

At Whitchurch, about two miles from the cathedral, a cross-inscribed stone known
as Maen Dewi stood near the church. Following the parish boundary from
Whitchurch via Dwrhyd by Llwybir Pererindod, sick pilgrims made their way to
Nine Wells, situated in a hollow beside the present A487. Of the eleven wells that
formerly existed only one, still sheltered by a stone hood, could now be called a
well; the location of the other wells is indicated by their metal covers. In the
Middle Ages mass was celebrated here and priests dipped their rosaries in the
water, which was also used to wash the sepulchre (*bedrodd*) in the cathedral.[6] Just
around the sharp bend in the road lies the hamlet of Llandrudion, where stand the
ruins of a building which may have been an early hospital, recorded in 1224.[7]

---

[6] It is unclear whether the sepulchre mentioned was, in fact, the shrine of St David.

[7] The 'Pembrokeshire Archaeological Survey' gives a description of this building as it then was. The
walls were up to six feet thick and clay or clom had been used to construct them. The north wall
contained three vaulted recesses, which were thought to have been sleeping places. Two more were
located in the south wall. There were also a number of cupboard-like recesses in each wall. A
number of windows remained, each one being a narrow aperture no more than three or four inches
wide. In later centuries, the building was said to have been the residence of Dr Jones, a generous
donor to charities.

This well at Nine Wells still retains its stone hood

Pilgrims were conveyed from Nine Wells to St Non's Well on carts called gambos. At St Non's, cures were sought for all kinds of complaints and once the cure had been successful the patients were taken to the cathedral to be blessed by a priest.

The precise route from Nine Wells is not known and pilgrims may have made their way back towards Whitchurch, turning westwards to follow the high ground towards St Davids. The stretch from Fachelich to Dŵr Cleifion follows the line of the ancient boundary of Ffos y Mynach (monk's dyke), which may have marked sanctuary land. At Dŵr Cleifion (the waters for the sick), pilgrims washed their feet in the stream.[8]

After a long and exhausting journey from their homes the pilgrims had now arrived at their desired destination. It only remained for them to enter the cathedral itself and to worship at the shrine containing the relics revered throughout Wales, the bones of St David himself.

At Dŵr Cleifion, near St Davids, pilgrims washed their feet in the stream

---

[8] The name Dŵr Cleifion, waters for the sick, is often taken to refer to the healing of leprosy.

Conclusion

Vacabounde Pilgremes

The past is another country, they do things differently there

L. P. Hartley

To study pilgrimage in the Middle Ages is to lift one thread of the tapestry of Christian belief and practice. As long as it was not disruptive or used as a political tool, pilgrimage was generally left alone by the authorities of church and state although it was not universally approved. The spiritually sophisticated thought that too much time and money were expended in going on long pilgrimages where it would have been better to attend to one's life and family at home. Wealth attracted more wealth: Bernard of Clairvaux observed 'wherever more riches are seen, the more willingly offerings are made'. As the Middle Ages progressed so too did censure of pilgrimage and its abuses, particularly of pilgrims who treated it as an evasion of work and duty or an opportunity to travel; motivation was as various as the pilgrims themselves and more control over pilgrims was exercised. In the 14th century legislation stipulated that any man or woman going on pilgrimage must have a Letter Patent 'containing the cause of his going, and the time of his return'. Censure became more strident in the 15th century. The written word in the eyes of some was a better communicator of the truth of scripture than the images so revered by pilgrims. The invention of the printing press meant that literature became more readily available. In the face of the Lollards, who preached against the manifestations of popular religion such as pilgrimages and veneration of images and relics of saints, the learned though sometimes controversial Bishop Reginald Pecock of St Asaph (1444–50) wrote in support of the legitimacy of pilgrimage and the use of images in worship in his work *Repressor of Over Much Blaming of the Clergy*, printed around 1455 but begun some six years previously. The total experience of pilgrimage and veneration of images was likely to achieve more than the cerebral process of reading even if one could read.

The religious and political complexities that brought about the Reformation are outside the scope of this book. The end of the order in Britain that acknowledged the Pope as head of the church was also the beginning of the end of pilgrimage as it was then known. In the early years of Reformation Henry VIII declared himself supreme head of the Church of England ordering the destruction of shrines, outlawing catholic practices and disestablishing monasteries. General orders were given for the destruction of shrines about the middle of 1538. The focus of pilgrimage was thus removed and much of what we know about individual shrines comes from the accounts of their destruction. The shrine of St David is unusual in that so much of a primary shrine should survive unbroken and this may have been due to the presence before the high altar of the tomb of Henry VIII's grandfather, Edmund Tudor, removed from Greyfriars church in Carmarthen to the cathedral at the Reformation. In 1544 the Court of Augmentations was informed that 'the price of the sepulchre called le shryne of St David in Wales was £66 13s 4d': no mean sum. In 1546 James Leach was granted £40 for recovering plate and jewels belonging to it. The unpopular Protestant bishop of St Davids, William Barlow (1536–47) forbade the canons to expose the 'fayned relics' or to observe 'unnecessary holy days'. The canons evidently did not consider that St David's Day fell into this category, after all it had been ordained a major feast day with nine lessons. They 'wilfully' solemnised the feast, setting forth the relics. Accordingly Barlow seized 'two heads of silver plate enclosing two rotten skulls stuffed with putrified clouts, two arm bones and a worm-eaten book covered with silver plate' and took them away: they were never seen again. Llandaf's costly shrine with images of St Teilo, Dyfrig and Euddogwy and numerous relics was broken up and 'three saints heads with their mitres in silver and double gilt' were among the items handed over by cathedral Chancellor, John Broxholme. Change began suddenly but its pace varied considerably throughout the Tudor period and it would be centuries before Catholic practices ceased and faded from memory.

In the geographically isolated, small rural communities of Wales change was slow, and a quiet and loyal persistence in local pilgrimages continued by country dwellers, uncomprehending of the niceties of theological argument and simply bewildered by the removal of the outward symbols and observances of their faith. The veneration of the Welsh saints was interwoven with local and national legend and genealogy. Just how disturbing this conservatism was to senior clergy and some of the land-owning families and how thorough the subsequent purges, can be seen through contemporary writings. Bishop Barlow of St Davids (1536–47) complained vociferously to Thomas Cromwell that St Davids was 'allwayes estemed a delycate doughter of Rome, naturally resemblinge her mother in shameless confucion . . .' and continued in 'ungodly ymage service, abhomynable ydolatrye . . . popish pilgremages, disceatefull pardons, and fayned indulgences . . .' added to which it suffered the severe disadvantage of 'being sytuated in soch a desolate angle and in so rare a frequented place (excepte of vacabounde pilgremes)' that cathedral and palace had best be removed to Carmarthen. In this the cathedral chapter bitterly opposed him and he only succeeded in removing the bishop's palace. Others, less vitriolic, were concerned for the welfare of their flock. Bishop Nicholas Robinson of Bangor (1566-84) wrote in 1566 'I have found since I came to the country, images and altars standing in churches undefaced, lewd and indecent vigils and watches observed, much pilgrimage-going, many candles set up in honour of saints, some relics yet carried about, and all the country full of beads and knots (rosaries).' He also wrote to Walsingham 'I have bene divers tymes in danger of my life in suppressing pilgramages, praying to Images, night watches at tombes of saints and other supstitions.'

A letter from George Owen of Henllys and other Justices of the Peace dated 14 July 1592, Haverfordwest, to certain gentlemen, clerks and parsons directed an enquiry into the continuing practice of pilgrimage in the county of Pembroke with particular reference to St Meugan's Well. 'Where in past times there have been pilgrimages, images or offerings whereunto . . . divers sorts of people do use to repair as well in the night season as other times of day, and that in great numbers, and that we should cause those idolatrous and superstitious monuments to be pulled down, broken and quite defaced, so as there be no monument, token or memory remaining of the same, and likewise to take order that thereafter there be no such unlawful resort to those supersititious places, but to appoint some discreet and well affected persons to have an eye and regard to those that, notwithstanding this inhibition, shall repair to those places and to see them apprehended and brought before us to be severally punished for their disobedience and lewd behaviour.'

A letter written in 1575 said of the Welsh: 'They doe still goe in heapes one pilgrimage to the wonted welles and places of superstition; and in the nightes after the feastes when ould offerings were used to be kept at anie chappell, albeit the church be pulled down, yet do they come to the place where the church or chappell was, by great journeys barefoots.'

A funeral oration preached by Bishop Richard Davies of St Davids in 1576, condemned those who 'defende papistrie, supersticion and Idolatrie, pilgrimages to Welles and blind Chappelles, procure the wardens of churches in tyme of visitacion to periure (perjure), to conceale images, roode loftes and aulters'.

In June 1592 Sir Thomas Jones and others were instructed by the Privy Council to take action to pull down 'superstitious and idolatrous monuments' and to examine strictly and severely punish those frequenting 'places where in times past there have been pilgrimages, images or offerings'.

In 1593 the Earl of Pembroke complained that the inhabitants of west Wales 'are in religion generally ill-affected, as may appear by their use of pilgrimages, their harbouring of mass priests, their retaining of superstitious ceremonies'.

David Powel, a Denbighshire cleric denounced Catholic practices in the late 16th century: 'Even to the present day, every single year multitudes superstitiously flock to places of pilgrimage: (such) as the holy well of St Winifred, Dyfnog's well in the vale of Clwyd, the church of King Einion in Arfon (Llanengan) and David's church in Dyfed'.

Ffynnon Gwyddfaen at Llandyfan (Carmarthenshire) was a popular centre of pilgrimage. Two hundred or more pilgrims were apprehended there (1594–5) but the local magistrate Morgan Jones of Tregib, refused to imprison or examine them because he considered their actions harmless and described them as 'poor, sickly persons who had gone to the well to bathe, hoping by the help of God to have their health'.

Later still in 1646, John Lewis commented 'I need not remind thee of that swarm of blinde supersitious ceremonies that are among us, passing under the name of old harmless custom; their frequent calling upon saints in their prayers and blessings, their peregrinations to wells and chappels.'

Erasmus Saunders, Bishop of St Davids in 1721, noted that the Welsh still prayed to the Saints – 'Mair-wen, Iago, Teilaw-Mawr, Celer, Celynog, and others are often thus remember'd as if they had hardly yet forgotten the use of Praying to them. And there being not only Churches and Chappels, but Springs and Fountains dedicated to those saints, they do at certain times go and Bath themselves in them, and sometimes leave small oblations behind them . . .'.

Bards who accepted the Protestant faith turned their former lavish praise of shrines, images and wells to vilification. With the exception of Holywell, where pilgrimages never really ceased and which continues as a Catholic shrine today, other late survivals of pilgrimage were exceptional. A remarkable one was to Wales's own St Michael's Mount. Skirrid Fawr, or Ysgryd, north-east of Abergavenny, rises to 1596 feet. According to one legend, the fissure and precipice to the north, were created by the earthquake at the time of the crucifixion. The soil itself was sacred and believed either to have been brought by St Patrick from Ireland, or from the Holy Land. It was placed in coffins and farmers scattered it on their fields to promote fertility. The Roman Catholic parish of Abergavenny has a Papal Brief of Clement X, dated 20 July 1676, granting a plenary indulgence to those who devoutly visited the chapel of St Michael on the Mount on the feast of St Michael between vespers and sunset. In 1680, John Arnold of Llanfihangel Crucornau revealed to the House of Commons that he had seen a hundred papists meet there. Even in 1813, the *Cambrian Travellers' Guide* observed that 'many Roman Catholics in the vicinity are said to repair annually on St Michael's Eve and perform their devotions'.

St Govan's Well, Pembrokeshire; engraving by H. Gastineau, *c.* 1830

Most of the pilgrimage chapels were completely destroyed or put to other purposes as indicated by the old Pembrokeshire couplet: 'When St Brides chapel a salt-house was made, St Bride's lost the herring trade'. Nevertheless, pilgrimages to holy wells continued by stealth and were almost impossible to eradicate. As the years passed, holy wells were tolerated as chalybeate springs with healing properties. The saints' day festivities that took place at wells continued into the 19th century entrenched as they were in folk belief and custom. The well cult was generally but not always associated with the lower orders of society: Richard Fenton remembered being often dipped in St Non's Well, and St Govan's Well drew patients 'even of the upper classes'. In the early years of the 20th century, St Non's Well was still resorted to, using a practice which followed a common ritual pattern: the affected limb was immersed and wrapped in a flannel shawl, if the limb warmed, then it would 'cure'. However much the pilgrimage element had been debased, these little visits for healing purposes by those who truly believed that the water from a holy well and the associated ritual could cure their aches and pains, were part of an unbroken link with medieval pilgrimage in Wales, when belief and ritual must have been transmitted orally from one generation to another.

Pilgrimage in Wales today continues but after an interruption. Many come to places like St Davids, Penrhys, Ynys Enlli and Pennant Melangell singly or in groups and some still try to follow the old pilgrim ways. The pilgrimages described in these pages belong to the old order, yet despite centuries of persecution and ostracism, the Catholic past and its practices peculiar to Wales survive in folklore and tradition and also, perhaps paradoxically, finds a living echo in some aspects of Nonconformity. Our recording methods have often been reliant on oral and local tradition which cannot easily be evaluated and we could say with John Aubrey 'These curiosities would be quite forgot did not such idle fellows as I am put them down.' But the situation is perplexing, more questions are raised than answers found and the image of the well, the last survivor, is peculiarly apt. It could describe our ideas today about medieval pilgrimage in Wales – as we peer down into the waters of a deep well, all we see there is our own reflection.

St Non's Well,
Pembrokeshire

Edudful ferch Gadwgan's pilgrimage to St Non's Well and Church (chapel)

Edudful Dduwsul a ddaw	On Sunday Eduful comes
ar Dduw i wir weddïaw;	to pray sincerely to God;
bwrw ei phwys yn eglwys Non,	She visits Non's church,
bwrw ei phen lle bo'r ffynnon,	puts her head in the well
dyrchaf dwylaw yn llawen	raises her hand merrily,
addoli oll i'r ddelw wen	worships the holy image,
ennyn y cwyr melyn mawr,	lights the large, yellow candles,
a'i roi oll ar yr allawr;	and puts all of them on the altar,
oddyno heibio'dd â hi	from there she passes to
I glos da eglwys Dewi;	the good close of St David's church;
offrymu, cusanu'r sant,	makes an offering of crimson wax and money
iddo gŵyr rhudd ac ariant;	and kisses the saint;

Lewis Glyn Cothi

Gwaith Lewys Glyn Cothi (ed) Dafydd Johnston CUWP 1995, p. 371. Translation by Dr Jane Cartwright, University of Wales, Lampeter.

Bibliography

Abbreviations

AC	*Archaeologia Cambrensis*
JWRH	*Journal of Welsh Religious History*
JWEH	*Journal of Welsh Ecclesiastical History*
NLW	National Library of Wales
NLWJ	*National Library of Wales Journal*
PRO	Public Record Office
RCAM	Royal Commission on Ancient Monuments
THSC	*Transactions of the Honourable Society of Cymmrodorion*
OUP	Oxford University Press
UWP	University of Wales Press

AC 1846, 1847, 1860, 1875, 1876, 1878, 1887, 1889, 1897, 1901, 1910, 1914, 1926, 1933
Acts of the Privy Council 1591/2

Adair, J.	*The Pilgrim's Way*	Thames Hudson 1978
'Antiquitates Parochiales'	VIII	*AC* 1848
'Arvona Mediaeva No 2, Beddgelert Priory'		*AC* 1847
Aubrey, J.	*Brief Lives*	London 1690
Bailey, A.	*The Legend of St Teilo's Skull*	Preseli Heritage Publications, Llangolman
Barber, R.	*Henry Plantagenet*	Purnell 1973
Baring Gould, S. & Fisher, J.	*The Lives of the British Saints*	London 1907–13
Barlow, F.	*Thomas Becket*	Wiedenfeld & Nicholson 1986
Baynes, E. Neil	'Capel Sant Ffraid, Porth y Capel (Trearddur Bay)'	*Anglesey Transactions* 1921
Birch, D.J.	*Pilgrimage to Rome in the Middle Ages*	Boydell Press 1998

BL MS Royal 13 c i folios 177v-180r a collection once belonging to William Worcestre (1415–*c*.1485), and probably compiled around 1405

Blackburne, H. & Bond, M.	*The Romance of St George's Chapel, Windsor Castle*	Windsor 1973
Bond, S.	*St George's Chapel, Windsor Castle*	Pitkin Pictorials 1973
Bowen, E.G.	*Britain and the Western Seaways*	Thames and Hudson 1972
Breeze, A.	'The Girdle of Prato and its Rivals'	*Bulletin of Board of Celtic Studies* XXXIII, 1986
Bromwich, R. (Ed.)	*Dafydd ap Gwilym: Poems*	Gomer Press
Bromwich, R.	*Trioedd Ynys Prydein*	UWP 1961
Buckley, K.	'The well and the skull of Llandeilo Llwydiarth'	*The Holy Wells Journal* New Series No 2 winter 1994
Butler, H.E.	*The Autobiography of Giraldus Cambrensis*	Jonathan Cape 1937
Butler, L. & Graham Campbell J.	'A lost reliquary casket from Gwytherin, North Wales'	*Antiquaries Journal* 1990

Calendar of Inquisitions Post Mortem xv
Calendar of Papal Petitions, i, iii, iv
Calendars of Entries in the Papal Registers relating to Great Britain and Ireland 6
Calendars of Inquisitions Post Mortem, Henry VII, 2

Cambrian Archaeological Association Meeting report		1922
Carpenter, Clive	*Kings, Rulers and Statesmen of the World*	Guinness Superlatives 1978

Carr, A.D.   *Medieval Anglesey*   Llangefni 1982
Cartwright, J.   Y *Forwyn Fair, Santesau a Lleuanod*   UWP 1999
Cathedrals   Great Western Railway 1924
Charles-Edwards, T.   *Saint Winefride and her well*   undated
Chaucer, G. ed. F.N. Robinson   *The Work of Geoffrey Chaucer;* second edition,   OUP 1957
Cheney, C.R. (ed.)   *Handbook of Dates for Students of*   London 1970
                                                  English History 110
Chitty, M.   *The Monks on Ynys Enlli* Part II,   W. Alun Jones, Aberdaron 2000
Clancy, J.P.   *Medieval Welsh Lyrics*   Macmillan 1965
Clarke, M.L.   *Bangor Cathedral*   UWP 1969
Cole, J.   'Some early hospitals in Wales and   *NLWJ* Vol XX No 2
                                                  the Border'
Conant, K.J.   *Carolingian and Romanesque Architecture*   Penguin 1959
                                                  800-1200
Cooper, J.C.   *Illustrated Encyclopaedia of Traditional Symbols* Thames and Hudson 1982
Correspondence, St Davids Cathedral Library
Cowley, F.G.   'A note on the discovery of St David's body'   BBCS 1960
Crockett, P.A.   'Pilgrimage', unpublished lecture in St Davids   1996
Cross, F.L. (ed.)   *Oxford Dictionary of the Christian Church*   OUP 1957
Crouch, D.   'Urban; first Bishop of Llandaf, 1107–34'   *JWEH* 6 1989
Culpepper, N.   *Culpepper's Complete Herbal*   Fonlsham & Co., London undated
Cunnane, J.   'Ceredigion and the old faith'   *Ceredigion Historical Society*
                                                                                                    Journal XII, no 2
Cunnane, J.   *Our Lady of the Taper*   church leaflet
Curley, M.J.   *Eleven Miracles of Saint David*   University of Puget Sound,
                                                                                                    unpublished manuscript
Daniel, C.   *Gate of Heaven*   Brython Press, Liverpool
David, C.   *St Winefride's Well*   undated
David, J.D.   *Historical notices of the parishes*   Part III Swansea 1885
                                                  of Llangenydd and Rhossili in the rural
                                                  deanery of West Gower.
David, P.R. & Lloyd-Fern, S.   *Lost Churches of Wales and the Marches*   Allan Sutton 1990
Davies, H.R.   *The Conway and the Menai ferries*   Board of Celtic Studies, University
                                                                                                    of Wales, History and Law Series
                                                                                                    No. VIII UWP 1942
Davies, H.W.C.   *Medieval England*   Bracken Books 1995
Davies, J. Barry.   'The Mathew family of Llandaf,   *Glamorgan Historian* 11
                                                  Radyr and Castell-y-Mynach'   Stewart Williams Publishers.
Davies, J.C.   *Folklore of West and Mid-Wales*   1911; Llanerch reprint 1992
Davies, N. Roberts, E.   *Pererindota, i Enlli, O Dywyn I Aberdaron.*   21b Cyfres Teithiau Llenyddol,
                                                                                                    Gogledd Cymru,
                                                                                                    Cyngor Celfyddydau Cymru.
Davies, N. & Roberts, E.   *Pererindota i Enlli, O Fangor Fawr*   21b Cyfres Teithiau
                                                  I Ynys Enlli.   Llenyddol, Gogledd Cymru
Davies, O.   *Celtic Christianity in early Medieval Wales*   UWP 1996
Davies, P.   *Historic West Wales*   Christopher Davies 1992
Davies, W.   *Wales in the Early Middle Ages*   Leicester Univ. Press 1982
Duffy, E.   *The Stripping of the Altars*   Yale Univ. Press 1992
Duffy, E.   *Saints and Sinners: A history of the Popes*   Yale Univ. Press 1997
Edwards, I.   '15th century alabaster tables and the   *AC* CXLI 1992
                                                  iconography of the bound rood
                                                  and St Armel'

Edwards, N & Gray Hulse, T.   'A fragment of a reliquary casket from   *Antiquaries Journal* 1992
                                        Gwytherin, north Wales'

Edwards N & Lane, A.   *The early church in Wales and the west*   Oxbow monograph 16 1992
Edwards, O.M.   'Holyhead and District'   *Wales* Vol II, Wrexham 1894
Edwards, O.M.   'The Nant Eos Cup'   *Wales* Vol II, Wrexham 1894
Elon, A.   *Jerusalem, City of Mirrors*   Weidenfeld & Nicholson 1990
Episcopal Registers of St Davids 1397–1518   Vol. I *Cymmrodorion Record
                                                                                        Series* 6 1917

Evans, D.S.   *Medieval Religious Literature*   Writers of Wales Series UWP 1986
Evans, G.N.   *Religion and Politics in mid-18th-*   UWP Cardiff 1953
                                        century Anglesey

Evans, H.   *Twr y Felin Guide*   1923
Evans, J.W.   *The Reformation and St Davids*   *JWEH* 7 1990
Fenton, R   *A Historical Tour through Pembrokeshire*   London 1811, Dyfed County
                                                                                        Council reprint 1994

Finucane, R.C.   *Miracles and Pilgrims*   J.M. Dent 1977
Fisher, Canon   'The Welsh Celtic bells'   *AC* 1926
Fisher, J.   'Bardsey Island and its Saints'   *AC* 1926
Fisher, J.B.D.   'The private devotions of the   *Transactions of the Liverpool
                                        Welsh in days gone by'   Welsh National Society* 1897–98

Flores, A.   *Medieval Age; specimens of European Poetry*   Phoenix, 1965
Fraser, A.   *The Gunpowder Plot; Terror and Faith*   Weidenfeld & Nicolson 1996
                                        in 1605

Gerard, J.   *Autobiography of John Gerard*   Longmans Green and Co. 1951
Gerald of Wales   *The Journey through Wales/*   Penguin 1978
                                        The Description of Wales trans. Lewis Thorpe

Gies, F & G   *Cathedral, Forge and Waterwheel*   Harper Collins 1994
Gilyard-Beer, R.   *Abbeys*   HMSO 1959
Gingras, G.E. (ed.)   *Diary of a Pilgrimage*   Newman Press, New York 1970
Glazebrook, F.H.   *Anglesey and North Wales Coast*   Bookland & Co., Bangor 1967
Grandsdon, A. (ed.)   *Chronicle of Bury St Edmunds 1212-1301*   London 1964
Green. F. (ed.)   'Cardiganshire Families'   *Historical Society of West Wales
                                                                                        Transactions* I

Green, F.   'Stedman of Strata Florida'   *West Wales Historical Records* VIII
                                                                                        1919–20, Spurrell 1921

Green, F. & Badger, A.B.   'Chapels of St Patrick and St Justinian'   *West Wales Historical Records* X
                                                                                        Carmarthen 1925

Gray, M.   *Penrhys; the Archaeology of a Pilgrimage*   unpublished manuscript
Haddan, A. & Stubbs, W.   *Councils I*   Oxford 1869
Halliwell, J.O. (ed.)   *An Ancient Survey of Pen Maen Mawr*   London 1859
Handbook to the Cathedrals of Wales   London 1873
Harris, S.   *St David in the Liturgy*   UWP 1940
Hartley, D.   *The Land of England*   Macdonald 1979
Hartley, D.   *Water in England*   Macdonald,1964
Hartwell Jones, G.   *Celtic Britain and the Pilgrim Movement*   *THSC* 1912
Harvey, P.D.A.   *Mappa Mundi, the Hereford World Map*   British Library 1996
Heal, F. & Holmes, C.   *The Gentry in England and Wales 1500-1700*   Macmillan 1994
Henken, E.   *Traditions of the Welsh Saints*   D.S. Brewer 1987
Henken, E.   *The Welsh Saints; a Study in Patterned Lives*   D.S. Brewer 1991
Hitt, J.   *Off the Road*   Aurum 1994
Hohler, C.   'The Badge of St James' in *The Scallop*   I. Cox (ed.) Courtauld Institute of
                                                                                        Art, University of London 1957

Hope Jones, P.   *Wales*   Gomer Press 1991
Howells, B.E. & K.A.   *Pembrokeshire Life 1572-1843*   Pembrokeshire Record Series 1
                                                                                           Pembs. Record Society 1972

Hughes, B.H.J.   *Jottings on the History of South   Pennar Publications 1993
                                            Pembrokeshire; St Daniel's Church*

Hughes, H.H.   'Llanerfyl reliquary and reredos'   *AC* 1932
Hughes, H. & North, H.L.   *The Old Churches of Snowdonia*   Bangor 1924
Hughes, W.   'Llanuwchlyn'   *AC* 1885
Hulse, T.G.   *Ffynnon Dyfnog;*   unpublished manuscript 1999
Hulse, T.G.   *Three Saints, Two Wells and a Welsh Parish*   unpublished manuscript
Hunt, R.S.   *The Way of St James, El Camino   Spanish Study Circle 1981–3
                                            de Santiago, España.*

Huws, D. & Roberts, E.   *Early Treasures*   Dean and chapter,
                                                                                           Bangor Cathedral 1996

James, H.   'The Cult of St David in the Middle Ages'   *Journal of Pembrokeshire
                                                                                               Historical Society* 7 1996–7

James, J.W.   *Rhygyfarch's Life of St David*   UWP Cardiff 1967
James, N.A.   Llandaf Cathedral postcard
Jarvis, J. Brynmor   *The Road from St David's in   unpublished manuscript
                                            Pembrokeshire to Holywell in Flintshire*

Jenkins, D.I. (ed.)   *Looking around Newport*   E.L. Jones & Sons, Cardigan 1970
Joel, J.   *Nanteos*   1995
Johnson, D. (ed.)   *Iolo Goch: Poems*   Welsh Classics Series,
                                                                                           Gomer Press 1993

Jones, F.   *The Holy Wells of Wales*   UWP 1954
Jones, F.   *Knights of the Holy Sepulchre*   Historical Society of the
                                                                                           Church in Wales 1979

Jones, G.T.   *Y Ffordd i Enlli*   Canolfan Genedlaethol Addysg
                                                                                           Grefyddol 1986

Jones, M.K., and   *The King's Mother*   Cambridge 1992
    Underwood, M.G.

Jones, T. (trans.)   *Brut Y Tywysogyon, Red Book of Hergest* version UWP 1955
Jones, T.P.   'Strata Florida Abbey'   *Ceredigion* i 31
Jones, W.B. & Freeman E.A.   *History and Antiquities of St Davids*   London 1856
Kendall, A.   *Medieval Pilgrims*   London 1996
Kempe, M.   *The Book of Margery Kempe*   Penguin Classics 1994
Kightly, C.   *A Mirror of Medieval Wales*   Cadw 1988
Kightly, C.   *Enjoy Medieval Denbighshire*   Denbigh County Council 1998
Knight, J.   'Excavations at St Barruc's Chapel'   *Cardiff Naturalists' Society
                                                                                               Transactions* 1976-78

Landsberg, S.   *The Medieval Garden*   British Museum Press undated
Laws, E. & Edwards, E.H.   *Church Book of St Mary the Virgin, Tenby*   John Leach, Tenby 1907
Letters relating to the suppression   No 26, 1843   Camden Society, Old Series.
    of the monasteries   Johnson Reprint Association of the USA 1968
Lewis, B.   *Llanddewi Brefi*   church leaflet
Lewis, B.   *Brynach's People*   church leaflet 1997
Lewis, H; Roberts, T; Williams, I.   *Cywyddau Iolo Goch ac eraill*   UWP 1972
Lewis, J. of Glascrug   *Parliament explained to Wales* 1646   1907
Lewis, L.S.   *Glastonbury, Her Saints*   Mowbray 1927
Lewis, M.R.   'The Pilgrimage to St Michael's Mount: *JWEH* 8 1991
                                            Catholic continuity in Wales'

Lewis, S.	*Topographical Dictionary of Wales*	London 1833
	'Llandaf Cathedral church'	*AC* 1887
Lhuyd, E.	'Parochalia'	*AC* Supplement 1090, 1910-11
Lloyd, D.T.	'Welsh Pilgrims at Rome 1471–1748'	*Trivium* vi 1971, vii 1972
Lloyd, E.	*Welsh Gazette*	September 1957
Lloyd, H.A.	*The Gentry of South West Wales 1540-1640*	UWP 1968
Lloyd, J.D.K.	'Two figures from the Rood at Mochdre, Montgomeryshire'	*Montgomeryshire Collections* 1953
Lloyd, L.	*Pwllheli, the Port and Mart of Llŷn*	Gwasg Pantycelyn, Caernarfon 1991
Lynch, F.	*Guide to Historic and Ancient Wales: Gwynedd*	CADW/London HMSO 1995
Matthews, E. Gwynn	*The Llanrhaeadr Jesse Window; its meaning and history*	Llanrhaeadr-yng-Nghinmeirch Parochial Church Council
Mayer, H.E.	*The Crusades*	OUP 1988
McKenna, C.A.	*The Medieval Welsh Religious Lyrics 1137–1282*	Ford and Bailie, Massachusetts 1991
Miles, D.	*The Ancient Borough of Newport in Pembrokeshire*	Haverfordwest Library 1995
Miles, D. (ed.)	*George Owen of Henllys: The Description of Pembrokeshire*	Gomer Press 1994
Miller, M.	*The Saints of Gwynedd*	Studies in Celtic History Series ed. David Dumville, Boydell Press 1979
Miscellanea	'Pilgrim's Flask from Meols'	*Journal of Chester and North Wales Architectural Archaeological and Historical Society* 43,48,49, 1956
Mitchell, R.J.	*The Spring Voyage*	John Murray, 1965
Montgomeryshire Collections 82	Special issue on Pennant Melangell	1994
Moore-Colyer. R.	*Roads and Trackways of Wales*	Moorlands Publishing 1984 and Landmark Publishing 2002
Morby, J.E.	*Handbook of Kings and Queens*	Wordsworth Reference 1994
Morgan, G. (ed.)	*Nanteos: A Welsh House and its Families*	Gomer Press 2001
MS Bodley 572		
MS Cardiff 26 1710	*Y Cymmrodor* xxiii	
MS Lansdowne iii Original Letters iii		
MS N 1559B NLW		
Muir, R.	*The Countryside Encyclopaedia*	Macmillan 1988
Naisby, E.	*A Section of the Pilgrim Road from Holywell to St Davids*	BSc thesis for Open University 1962, NLW Aberystwyth
	New Catholic Encyclopaedia	New York 1967
Nilson, B.	*Cathedral Shrines of Medieval England*	Boydell and Brewer 1998
North, F.J.	*Sunken Cities*	UWP 1957
O'Malley, B.B.	*A Pilgrim's Manual* containing translations of Dafydd ap Gwilym by Nigel Heseltine	Paulinus Press 1985
Ogilby, J.	*Britannia: An Illustration of the Kingdom of England and Dominion of Wales* 1675	
Owen, E.	'Meini cred'	*AC* 1897
Owen, E.Y.	'Private devotions of the Welsh in days gone by'	*Y Cymmrodor* II 1878
Owen, G.	*Description of Pembrokeshire*	Part II ed. H. Owen, London 1897
Owen, G. ed. Dillwyn Miles	*The Description of Pembrokeshire*	Gomer 1994
Owen, H.	*Llanddwyn Island*	*Anglesey Transactions* Antiquarian Society and Field Club 1920–22

Packer, A.	'Welsh Medieval Spirituality'	*JWRH* 4 1996
Papal Letters vii		
Papal Registers and Letters	Descriptive Calendar	1399
Payne, H.T.	*Collectanea Menevensia*	NLW SD/CH/B 1815
Pembrokeshire Antiquities	*Cantref y Gwaelod*	H.W. Williams, Solva 1897
Penmon Priory	Church leaflet	
Pennant, T.	*A Tour in North Wales, 1778*	London 1810
Pennick, N.	*The Celtic Cross*	Blandford 1997
Price, P.	*Bells and Man*	OUP 1983
PRO SP12/44/27		
PRO Star Chamber Proc. G 45/3, 37 Eliz		
Protevangelium of James, a second-century apocryphon		T. Bibliander, Basle 1552
Prys-Jones, A.G.	*The Story of Carmarthen 2*	Christopher Davies 1972
Randall, A.	'Recusancy in Carmarthenshire'	*Carmarthenshire Antiquarian* 1997
RCAM	*South Caernarfonshire*	1918
RCAM	*Merioneth*	1921
Read, P.P.	*The Templars*	Weidenfeld & Nicholson 1999
Rednap, M.	*The Christian Celts*	National Museum of Wales 1991
Rees, J.R.	*The Slebech Commandery and the Knights of St John*	Bedford Press London 1900
Rees, N.	*The Medieval Shrines of St Davids Cathedral*	St Davids Cathedral 1998
Rees, W.	*A History of the Order of St John of Jerusalem in Wales and on the Welsh Border*	Cardiff 1933
Rees, W.	*South Wales and the Border in the Fourteenth Century*	Cardiff 1947
Richard, E.	'A short history of Bardsey'	*The Cambrian Register* Vol III London 1818
Riley Smith, J.	*Hospitallers; the History of the Order of St John*	Hambledon 1999
Roberts, E.	*A'u Bryd ar Ynys Enlli*	Lolfa 1993
Roberts, R.D.	*Clynnog, its Saint and its Church*	CM Book Agency Caernarfon
Robinson, J.R.	*Dungeon, Fire and Sword; the Knights Templar in the Crusades*	Michael O'Mara 1994
Saul, N.	*Richard II,* Appendix	Yale University Press 1997
Saunders, E.	*A View of the State Religion in the Diocese of St David's about the Beginning of the 18th Century*	UWP Cardiff 1949
Skidmore, I.	'Ian Skidmore on Saints'	*Window on Wales* No 4
Soulsby, I.	*The Towns of Medieval Wales*	Phillimore 1983
Spencer, M.R.	*Annals of South Glamorgan*	Spurrell, Carmarthen
Stratford, N.	*Catalogue of Medieval Enamels in the British Museum, London*	British Museum Press 1993
Streeter, B.H.	*The Chained Library*	Hereford 1931
Stephens, M.	*The New Companion to the Literature of Wales*	UWP Cardiff 1998
Stopford, J.	'Some approaches to the archaeology of Christian pilgrimage'	*World Archaeology,* 26 No 1. Routledge 1994
Sumption, J.	*Pilgrimage: an Image of Medieval Religion*	Faber & Faber 1975
Taylor, A.	*Castles and Castle-building*	Hambledon Press 1986
Tennant, W.C.	'Croes Naid'	*NLWJ* VII 1951-2
Thomas, D.A.	*The Welsh Elizabethan Martyrs*	UWP 1971

Thomas, D.R.	*History of the Diocese of St Asaph* in three volumes	AC 1873, 1908, 1911
Thomas, F.	*Down the Line – St Davids, Ancient and Modern*	W. Spurrell & Son, Carmarthen 1927
Thomas G.C.G.	'A lost manuscript of Thomas Saint'	*NLWJ* XXIV 1966.
Thorpe, B.	*Ancient Laws*	London 1840
Tyrell, G.	*Christianity at the Cross-Roads*	G. Allen & Unwin 1963
Upton-Ward, J.W.	*The Rule of the Templars*	Boydell Press 1998
Virgoe, R.	*Illustrated Letters of the Paston Family*	Guild 1989
Walker, D. (Editor)	*A History of the Church in Wales*	Church in Wales Publications, Penarth 1976
Walker, D.G.	'Cardiff', an essay contained in *Boroughs of Medieval Wales* ed. R.A. Griffith	UWP 1978
Walker, R.F.	'Tenby', an essay contained in *Boroughs of Medieval Wales*	UWP
Wall, J.C.	*Shrines of the British Saints*	London 1925
Ward, J. (ed.)	'Our Lady of Penrhys'	AC 1914
Webb, D.	*Pilgrimage in Medieval England*	Hambledon 2000
Webb, D.	*Pilgrims and pilgrimages in the Medieval West*	Tauris 1999
William of Malmesbury	*The Antiquities of Glastonbury* translated by F. Lomax	1908
William of Malmesbury	*Gesta Regum Anglorum* Vol 1 trans. Mynors, R.A.B.	Clarendon Press Oxford 1998
William Worcestre	*Itineraries*	ed. J.H. Harvey, Oxford 1969
Williams, D.	*The Welsh Cistercians,* Vol 1	Norwich 1983
Williams, G.	*Henry de Gower, Bishop and Builder*	Address given to the friends of St Davids Cathedral, St Davids Press
Williams, G.	'Poets and pilgrims in fifteenth- and sixteenth-century Wales'	*THSC* 1991
Williams, G.	*Religion, Language and Nationality in Wales*	UWP 1979
Williams, G.	*The Welsh Church, Conquest to Reformation*	UWP 1978
Williams, G.	*Wales and the Reformation*	University of Wales, 1997
Williams, J.	*History of Radnorshire*	AC 1858
Williams, W.	*Some traces and traditions around Llangybi*	AC 1904
Willis, Browne	*St Asaph Cathedral*	London 1721
Willis, Browne	*Survey of the Cathedral Church of St Davids*	London 1717
Wise, T. & Scollins, R.	*The Knights of Christ*	Osprey 1999 reprint
Wood, J.	'Nibbling pilgrims and the Nanteos Cup: A Cardiganshire Legend'	*Nanteos: A Welsh House & its Families* ed. Gerald Morgan, Gomer Press 2001
Yardley, E.	*Menevia Sacra*	London 1927

Acknowledgements

The authors are most grateful to the following for their time and expertise, which has been most generously given, both in research and advice on the manuscript. Their suggestions have been valuable, the errors are the authors'. Dr A.D. Carr, Mr and Mrs Hugh Charles-Jones, Archdeacon A. Crockett, Canon J. Cunnane, Dr Michael Curley, The Very Rev J. Wyn Evans, Mr Michael Freeman, Brother Gildas OCSO, Caldey Abbey, Dr Madeleine Gray, Mr Tristan Gray Hulse, Mr Daniel Huws, Mrs Heather James, Mr Nevil James, Mr F. Stedman Jones, Mr Laurence Main, Professor R. Moore-Colyer, Dr John Morgan-Guy, Mr and Mrs E. Naisby, Dr E. Pierce Roberts, Canon Martin Riley.

Information relating to the various places has been given by courtesy of the following:
    Dinas: Mr Geoffrey Green, Mr Stewart Hall and the late Mr Victor James.
    Ffynnon Fair, Aberdaron: Mr Gareth Jones.
    Harmony Chapel: Henner Women's Institute
    The site of Hen Fynwent by courtesy of Mr Ian Jamieson, Hendre Eynon Farm, St Davids.
    Keeston Hospice site: Mrs Jean Llewellyn
    Maen Dewi, St Davids: Mr Graham Dove, quoting his mother, once of Hendre Eynon.
    Mathry Church: Solva Sisterhood.
    Santiago de Compostela: Canon and Mrs Martin Shaw, St Edmundsbury Cathedral.

The authors would like to thank the following for their kindness in allowing photography of various sites in this book:
    Canon J.F. Butterworth for Abbey Dore;
    The Dean and Chapter, St Davids Cathedral for the images of Giraldus Cambrensis, pilgrim graffiti, procession of Knights of St John, St James, 'sea-sickness' misericord, shrine of St David (photographed by Mr John Stark);
    Dean and Chapter, Llandaf Cathedral, for St Teilo's Reliquary (photographed by Janet Bord);
    Sir Edward Dashwood of West Wycombe Park, for the Sisters' House, Minwear;
    Rev. P. Dixon for Llanfilo Church;
    Mr & Mrs M. Eastham, for the ancient bridge at Dolau;
    Canon G. Edwards for Llaneilian Church;
    Rev G.M. Edwards for Penmon Abbey Church;
    Rev John Esau for St Mary's Church, Cydweli;
    Rev B. Hall for Pennant Melangell;
    Mr Stuart Hall, for the old chapel, Dinas;
    Rev G.M. Hughes, for Penmon Abbey Church;
    Canon A. Jones for Llangwnadl;
    Llanerfyl Parochial Church Council;
    Mr Mrs Peters of Sunny Hill, Crundale, for St Leonard's Well;
    Mr Mrs G. Philipps of Slebech Park, for St John's Church, Slebech and the offshore island;
    Rev S. Roberts for Llandderfel;
    Rev I. Thomas for Clynnog Fawr.

The following images appear by courtesy of:
    Mostyn Christ, Dean and Chapter, Bangor Cathedral and Mr Gomer Roberts, photographer;
    sketch for Edward Lhuyd of the Gwytherin Casket, Oxford MS Rawl B 464 fol r, Bodleian Library;
    St Teilo's Reliquary, Janet and Colin Bord, Fortean Picture Library;
    manuscript illustration of the priest Bernard blowing St Patrick's Horn, MS Royal 13 B VIII fol 30, British Library;

drawings of St Caradog's shrine and recess containing reliquary, St Davids Cathedral, Mr
  Michael Eastham;
Penrhys Holy Well and statue of Our Lady of Penrhys, Dr Madeleine Gray:
Twll y Dillyn, Pembrokeshire, Anne Humble;
the pilgrim ampullae, Mr Roy Lewis;
title page of St Luke's Gospel and Carpet Page from the Book of St Chad, Dean and Chapter,
  Lichfield Cathedral;
Llanrhaeadr Jesse Window, Llanrhaeadr-yng-Nghynmeirch Parochial Church Council and Mr
  Gwynn Matthews;
Capel Sant Ffraid, Trearddur Bay 1776, Strata Marcella Printed Indulgence 1528-29, Rood
  screen in Pennant Melangell Church drawn by John Parker 1837, National Library of Wales;
20th century pilgrim at Ffynnon Fair, Aberdaron, Sister Cintra Pemberton;
Mair o Cydweli, Mrs Alison Price;
St Justinian's, St Davids Head and Ynys Enlli from Mynydd Mawr, Mr Sion Rees; Nanteos
  Cup, Royal Commission on the Ancient and Historical Monuments of Wales; pilgrim badges
  and pilgrim necklace, Mr Colin Scale (photographed by Mrs Anne Eastham);
Croes Nawdd, Dean and Canons St George's Chapel, Windsor;
14th century cross St Davids, Bishop's Palace St Davids, Porth Clais, Ramsey Island, Mr
  Martin Treacey.

Unless otherwise stated, copyright of drawings belongs to Terry John and photography to the
authors.

The authors wish to express their gratitude to the following for help, information, constant interest
and encouragement;
  Canon A. Allchin; The Rev and Mrs Christopher Armstrong for giving Nona the opportunity to
  spend an unforgettable week on Ynys Enlli; David and Glenys Bennet; Janet Bray; Dr Trevor
  Broom; Dr Jane Cartwright; Mr Peter B.S. Davies: Rev Roger Donaldson, Llanbeblig: Mr and
  Mrs M Eastham; Doris Edwards; Dr and Mrs John Etherington; Anne Eynon; Sr Juan Antonio
  Ginere; Mrs Anona Gray for help with the translation; Mike and Thelma Golden for some
  timely nagging; Llywela Harris; the late Mr D.W. James; Sian James of Llanerfyl; Rev Roger
  Jones of Pembroke; Nesta Kirk; Mr Marley Lippiatt; Mrs Anne Marks; Mr Peter Marks: Miss
  Fiona Mirylees; Rev Glyn Morgan: Helen Parry; Sister Cintra Pemberton OSH, for opening up
  a world of pilgrimage; Pembrokeshire Prospectors Society; Miss Poyner and Mr Jones of
  Clynnog Fawr; Judy Pratt for tea and sympathy; Canon D.T.W. Price; the late Mr and Mrs
  Brinley Rees, now sadly missed, for the warmth of their welcome in Bangor over the years;
  Frieda Rowe; Mr C.D. Samuel, Representative Body of the Church in Wales: Mrs Jo-Jo
  Sieroslawski; Mr and Mrs Chris Taylor of St Davids for providing ideal writing conditions; the
  Rev Eirwyn Thomas of Pistyll; Canon Patrick Thomas; Sean and Mandy Tilling; Miss Kathleen
  Timmis; Mr Rye Wallace; Jean and Gordon Wheatley; Canon Aled Williams; Hilary Wylde; a
  special thanks is due to an unknown American lady who had faith enough to donate £100 to the
  task of writing a book on pilgrimage in Wales ten years ago – the gift has been spent many
  times over and we hope she will see the result; the staff of Haverfordwest Library, The National
  Library of Wales Aberystwyth, the Pembrokeshire Record Office and the Royal Commission on
  the Ancient and Historical Monuments of Wales for their patience and courtesy; and to Nona's
  sons Dafydd and Padrig and her daughter Ffion; and to Terry's godsons, Glenn and Liam
  Hewer and Sam Kirkhouse.

The authors are most grateful to the Welsh Church Fund, Isla Johnston Trusts for generous
assistance towards the production costs of this book.

Index

ADDENDUM

St David, Cult, Church and Nation, Conference held at University of Wales, Lampeter, June 2002.

Dr Nancy Edwards drew attention to two Pembrokeshire stones on which small pilgrim crosses appear to have been cut. Maen Dewi, north of Fishguard, on the border of Cemais, close to an old road to Llanychaer, is heavily lichened but at least one small cross is discernible. The other stone is set into the external east wall of Llawhaden church and once had a ring cross carved on its upper half. There are three evenly spaced crosses down the cross shaft and others randomly placed. It is drawn by J. O. Westwood in *Lapidarium Walliae*, Oxford 1876-79 and described by V. E. Nash Williams, *Early Christian Monuments of Wales*, Cardiff 1950.